T0229872

Artificial Intelligence and Literary Creativity

Inside the Mind of BRUTUS, a Storytelling Machine

Artificial Intelligence and Literary Creativity

Inside the Mind of BRUTUS, a Storytelling Machine

Selmer Bringsjord
Rensselaer Polytechnic Institute

David A. Ferrucci
IBM T. J. Watson Research Center

Psychology Press
Taylor & Francis Group

NEW YORK AND HOVE

First published by Lawrence Erlbaum Associates, Inc., Publishers
10 Industrial Avenue
Mahwah, NJ 07430

This edition published 2013 by Psychology Press

Psychology Press   Psychology Press
Taylor & Francis Group   Taylor and Francis Group
711 Third Avenue,   27 Church Road
New York, NY 10017   Hove
                                East Sussex BN3 2FA

Psychology Press is an imprint of the Taylor & Francis Group, an informa business

Cover layout and type design by Kathryn Houghtaling Lacey

Library of Congress Cataloging-in-Publication Data
Bringsjord, Selmer.
    Artificial intelligence and literary creativity: inside the mind
of BRUTUS, a storytelling machine / Selmer Bringsjord, David A.
Ferrucci.
        p.   cm.
    Includes bibliographical references and index.
    ISBN 0-8058-1986-x (alk. Paper) . -- ISBN 0-8058-1987-8 (pbk :
alk. Paper)
    1. Creation (Literary, artistic, etc.). 2. Artificial intelligence. I. Ferrucci, David, A.   II. Title.

  BF408.B773   1999
  006.3--dc21   99-13748
                                                         CIP

The final camera copy for this work was prepared by the author, and therefore the
publisher takes no responsibility for consistency or correctness of typographical style.
However, this arrangement helps to make publication of this kind of scholarship possible.

10 9 8 7 6 5 4 3 2 1

To Katherine and Alexander,
who show me super-computational creativity every day (S.B.)

and

To my parents, Antonio and Connie,
for their unyielding love, support, courage, and intellectual energy,
which have inspired me for as long as I can remember (D.F.)

Contents

Acknowledgments

This book and BRUTUS/BRUTUS$_1$ are the result of years of effort on our parts, but lots of people helped, and, accordingly, we have lots of debts. They are too many and too great to pay, but we'll try at least to mention most.

Thanks are due to Harriet Borton for her matchless LaTeX and TeX expertise, without which there would be no book. LaTeX and TeX are amazing things, and Selmer now wonders how he ever wrote a syllable without them. (Selmer assumes that Dave is now entirely converted to the notion that precise writing should be like computer programming.)

We thank the tremendous team at Lawrence Erlbaum for their patience and professionalism: Anne Duffy, Art Lizza, Linda Eisenberg, and copy editors we know only by meticulous marks. Before leaving LEA, Ray O'Connell signed us up for this project, and gave valuable guidance when the following pages were but hazy dreams.

Thanks are due to the *Journal of Experimental and Theoretical Artificial Intelligence* for permission to use, in Chapter 2, parts of the paper "The Case Against AI From Imagistic Expertise" [30]. We are likewise grateful to *Behavioral and Brain Sciences* for permission to use, in Chapter 1, parts of the review [35] of Margaret Boden's *The Creative Mind: Myths and Mechanisms* [20], and to the French publisher Arras for allowing us to use, in Chapter 1, translated parts of "Pourquoi Hendrik Ibsen Est-Is Une Menace pour La Littérature Générée Par Ordinateur?" [33].

Dave is indebted to IBM and, specifically, IBM's T.J. Watson Research Center, for time to work on BRUTUS and BRUTUS$_1$, and the book itself. Likewise, Selmer is grateful for the support Rensselaer has given him through the years. The Minds & Machines Laboratory, which Selmer directs at Rensselaer, has in particular been and continues to be a great resource. This lab only runs at present because students like Tom Poltrino, Clarke Caporale, Micah Clark, Faris Gammoh and others (e.g., Jack Yuzyenko and Claudia Hunter) make it possible. (In addition to his lab responsibilities, Tom Poltrino graciously helped with some of the images that follow.) The world has heard about BRUTUS and all the "big" questions he raises about the human mind in large part because people at RPI like Megan Galbraith and Nancy Connell and Tom Torello are gifted at securing opportunities for us to communicate through the mass media. Of course, we are indebted as well to the media itself, who to their considerable credit realize that there is a thirst out there in the laic world for answers to "big" questions. Will the machines we humans build eventually leave us in the dust? Will even our great feats of creativity fall as Kasparov's achievements have fallen? How is it that machines will eventually match us, given that we have *originated* such things as *Julius Caesar*? These are questions for the new millennium; arguably, these are *the* questions for the next century.

Many colleagues have helped with research related to this book. In particular, a number of colleagues have worked in the "Autopoeisis Project," initiated by Selmer Bringsjord and Dave Porush in 1990 with the aim of getting a machine to autonomously[1] write sophisticated fiction by the turn of the century. In the years before our work on BRUTUS, Dave Porush provided innumerable insights about "rule-breaking" belletristic literature. These insights helped move us toward rejecting Church's Thesis. (See Chapter 5.) Having Marie Meteer at Rensselaer for three years to specialize in natural language generation as part of the Autopoeisis team was invaluable. BRUTUS1, unfortunately, lacks the genuine NLG capability (e.g., as described in [163]) that Marie can bring to a system. Our hope is that future incarnations of the BRUTUS architecture will have such capability. Chris Welty participated in Autopoeisis before going to Vassar and

---

[1]BRUTUS1 doesn't represent success for Autopoeisis, because BRUTUS1 is not autonomous. BRUTUS, the architecture of which BRUTUS1 is a partial implementation, has no provision for autonomy, or what might be called "free will." Hofstadter has suggested 6 requirements for a computational artifact to be deemed truly creative (see p. 411 of [111]). It seems to us that BRUTUS easily allows for implementations that satisfy this list — but these implementations would not have anything like real free will. So Hofstadter must be wrong. One of us has argued at length that no computational entity can have true autonomy: see the chapter "Free Will" in [40].

made many brilliant contributions; he was involved in the original discussions about betrayal. Many student researchers in Autopoeisis came up with many helpful ideas through the years. Finally, thanks are due to the Henry R. Luce Foundation for the $300,000 that launched Autopoeisis. Support along the way also came from IBM, AT&T, and Apple Computer.

In recent years, trenchant comments have come from Ron Noel, whose "non-parameterized" approach to creativity (as reported, e.g., in [22]) is the opposite of ours, and has made Selmer think long and hard about the logicist approach to machine creativity advocated and exemplified herein. Ingenious ideas about human creativity have come from Michael Zenzen and Jim Fahey over the last 11 years. Michael has as keen a grasp of the nature of creativity as anyone on this planet. Others in the Creativity Circle at Rensselaer have been very helpful: Elizabeth Bringsjord, Ellen Esrock (whose unique and substantial contributions, courtesy of her fascinating book *The Reader's Eye*, will be discovered later by our readers), and Kathy Voegtle.

We are indebted to Spiral Design Inc. for the smashing image used on the cover. Observant and patient readers will find therein not only relevant technical elements seen later in the book, but also visual expression of the kind of serenity enjoyed by our BRUTUS, but definitely *not* by Shakespeare's Brutus. This image is also the core image for the aforementioned Minds & Machines Laboratory and Program at Rensselaer.

We are grateful to all those who have reacted to demos of implementations of BRUTUS that preceded $BRUTUS_1$. One particularly profitable demo took place at Brown University, sponsored by the Department of Cognitive Science and the Department of Philosophy. It was here that we were encouraged to turn to reader response theory for insights into how prose can be "engineered" to trigger desired psychological states in readers.

Finally, the debates. We are indebted to many debates and discussions with many people on the issues touched upon in this book. The majority of these thinkers advanced positions at odds with our own, and thereby helped sharpen our thoughts. They include: Margaret Boden, whose optimism about reducing creativity to computation stands in stark contrast to our calculated engineering; Marie Meeter, whose bottom-up approach contrasts with our top-down approach; Chris Welty, whose grasp of the undeniable fact (which we gleefully affirm herein) that BRUTUS$_1$ mirrors the minds of his two creators produces a stimulating cynicism; John McCarthy, who at *IJCAI 91*, in argument with Selmer, defended a view (viz., that explicit, formal definition of such concepts as betrayal is superfluous) that this book is in large part designed to overthrow; Jim Fetzer, whose semiotic brand of non-computationalism stands in contrast to BRUTUS' underpinnings; Pat Hayes, Stu Shapiro, Marvin Minsky, Ken Ford, four who have staunchly articulated the view that, despite Selmer's arguments to the contrary, cognition *is* computation; and Jim Moor, Robert Cavalier, Marvin Croy, and many others in the national "Computing and Philosophy" group, who pretty much every year supply objections to the kinds of arguments in this book.

After BRUTUS$_1$ will come BRUTUS$_2$, and then BRUTUS$_3$, and so on. That, at least, is the plan — a plan which, given all the help we've needed to this point, will, alas, require another wave of support to carry us on. Our debts will therefore mount. However, all errors herein and hereafter are decidedly our own.

Preface

The Marriage of Logic and Creativity

This book marks the marriage of logic and creativity.

While it may be true that incompatible humans often wed, there are doubtless unions of a less palpable sort that can never even come to pass. Such is the case, by the lights of many, for precisely what we are about herein. Creativity and logic? *Married*? Upon hearing of our plans, 7 years ago, to harness theorem-proving technology in order to create a computer program able to generate belletristic fiction, a rather famous novelist informed us that creativity and logic are as far apart as the east is from the west (and he proudly quipped that even such a metaphor is beyond logic, and hence beyond machines). Just an anecdote, yes, and just the opinion of one, but the truth of the matter is that this attitude is widely (and often fiercely) affirmed. Creativity is generally regarded to involve breaking the kind of rigid rules standing at the heart of logic; creativity, at least of the artistic variety, is commonly identified with the emotions and the "irrational." Freud, whose specific claims are today a bit tenuous, remains a seminal figure for often getting at least the tenor of things right. Freud believed that creativity is the link between art and play, and requires the "suspension of rational principles." He wrote that "The creative writer does much the same as the child at play. He creates a world of phantasy which he takes very seriously — that is, which he invests with large amounts of emotion — while separating it sharply from reality" ([93], p. 144). However problematic Freud's rather dark theories may be today, here he is simply making an observation that cannot be doubted. But the issue is whether such sophisticated play can in the end be reduced to logic. Is the play of Joyce and Tolstoy and Updike and Helprin and Morrison at bottom logic in action?

Many used to ask a different question: Could a computer ever beat the best human chess player? With Kasparov brooding and Deep Blue and his silicon cousins improving every week, many are *now* asking: Could a computer beat all human grandmasters *time and time again in normal tournament play?* To this the both of us unhesitatingly answer in the affirmative (as should, we daresay, anyone who knows a thing or two about the dizzying ascension of raw computing power on this planet — though by our calculations it will nonetheless take a decade for machines to achieve such metronomic triumph).

Will Robots Soon Be Smarter Than Us?

So computers will soon be smarter than us at chess; nothing controversial here. What about everything else, creative activities included? Well, according to a quartet of recent books, there will soon be *nothing* that computers and robots can't beat us at. The books are

1. *Robot: Mere Machine to Transcendent Mind*, by Hans Moravec [165]

2. *The Age of Spiritual Machines: When Computers Exceed Human Intelligence* by Ray Kurzweil [142]

3. *When Things Start to Think* by Neil Gershenfield [97]

4. *March of the Machines: Why the New Race of Robots Will Rule the World* by Kevin Warwick [243]

We find many of the predictions in these books to be laughable.[2] For example, Moravec predicts that robots will get smarter and smarter so fast that 2040 will mark the advent of "fourth generation" robots, which will exceed us in all respects. They will not only do the kind of work we currently associate with robots (inflexible physical work; e.g., manufacturing) but will "run the companies and do the research" ([165], p. 125). The chief problem with predictions like this is that they are flatly inconsistent with the utter absence of

---

[2]The first three of these books have been recently reviewed by Colin McGinn [156]. McGinn explains that there is no reason to think that robots will have (to use the terminology of our Chapter 3 in this book) a point of view, and so it would be rather stupid to agree to have your "mind" downloaded into a machine.

machine creativity in the world today. The Index in Moravec's book contains not a single entry for creativity, and yet it takes some creativity to do research, does it not? And how about running IBM? Does that take some creativity? Every single piece of technology today is due to many creative humans who lived yesterday. Look around you now. How many artifacts can you count whose origins can be traced to one or more highly creative human beings? I'm (Selmer) typing this on my laptop at a favorite restaurant. In my laptop I see the reflections of Turing, and the entrepreneur Steven Jobs. I'm sipping a "Fresh Samantha" fruit smoothie from a multi-color jug, sold by a company whose Maine-based founders had a creative idea about bottling expensive smoothies with a hip label. The watch I'm wearing has the ancestral fingerprints of a thousand engineers. There is a light above me; in it I see Edison. There is a phone beside me; in it I see Bell. Obviously, I could go on — and on. So could you, we wager.

In particular, it's safe to say that we simply wouldn't have computers and robots around today were it not for countless strokes of human creative genius. And yet Moravec, whose vision is a computation-driven one, is silent on creativity. Very interesting. Where are the AI labs in which computers are creating things? Where are the labs in which computers are creating new branches of mathematics, new modes of music, great novels, novel scientific theories, and so on? Where are they? They do not exist.[3]

We do not want to give you the wrong idea, reader. The two of us are quite optimistic about what AI can achieve. For example, we're inclined to believe that

- NASA will run successful missions to Mars and other planets largely on the strength of "immobots," HAL9000-like AIs that will control

---

[3]Selmer is at work on a book-length antidote to the fanatical sanguinity seen in these four books. Part of this antidote consists in good old-fashioned fact-checking. For example, Warwick tells us that machines that can beat us on IQ tests already exist. Really? Selmer is willing to compete against any present-day machine on the Weschler adult intelligence test, and to wager serious money that he can win. This test includes a task in which the test taker must assemble a coherent story from jumbled diagrams that represent snapshots of the action. What machine can do *that*? The test also includes general commonsense reasoning questions that even CYC would have trouble with. Nonetheless, a robot able to excel on this IQ test is under construction in Bringsjord's Minds & Machines Laboratory.

the ships in question.

- AI-controlled cars, safer than their human-controlled counterparts, will be available sooner rather than later.

- General house-cleaning robots will arrive — again, sooner rather than later.

- Even now, the bulk of medical diagnosis can be carried out by computers, at an accuracy level surpassing all but a small number of human diagnosticians. In the future, machine diagnosis will reach a point where it is downright *irrational* to consult a human M.D. first.

And so on. But notice that the kind of list we have in mind doesn't require any creativity to speak of. (Sorry, diagnosticians.) So we still have the question before us: What about creativity? Robotic drivers may be securely in our future, but Einstein, Gödel, Tolstoy, Turing, Shakespeare, Plato, Cantor, ... — could machines ever reach *their* rank? Could we ever build a genuinely creative machine?

We seek to answer "the creativity question" not from the comfort of our armchairs, but from the workbenches in our laboratories. Specifically, we seek to ascertain whether or not literary creativity is the sole province of humans by attempting to *build* artificial authors. The first fruit of our labor, 5 years in the making (with another half-decade prior to this one devoted to less ambitious systems), is BRUTUS, a storytelling agent specializing in narrative that involves betrayal first and foremost, and also self-deception and other literary themes. The mind of BRUTUS is revealed in the book you're holding.

From Chess to Literary Creativity

In our experience, the public is quite comfortable with the notion that a machine can play invincible chess — because even those who know nothing of the niceties of search algorithms intuitively grasp the mathematical fact that chess, at bottom, is utterly mechanical, that if one can "look far enough ahead" the game becomes trivial. On the other hand, given the reaction of the public to BRUTUS$_1$'s prowess as reported in the media (as evidenced by a persistent stream of rather emotional communication we receive), we think it's safe to say that while we (and many other AIniks, e.g., Douglas Hofstadter [111]) merrily press ahead in the attempt to reduce creativity to computation, the lay mind is fundamentally disturbed by the prospect of creative machines.[4] This is probably because they realize, intuitively, that the future described in the quartet of books cited earlier can come to pass *if* machines become creative. In presenting the anatomy of BRUTUS's brain herein, we will soothe the souls of those who, hearing about his exploits, fear that humans will soon have nothing over machines. It will become crystal clear in what follows that BRUTUS should give his human creators rather a lot of credit. Put in terms of our terminology, we say that BRUTUS has weak, rather than strong, creativity. (Of course, there are people out there at the other end of the spectrum: people who think that a machine that creates genuine literature is right around the corner. Figure 1 encapsulates this attitude.)

What we call "strong creativity" is what might be called "raw origination." Raw origination is akin to creation *ex nihilo*, and though this form of creativity may well be impossible, the fact of the matter is that the *concept* of creating something from nothing is very real not only to monotheists, but also to many hardheaded scientists who have pondered creativity. The paradigmatic example is Margaret Boden, arguably the world's leading authority on computational creativity. Boden [19] distinguishes between a brand of creativity associated with the novel combinations of old ideas (she gives the example of the Lennon/McCartney arrangement of "Yesterday," marked by the unprecedented combination of a cello with music of this type), and a type of creativity in which something utterly and completely new is produced (e.g., non-Euclidean geometry, wherein the sum of the interior angles of a triangle is *not* 180 degrees). Computers, of course, have no trouble with the former type of creativity. The latter type is somewhat more difficult for them. It's exceedingly hard to see how a computer could, say, autonomously discover a new class of numbers through new proof techniques, which was one of Cantor's novel achievements.

The distinction between strong and weak creativity isn't a new one. When Alan Turing, one of the grandfathers of computer science and AI, proposed that if a machine could pass his famous "imitation game" (in which a computer passes if it's linguistically indistinguishable from a human; the game is now known as the "Turing Test"), we humans should immediately conclude that such a machine can gen-

---

[4]It's important to note that we don't think the reduction can be pulled off. Hofstadter does.

Figure 1: Nonchalance Regarding BRUTUS$_1$'s Descendants. Roz Chast © 1996 from The New Yorker Collection. All Rights Reserved.

uinely think, he considered an objection from Lady Lovelace that was given on the strength of raw origination. She argued: "Computers will never be creative, for creativity requires *originating* something, and this is something computers just don't do. Computers do what they are programmed to do, nothing more." (Turing presents his imitation game, and discusses the Lovelace objection, in his [236].)

Suppose for the sake of argument that Lovelace is correct. Even so, the other sense of creativity, "weak creativity," remains intact. Weak creativity has its roots in the "operational" notion of creativity devised by psychologists. For example, E. Paul Torrance, who more than any other psychologist has probed the nature and concrete signs of creativity, holds that x is to be deemed creative just in case x scores well on the dominant test for creativity in children and adults: The Torrance Tests of Creative Thinking.[5] This test comes in both "visual" and "verbal" forms. In the visual form, test takers are asked to draw pictures (often by enriching existing sketches); in the verbal form, test takers are asked to write — creatively. For example, one of the activities subjects engage in on the verbal test is the following.

> Most people throw their tin cans away, but they have thousands of interesting and unusual uses. In the spaces below and on the next page, list as many of these interesting and unusual uses as you can think of. Do not limit yourself to any one size of can. You may use as many cans as you like. Do not limit yourself to the uses you have seen or heard about; think about as many possible new uses as you can. (From the verbal version of [233].)

After the Torrance Test is administered, one can send it out to be professionally judged. Our aim on the problem of literary creativity is to build an artificial agent capable of producing stories that would be scored as highly creative by human judges in the dark as to whether or not the stories they receive are from humans or machines. One of us (Bringsjord) has refined this scenario into what he calls the "short short story game," or just S³G for short. The idea is simple; it is summed up in Figure 2. A human and a computer compete against each other. Both receive one relatively simple sentence, say: "Barnes kept the image to himself, kept the horror locked away as best he could." (For a much better one, see

---

[5]See [233] for the test itself. For reviews of the test, see [50], [227], [235].

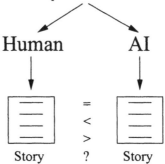

"When Gregor woke, he found
that his arm was hard and
skinless, and where his hand
had been, there was now some
kind of probe."

Human   AI

Story   ?   Story

Figure 2: The Short Short Story Game, or S^3G for Short.

the "loaded" sentence shown in Figure 2.[6]) Both mind and machine must now fashion a short short story (about 500 words) designed to be truly interesting; the more literary virtue, the better. Our goal, then, is to build an artificial author able to compete with first-rate human authors in S^3G, much as Deep Blue went head to head with Kasparov.

Unfortunately, this goal is too tough to reach, at least for the foreseeable future; it may even be a goal that is forever beyond the reach of a machine. (Consider the process of writing something like *David Copperfield* from a picture like that shown in Figure 3, which is taken from an illustrated version of this classic [74].) Our more immediate goal is therefore to build a machine capable of passing

---

[6]The actual opening, which we visit in Chapter 2, is as follows:

As Gregor Samsa awoke one morning from uneasy dreams he found himself transformed in his bed into a gigantic insect. He was lying on his hard, as it were armor-plated, back and when he lifted his head a little he could see a dome-like brown belly divided into stiff arched segments on top of which the bed quilt could hardly keep in position and was about to slide off completely. His numerous legs, which were pitifully thin compared to the rest of his bulk, waved helplessly before his eyes. ([122], p. 67)

a less demanding Torrance-like test; that is, a silicon author able to generate stories that would be regarded creative, even if these stories are well below what a muse-inspired member of *Homo sapiens sapiens* can muster.

"Your Mother and Brother Have Died."

Figure 3: Possible "Dickensian" Input for S^{3}G. (Reprinted with kind permission from Waldman Publishing Corporation.)

How Do You Build an Artificial Author?

How does one go about building such artificial author? Our answer comes in the following pages. At this point we mention only one property we believe a good story generator must have: **wide variability**.

There are many dimensions over which a story can vary. Plot is only one of them. Characters, settings, literary themes, writing style, imagery, etc. — these are other dimensions, and there are many more. Generally speaking, belletristic fiction has very wide variability across these dimensions. Mark Helprin's latest novel is likely to have a rather unpredictable plot traversed by rather unpredictable characters in rather unpredictable settings tossed by unpredictable mixtures of love, revenge, jealousy, betrayal, and so on, as reported in prose with a cadence and clarity rarely seen. One of the chief effects of it all is to conjure unforgettable images in the reader's mind. (One of us is haunted weekly by the image of the lost gold in Helprin's *Memoirs From the Antproof Case*.) At the other end of the spectrum fall formulaic fiction and film; here the variability is narrow. Some romance novels, for example, fail to offer wide variability of plot and characterization: It's the same character types time and time again, dancing hot and heavy to the same choreography. (If $BRUTUS_n$, some refined descendant of $BRUTUS_1$, is to soon find employment at the expense of a human writer, in all likelihood it will be as an author of formulaic romance and mystery.)

Whether or not a story generator can be implemented to achieve wide variability hinges on what we call **architectural differentiation**. A story generation system has architectural differentiation if for each substantive aspect of the story that can vary, there is a corresponding distinct component of the technical architecture that can be parameterized to achieve different results. While we owe many debts to the pioneers who have come before us in the field of story generation, it's safe to say that their systems failed to enable wide variability via architectural differentiation.

From the start, our approach has been to bestow the BRUTUS architecture with a counterpart to *every* substantive aspect of human literary genius. While our first implementation of this architecture, $BRUTUS_1$, has quite limited variability, ancestors will implement more and more of those parts of the architecture designed to secure wide variability.

Wide variability is an important property, but there are others that are equally important. One of the ways to encapsulate all of them, and to quickly characterize our approach, is to say that BRU-

TUS is designed to satisfy what we call the seven magic desiderata for a successful story generator, namely:

MD1 *Give proposed rigorous accounts of strong creativity a run for their money.* An impressive storytelling AI is one that satisfies, or at least comes close to satisfying, proposed sophisticated accounts of *strong* creativity. BRUTUS₁ does this: As we show later, the system qualifies as capable of raw origination on Margaret Boden's definition of this concept.

MD2 *Generate imagery in the reader's mind.* An artificial agent aspiring to be counted among the literati must be able to spark significant readerly imaging. (Sometimes even literary fiction can earn classification as such despite displaying ordinary prose. Victor Hugo's *Les Miserables* is a case in point: The writing is simple, relative to other immortals, anyway, but what readers can forget the scenes set in the sewers beneath Paris?)

MD3 *Situate the story in "landscape of consciousness."* A good storytelling AI must produce stories having not only a landscape of action, but also a landscape of consciousness, that is, a landscape defined by the mental states of characters.

MD4 *Mathematize concepts at the core of belletristic fiction.* No artificial agent will lay claim to being counted literarily creative unless it processes the immemorial themes (e.g., betrayal) at the heart of literature; and such processing can presumably come only if the themes in question have been formalized.

MD5 *Generate genuinely interesting stories.* A true artificial storyteller must produce genuinely interesting stories. Among the things that readers find interesting are particular topics like sex and money and death (as the well-known cognitive scientist Roger Schank has explained [205]), and also classic themes like betrayal, ruthless ambition, and unrequited love.

MD6 *Tap into the deep, abiding structures of stories.* Any truly impressive artificial author must be in command of story structures that give its output an immediate standing amongst its human audience. For BRUTUS₁, these structures take the form of what are called 'story grammars.'

MD7 *Avoid "mechanical" prose.* Last but not least: An artificial author must produce compelling literary prose.

The seven magic desiderata are cashed out in BRUTUS, a rich and highly differentiated system architecture for story generation.

BRUTUS₁ is the current implementation of the BRUTUS — notice the absence of the subscript — architecture.

Why Build an Artificial Author?

Finally, a question interviewers and members of the audience and out-of-the-blue e-mailers have asked us time and time again through the years: Why do it? There are at least three general reasons, two theoretical, one practical.

The first theoretical reason for investing time, money, and talent in the quest for a truly creative machine is to work toward an answer to the question of whether we ourselves are machines. If the creative side of human cognition can be captured by computation, then it's surely likely that we are at bottom computers. (The more quotidian side of human mentation can presumably be mechanized, and "lower level" sensing and effecting in interchange with the environment should present no insurmountable obstacles to AI's upward march through the next century.) As you will see in the coming pages, we follow a singular method: As we uncover reasons for believing that human creativity is in fact beyond the reach of computation, we will be inspired to nonetheless engineer systems that dodge these reasons and *appear* to be creative. A side effect of our approach is perhaps to furnish AI with at least an early brick or two in a theoretical foundation for machine creativity. Absent such a foundation (whose mortar, to be effective, would presumably have to be somewhat mathematical in nature), artificial creative agents will never arrive.

The second theoretical reason for our work is stark and simple: to silence those who believe that logic is forever closed off from the emotional world of creativity. BRUTUS is Vulcan through and through, utterly devoid of emotion, but he nonetheless seems to have within his reach things that touch not only our minds, but our hearts.

The practical rationale for our endeavor is that machines able to work alongside humans in arenas calling for creativity would have incalculable worth. A machine able to write a full, formidable novel, or compose a feature-length film, or create and manage the unfolding story in an online game, would be, we suspect, pure gold.

S.B. Troy NY / D.F. Yorktown Heights NY — June 1999

On Silicon Wings

Granite majesty rises our vision to heaven and bound
Crushed and ground, smashed and spread,
Bed our mother's ebb and tide.
The push and pull delivers a grainy pebble ride.
Beneath our feet, cushioning our journey
From slimy cellular slop to pensive petitioners of paradise.

The mat of our birth and the walls of our demise.

Stretching through time, small and broken pieces of dirt
The fallen and the forgotten, the plenty and the bare –
Rise to cup the water to our lips,
Rise to clear our vision of things far and small,
Rise to road our passage from home to home,
Rise to bridge our thoughts from sun to sun.

And the splendid, seemingly solid, visions of heaven,
Humbly laid down to bed our birth and our play,
Rise again to lift us above the somatic images of paradise lost,
Mimicking our minds to clear sight of our souls.

On Silicon wings we will fly.

David A. Ferrucci ©1992

List of Tables

List of Figures

Chapter 1

Setting the Stage

1.1 The Turing Test Sequence

Lady Lovelace famously pressed against Alan Turing and his "Turing Test"[1] (hereafter T_1) a short but powerful argument; charitably paraphrased, it runs as follows.

> Computers can't create anything. For creation requires, minimally, *originating* something. But computers originate nothing; they merely do that which we order them, via programs, to do. (see [236])

Let's agree to momentarily postpone the issue of whether this reasoning is sound — in favor of the observation that Lovelace apparently believed T_1 *would* in the future be passed by a computing machine, even if the judge running the test asked questions designed to be

---

[1]The test was discussed in the Preface, and is part of the canon of AI and cognitive science. Turing's scheme was simple, but seminal. A human judge is able to communicate (only) by — to modernize a bit — e-mail with two players, each concealed in a separate room. One player is a woman, the other a computer. Turing said that when we reach the point at which human judges do no better than 50/50 when rendering verdicts as to which player is in fact a woman, we will have machines that can truly think. He believed this point would arrive before the turn of the century. Bringsjord believes that his [32] refutes Turing's position. Our next, more robust implementation of the BRUTUS architecture, BRUTUS2, will reflect our doing for mendacity what we have done for betrayal; that is, BRUTUS2 will be armed with an account of mendacity like the account of betrayal described in Chapter 4. Mendacity would seem to be at the heart of the Turing Test.

answerable only by truly creative systems. Lovelace's belief presupposes some world-beating engineering: Something that isn't creative, but *appears* to be creative to the degree that it passes T_1 — well, that something is *really* something. In this book we endeavor to share with you what the engineering in question would be like, by, in part, *doing* it. The result of our engineering is the architecture we refer to as BRUTUS, and BRUTUS$_1$, the first implementation of part of that architecture, an artificial storyteller who certainly *appears* to be creative. Though BRUTUS$_1$ cannot himself pass T_1, we intend to build a descendant who can. So, for some $n > 1$, BRUTUS$_n$ would pass T_1; and were this clever agent to arrive, Lovelace's argument would be of intense interest. Our race would very much want to know whether BRUTUS$_n$ is super-elaborate prestidigitation, or a creature with emotions on par with those exploited by Tolstoy and his peers. This book will help you to see why the design and construction of BRUTUS$_n$, from where we currently stand in AI and cognitive science, is difficult almost beyond belief.[2]

You may be thinking: "Creativity? I thought the Turing Test, what you call T_1, was just about plain old *thinking*. Wasn't Turing's claim simply that if something passes T_1, then that thing is, or at least ought to be treated as, a thinking thing? Besides, I read the cover of your book, guys, and your interests are quite specific: *Literary* creativity is what you're about. This is a topic much narrower than Turing's concern, no?"

Well, as a matter of fact, in Turing's seminal paper [236], creativity, specifically *literary* creativity, proves to be irrepressible. For example, in response to the objection that something can pass T_1 without being conscious, Turing claims that a computing machine able to converse with the judge as in the following would have to be counted as conscious.[3]

> **Judge:** In the first line of your sonnet which reads "Shall I compare thee to a summer's day," would not "a spring day" do as well or better?

---

[2]Note that one can sincerely intend to bring about p, even though one isn't convinced that p can come about. Sports are filled with situations like this: One of us regularly intends to carve every turn smoothly in a top-to-bottom alpine run, even though it may not be possible for his skis to behave as intended.

[3]Actually, Turing considers the following exchange between an "Interrogator" and a "Witness." See [236], p. 17.

Computer: It wouldn't scan.

Judge: How about "a winter's day." That would scan all right.

Computer: Yes, but nobody wants to be compared to a winter's day.

Judge: Would you say Mr. Pickwick reminded you of Christmas?

Computer: In a way.

Judge: Yet Christmas is a winter's day, and I do not think Mr. Pickwick would mind the comparison.

Computer: I don't think you're serious. By a winter's day one means a typical winter's day, rather than a special one like Christmas.

At the moment, though, neither BRUTUS$_1$ nor his successors are intended to engage in repartee. They are designed to generate stories, *good* stories. However, it's easy enough to adapt T_1 to focus on the literary realm. In fact, as mentioned in the Preface, one of us (Bringsjord) has proposed such an adaptation, in the form of what he calls the "short short story game," or just S^{3}G for short [25]. The idea is simple; it's summed up in Figure 1.1. A human and a computer compete against each other. Both receive one relatively simple sentence, say: "Barnes kept the image to himself, kept the horror locked away as best he could." (For a more interesting sentence, see the "loaded" one shown in Figure 1.1.) Both mind and machine must now fashion a short short story (about 500 words) designed to be truly interesting; the more literary virtue, the better. Down the road, we do intend to build an artificial author able to compete with first-rate human authors in S^{3}G, much as Deep Blue went head to head with Kasparov. But for now our efforts are devoted to building systems that generate stories on the basis of knowledge and reasoning power directly imparted by humans.

To be fair, we probably should not expect Shakespearean flourish from BRUTUS$_1$. If we could get something solid but well short

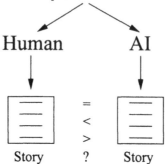

Figure 1.1: S^{3}G.

of *Julius Caesar*, something, perhaps, like the following, then our
project could arguably be said to be swimming along.

"Betrayal in Self-Deception" (conscious)

Dave Striver loved the university. He loved its ivy-covered
clocktowers, its ancient and sturdy brick, and its sun-splashed
verdant greens and eager youth. He also loved the fact that
the university is free of the stark unforgiving trials of the business world — only this *isn't* a fact: academia has its own tests,
and some are as merciless as any in the marketplace. A prime
example is the dissertation defense: to earn the PhD, to become a doctor, one must pass an oral examination on one's
dissertation. This was a test Professor Edward Hart enjoyed
giving.

Dave wanted desperately to be a doctor. But he needed the
signatures of three people on the first page of his dissertation,
the priceless inscriptions which, together, would certify that
he had passed his defense. One of the signatures had to come
from Professor Hart, and Hart had often said — to others and
to himself — that he was honored to help Dave secure his
well-earned dream.

Well before the defense, Striver gave Hart a penultimate copy
of his thesis. Hart read it and told Dave that it was abso-

lutely first-rate, and that he would gladly sign it at the defense.
They even shook hands in Hart's book-lined office. Dave noticed that Hart's eyes were bright and trustful, and his bearing
paternal.

At the defense, Dave thought that he eloquently summarized
Chapter 3 of his dissertation. There were two questions, one
from Professor Rodman and one from Dr. Teer; Dave answered
both, apparently to everyone's satisfaction. There were no
further objections.

Professor Rodman signed. He slid the tome to Teer; she too
signed, and then slid it in front of Hart. Hart didn't move.

"Ed?" Rodman said.

Hart still sat motionless. Dave felt slightly dizzy.

"Edward, are you going to sign?"

Later, Hart sat alone in his office, in his big leather chair,
saddened by Dave's failure. He tried to think of ways he could
help Dave achieve his dream.

This story is in fact "authored" by BRUTUS. And, as we shall see,
BRUTUS has other interesting narrative within his reach. Note, however, that we have placed the term 'author' in scare quotes. Why?
The reason is plain and simple, and takes us back to Lady Lovelace's
argument, presented at the start of the chapter: BRUTUS didn't *originate* this story. He is capable of generating it because two humans
spent years figuring out how to formalize a generative capacity sufficient to produce this and other stories, and they then are able to
implement part of this formalization so as to have a computer produce such prose. The engineering method followed here is known as
reverse engineering.

1.2 The Midwife

The midwife responsible for BRUTUS$_1$'s arrival is philosophy: Philosophical analysis and argument, as you will see, have played an in-
dispensable role in bringing BRUTUS$_1$ to life. In this regard our work
conforms to an approach according to which AI systems, at least *ambitious* AI systems, need to be born, at least in significant part, out
of rigorous philosophizing; and they need to be cultivated with help
from ongoing philosophical scrutiny. The paradigmatic case of this

approach at work is John Pollock's OSCAR project [182]. However, unlike Pollock's plans for OSCAR, we don't intend BRUTUS₁ to be a person; we don't even intend that BRUTUS₁ enjoy *any* of the properties at the core of personhood.[4] It may turn out that BRUTUS₁ approximates some of the properties Pollock and others regard to be at the heart of personhood (e.g., BRUTUS₁ certainly possesses some of the reasoning power of OSCAR), but from our perspective this would be an accident. Our objective is to engineer, by hook or by crook, a system that qualifies, in "Turing Testish" terms, as a genuinely creative agent. It follows that we drive a wedge between those systems capable of passing T_1 and those systems which *truly have* the underlying mental properties normally ascribed to things capable of passing such a test.

One of us (Selmer) has presented a book-length case ([40]: *What Robots Can and Can't Be*) for driving this wedge — a case for the two-part view that

(1) It's mathematically impossible to build persons via computational techniques.

(2) It's humanly possible to build robots (or androids, etc.) whose overt behavior is in large part indistinguishable from persons.

Most of the case presented in *What Robots Can and Can't Be* is devoted to demonstrating (1). The part of it concerned with substantiating (2) is, as Bringsjord readily admits in the monograph in question, inchoate. The book you are reading now, in conjunction with the BRUTUS₁ system at its heart, develops the case for proposition (2).

Actually, (2) is short for a thesis that makes crucial reference not only to the Turing Test (T_1) but to what one of us [40] has called the **the Turing Test sequence**. There are obviously tests easier to pass than T_1 that still capture Turing's empiricist spirit. For example, we might index T_1 to some particular domain — golf, say — and stipulate that questions moving significantly beyond this domain aren't fair game.[5] We might insist that the syntax of queries,

---

[4] In a recent book, one of us (Selmer; [28]) offers a list of properties constitutive of personhood. The list includes the capacity to reason, to communicate, to will, to be conscious and self-conscious, etc.

[5] Admissible question: "What is 'Hogan's dream'"? (Answer: A round of golf with a birdie on each hole.) Inadmissible: "Is the feeling one gets from scoring

and the syntax of responses, conform to a certain range of patterns. Or we might decide to modify the scoring that is part of Turing's original proposal — so that, for example, if a system can fool the judge 25% of time, rather than the full 50%, it is deemed to have passed.

It's also easy enough to devise tests more stringent than T_1. The most famous of these tests is Stevan Harnad's [106] intriguing "Total Turing Test," which we can baptize as T_2. In this test not only is the linguistic behavior of a robot (or android) scrutinized, but its sensorimotor conduct is evaluated as well. In order to pass T_2, a robot must not only have the capacity to be a (to use one of Harnad's terms) pen-pal; it must also *look* human. In the same paper, Harnad considers more stringent tests than T_2, for example tests in which the judge is allowed to "look under the hood," that is, to look at the physical stuff out of which the synthetic contestant is made. Other thinkers, for example Peter Kugel [140], have proposed tests so demanding that they cannot, as a matter of mathematics, be passed by finite state automata. And so on. Let's suppose, accordingly, that there is indeed some sequence

$$T_0, T_{.25}, \ldots, T_1, T_2, \ldots$$

which underlies the relevant modification of (2), namely,

(2') It's humanly possible to build robots (or androids, etc.) capable of ascending (perhaps all of) the Turing Test sequence.

This book is an attempt to lend credence to (2').

Of course, in T_i, $i \geq 1$, the subject matter that is fair game in the test is unlimited. *Our* subject matter, however, will be quite narrow: We will be concerned with creativity, and specifically with *literary* creativity. Though we are quite prepared to concede that this focus thins the connection between our work herein and (2'), the truth of the matter is that we believe the toughest nut to crack in an attempt to build AIs capable of ascending the Turing Test sequence will be human creativity.[6] If this is right, and if we're successful, it follows

---

an eagle on a par 5 anything like what it feels like to slam down on your car's accelerator in order to successfully avoid an accident?"

[6]We also believe that literary creativity will be the hardest kind of creativity to crack. For a report on some remarkable progress in the attempt to engineer artificial *musical* creativity, see [117].

that our work does significantly contribute to an attempt to climb the Turing Test sequence.

Of course, there are those who seem to believe that building a creative agent presents no special challenges — challenges above building, say, an expert system for automating air traffic control. (Recall Figure 1, shown in the Preface.) Even readers of this persuasion should find our work illuminating. This is so because our work is undeniably all about the interconnections between cognition, computation, and narrative; and it seems plausible that narrative does stand at the heart of cognition in *any* domain, whether it's air traffic control, medical diagnosis, pedagogy, or corporate decision making. This view — the view that narrative is central and ubiquitous in human cognition — is affirmed, for example, by Roger Schank: In their lead target chapter in *Knowledge and Memory: The Real Story* [251], Schank and Robert Abelson boldly assert on the first page that "virtually all human knowledge" is based on stories.[7] Schank and Abelson go on to declare that since the essence of cognition inheres in narrative, we can jettison propositional, logic-based, rule-based, formal ... schemes for knowledge representation. (This view is of course ridiculous, as is revealed by the fact that Schank and Abelson represent narrative using the formalisms they would defenestrate.) Among the 17 commentators who react to the target piece, 13 affirm the story-based view (the remaining 4 authors are skeptical).[8] And Schank and friends are not alone: Daniel Dennett's *Consciousness Explained* [70] can be read as a defense of the view (his "multiple drafts" conception of consciousness) that thinking is at bottom the spinning out of parallel *stories*.

1.3   Philosophy as Engineering

Our case for (2′) will be in significant part *helped* by reasons for affirming (1). In fact, reasons for affirming (1), when compelling, point the way to prudent "retreats" to certain engineering techniques. For example, in Chapter 2 we explain why building a computational system with the imagistic powers of a human author is, at least for the foreseeable future, impossible. As a result, we retreat to giving

---

[7]An insightful review of this book has been written by Tom Trabasso [234].

[8]Schank has devoted a book to the view that stories are at the very heart of human cognition [204].

BRUTUS$_1$ rules for generating narrative that produces mental images in the minds of *readers*.

All known tests in the Turing Test sequence are discussed and found to be inadequate in a paper written recently by one of us: Bringsjord [32]. In that paper there appears a prediction that, in the future, attempts to build systems capable of passing T_1 will increasingly rely upon engineering tools and techniques and tricks that have little to do with a scientific understanding of human cognition. Underlying our work herein is the belief that such a future will in large part unfold because AIniks will face up to the fact that AI's scientific side, the attempt to understand cognition in terms of computation (and related phenomena), has hit a brick wall. In this book we show you part of that brick wall, and we show you how to retreat productively from it, and then "sneak" around it. Of course, our discussion is limited to literary creativity: We explain why attempts to explain the human brand of such creativity in computational terms are doomed; and we describe our approach to engineering *seemingly* creative artificial authors.

1.4 Lovelace's Argument From Creativity

But what about Lady Lovelace's argument? Do we have in it our first piece of evidence for the view that human creativity will resist computational science?

In her stimulating book on computers and creativity, *The Creative Mind: Myths and Mechanisms*, Margaret Boden — who has of late devoted much thought to the AI–creativity connection — pronounces Lovelace's argument "too quick and too simple" ([20], p. 6), and she decomposes Lovelace's attack into four questions:

Q1 Can computational ideas help us understand how human creativity is possible?

Q2 Could computers (now or in the future) ever do things which at least *appear* to be creative?

Q3 Could a computer ever appear to *recognize* creativity?

Q4 Could computers themselves ever *really* be creative?

Boden's answers to these questions, and her defense of those answers, constitute her book. Her answers are not ours. Table 1.1

Table 1.1: Bringsjord/Ferrucci versus Boden on Creativity.

	Boden	**Us**
Q1	Yes.	No, not really.
Q2	Yes — but a *guarded* yes.	Yes, obviously!
Q3	Yes — but a *guarded* yes.	Yes, obviously!
Q4	No, probably not.	No.

sums up the clash.[9]

Q4, Boden tells us, is actually beside the point, and she relegates discussion of it to the final chapter:

> For reasons explained in the final chapter, I would probably answer "No" to the fourth question. Perhaps you would, too. However, this hypothetical moral decision-making about imaginary artificial creatures is irrelevant to our main purpose: understanding human creativity. For even if we answer "No" to the fourth Lovelace-question, the affirmative answers to the first three questions can stand. ([20], p. 11)

Ah, but when we reach the final chapter of her book, we find Boden's big surprise (p. 274): She concedes that John Searle's [208] Chinese Room[10] (CR) answer to Q4 is a negative one which im-

---

[9]There would seem to be a question missing from Boden's quartet, viz.,

Q2′ *Will* a computer ever do things which at least *appear* to be creative?

Note that if the answer to Q2′ is "Yes" then Q2 should likewise be answered in the affirmative, that is,

$$\text{Q2′-Y} \rightarrow \text{Q2-Y}.$$

And note as well that Q2′-Y seems to follow from the fact that BRUTUS₁ exists.

[10]We assume readers to be acquainted with Searle's Chinese Room thought-experiment, in which he is locked alone in a room but is nonetheless able to converse with native speakers of Chinese by correlating Chinese queries from them (passed in to him on cards) with appropriate answers solely on the strength of a rulebook that tells him which "squiggle-squoggles" to output based on which "squiggle-squoggles" come in. Searle himself doesn't understand any Chinese; hence the term 'squiggle-squoggles' to refer to the Chinese inscriptions he manipulates. Searle claims that in this scenario he is doing everything a conversational computer would do (he and the machine do nothing more than move meaningless symbols around), and since he fails to understand, so would such a computer. One of us (Bringsjord) has attempted to produce a strengthened version of Searle's argument in Chapter V: Searle in [40]. A pre-print of Selmer's

plies that his answer to Q1 be "Perhaps, but not at a fundamental level." The point is a twofold one: Searle's negative answer to Q4 implies, contra page-11-Boden, an anti-Boden answer to Q1; and, this implication is one Boden herself affirms (p. 274). The implication is straightforward: CR supposedly shows that executing a computer program can't give to that which executes it bona fide understanding; such execution can only bestow a mindless ability to move symbols around. An affirmative answer to Q1 presupposes that "computational psychology" (which comprises for Boden the writing of programs Searle parodies) can provide genuine insights into human creativity, so embracing CR means at best a half-hearted "Perhaps" on Q1, or, as we put it on our side of Table 1.1, "No, not really" — since mindlessly moving squiggle-squoggles around is somewhat unlikely to reveal how *Hamlet* came to be.

Let '$Qn\text{-}X \to Qm\text{-}X'$,' abbreviate the form of the implication we've just isolated. What other relations of this sort are true? Boden herself affirms (p. 10)

$$Q2\text{-}Y\text{-guarded} \to Q3\text{-}Y\text{-guarded}$$

by reasoning which would also sanction

$$Q2\text{-}Y\text{-obviously!} \to Q3\text{-}Y\text{-obviously!}$$

These conditionals, conjoined with the one we just unearthed,

$$Q4\text{-}N \to Q1\text{-}N, \text{ not really,}$$

imply that if the answer to Q4 is "No," and if the answer to Q2 is "Yes, obviously!", Boden's entire project (which is in large part an attempt to demonstrate that Q2 and Q3 are to be answered with a sedulous, reflective "Yes") is threatened by inferences of a sort non-creative computers of today can effortlessly perform.

But why is the answer to Q2 an emphatic and obvious affirmative? The argument is short and simple: First, note that the 'could' in Q2 is for Boden an "in principle" could (e.g., see p. 10). Well, it's

---

soon-to-be-published "Real Robots and the Missing Thought-Experiment in the Chinese Room Dialectic" (in a volume on Searle edited by John Preston and Mark Bishop) is available on his web site at

- `www.rpi.edu/~anderf/SELPAP/SEARLEBOOK/searlebook.html`

surely in principle possible that computers of the future be judged creative on purely behavioral grounds. This can be established by a thought-experiment in which computers ostensibly do all sorts of creative things — an imagined future in which our silicon-based friends generate Balzacian novels, engage in conversations with the literati about Shakespearean sonnets, and generate symphonies that would have Beethoven himself salivating. Remember, the point isn't that such a future will as a matter of fact arrive (on that score Boden is herself prudently agnostic, hence the guarded affirmative to Q1 and Q2); the point is that it's surely *in principle* possible that our future holds AIs which appear, on behavioral grounds, to be creative. Indeed, as will be seen, BRUTUS$_1$ is, or at least points the way to, such an AI.

"Hold on," you say, in synchrony with Boden, "for a computer to appear to be creative in the sense intended, its internal workings would have to be of the right sort." True enough, but the objection is surmounted by adding to our gedanken-experiment a pinch more imagination: We have only to watch the innards of our "creative" computers being probed by skeptical cognitive scientists, the result being that therein are found unbelievably complex systems, the details of which are impenetrable, but the broad strokes of which suggest that these systems are n^{th} generation descendants of today's AI systems. (Traditional symbolicist systems like OSCAR and SNePS were augmented with domain-specific skills like those enjoyed by BRUTUS$_1$, and were in 1997 given the capacity to evolve in unanticipatable ways with help from connectionist-based sensors and effectors; and by 2005 our synthetic rival to Beethoven arrives.)

But doesn't Boden dispose of Searle's CR? Perhaps.[11] But another Q4-X rationale, which Boden touches upon in her final chapter, may well support the 'Q4-$X \rightarrow$ Q1-X, not really' conditional. This

---

[11]Boden argues in [18] that computers are causal systems, not abstract sets of rules, and so, contra Searle, CR isn't an instantiation of a computer (at work). (Pat Hayes long ago articulated essentially the same objection to one of us — Bringsjord — in conversation.) Unfortunately, Searle's CR is easily adapted so as to destroy this objection. We have merely to imagine that Searle — or Jonah, the *mono savant* imagined in Bringsjord's [40] variant of CR — instantiates a causal system. For example, when a card holding a Chinese inscription comes in, Searle's hands, fingers, and arms move in accordance with a causal chain. Now we can still ask the question: Where is genuine understanding of Chinese, seeing as how Searle certainly doesn't have any?

rationale for Q4-X is a variant on what Boden calls (pp. 278–281) the "consciousness argument"; put roughly, it runs as follows.

Arg₁

(3)   Creativity requires inner, first-person-point-of-view, something-it's-like-to-be consciousness.

(4)   No computer could ever be conscious in this sense.

∴ (5)   No computer can ever be creative.   (3), (4)

Boden would probably pronounce this line of reasoning "iffy" (p. 281) and go her merry way. But as we see in Chapters 2 and 3, where **Arg₁** is explored in some detail, the reasoning is quite powerful. In a nutshell now, (3) is true (for *literary* creativity) because in order to produce sophisticated fiction, an author, whether human or artificial, must adopt the points of view of the characters involved. But if x adopts the point of view of y, then x must itself have a point of view. Proposition (4), as we see, is the conclusion of an argument derived from Jackson's [115] case against physicalist explanations of inner, subjective states (often called "qualia"). This derivation was initiated in [40], defended (against objections given by Dennett [70]) in [37], and is refined later in Chapters 2 and 3.

1.4.1   Moravec's Response to Lovelace

In his *Robot: Mere Machine To Transcendent Mind* [165] Hans Moravec counters Lovelace's argument as follows:

> Lady Lovelace, the first programmer, never had a working computer to trouble her programs. Modern programmers know better. Almost every new program misbehaves badly until it is laboriously debugged, and it is never fully tamed. Information ecologies like time-sharing systems and networks are even more prone to wild behavior, sparked by unanticipated interactions, inputs, and attacks. ([165], p. 85)

This is a pitiful rejoinder, alas. Sure, we all know that computers do things we don't intend for them to do. But that's because we're not smart and careful enough, or — if we're talking about rare hardware errors — because sometimes microscopic events behave in unforeseen ways. The unpredictability in question does *not* result from the fact that the computer system has taken it upon itself to *originate* something. Think about the point in connection with BRUTUS₁. Suppose that while carrying out the inferences that underlie the production of its prose, BRUTUS₁ generates the word 'automatic' instead of 'automaton.' The cause of the error, assume, is either a fluke low-level hardware error or a bug introduced by Ferrucci when programming. And suppose for the sake of argument that as serendipity would have it, the former word fits the context, and therefore a "new" story is produced. Would we want to credit BRUTUS₁ with having *originated* a new story? Of course not.

1.5   Is BRUTUS **Creative After All?**

We cheerfully conceded earlier that BRUTUS₁ *appears* to be creative, but isn't really. It's interesting to note, however, that perhaps the most sophisticated account of creativity in the literature seems to imply that BRUTUS₁ *is* creative. This account is given by none other than Margaret Boden [18]. In this section we analyze and charitably reconstruct this account, and consider as well a prominent psychometric approach to creativity due to E. Paul Torrance.

1.5.1   BRUTUS **and Bodenesque Creativity**

Boden begins by rejecting the view that creativity merely consists in combining, in novel fashion, old ideas. As she puts it: "The inadequacy of the combination-theory lies in the fact that many creative ideas ... concern novel ideas which not only *did* not happen before, but which — in a sense that must be made clear — *could* not have happened before" ([18], p. 53). In preparation for clarifying this mysterious "could not," Boden distinguishes between two senses of creativity:

> One is psychological (let us call it P-creativity), the other historical (H-creativity). An idea is P-creative if the individual person (or robot) in whose mind it arises could not have had it before; it does not matter how many times other people (or other androids) have already had the same idea. By contrast, an idea is H-creative if it is P-creative *and* no one else — whether person or robot — has ever had it before. ([18], p. 53)

Boden's first step toward clarifying her "could not" phrase is to point to an example of behavior that *fails* to be P-creative, namely, our ability to generate novel sentences. Here's one such sentence: "Ferrucci likes to sniggle in Lyngdal." (This means that Dave likes to catch eels in Lyngdal, a small town on the southern coast of Norway, Selmer's ancestral home. The sentence is false — but true if 'Ferrucci' is supplanted with 'Bringsjord.') The ability to generate novel sentences is traditionally formalized in terms of formal grammars, but the format can instead be a logic-based one related to capacities possessed by BRUTUS$_1$, that is, the ability can easily be redescribed in such a way that it's clearly enjoyed by a theorem prover. For example, suppose that Φ is some sizable collection of first-order formulas. Then there is some formula ϕ which can be derived from Φ (written $\Phi \vdash \phi$) for the first time; and the derivation is trivial. Indeed, BRUTUS$_1$ has this ability. As Boden rightly says, "Any native speaker, and any robot too, could produce novel sentences using the relevant grammar" ([18], p. 54).

What then about real cases of P-creativity? Boden informs us that in order for an idea ϕ to count as genuinely P-creative there must be in the picture a set of "generative principles" or a "conceptual space" from which it is impossible to obtain ϕ. Creativity then consists in changing the conceptual space and generating from the result some creative output ϕ. Boden gives as examples Schoenberg's dropping of the home-key constraint to create the space of atonal music, and the dropping of Euclid's fifth axiom in order to produce results in non-Euclidean geometry. Anchored by (Boden-sanctioned, given the Euclidean example) reference to deduction in ordinary first-order logic, the following is a sharpening of Boden's account of P-creativity:

Def$_C$ 1 Agent s is P-creative with respect to ϕ at t if and only if there is a time t' prior to t and knowledge-bases Φ_s and Φ'_s such that

  1 $\Phi_s \nvdash \phi$ at t';

  3 $\Phi'_s \vdash \phi$ at t, where s changes Φ_s to Φ'_s at some time t'' later than t' but not later than t.

This account is clearly unacceptable. This is so because there are cases where the change from Φ_s to Φ'_s consists in simply adding information that is the product of passive learning. Suppose that Smith knows only that the cat is on the mat; from this he certainly cannot deduce that the cat wants to come in. However, if he knows not only that the cat is on the mat, but also, courtesy of Jones telling him, that when the cat is on the mat it wants to come in, Smith can deduce that the cat wants to enter. But could anything P-creative be going on here? Of course not. Boden must surely intend that s changes Φ_s to Φ'_s (see clause 3) in some "significant" way, in some way that goes beyond "mere" addition. For that matter, Boden probably has in mind a change that goes beyond simple deduction: She probably would require more than that Φ_s is changed to Φ'_s by deducing things from Φ_s in first-order logic and adding them to yield Φ'_s.[12] So let's try:

Def$_C$ 2 Agent s is P-creative with respect to ϕ at t if and only if there is a time t' prior to t, a time t'' later than t' but not later than t, and knowledge-bases Φ_s and Φ'_s such that

1 $\Phi_s \not\vdash \phi$ at t';

2 s transforms Φ_s to Φ'_s at t'' via some operation $\mathcal{O}$ that goes beyond both passive learning and is such that $\Phi \not\vdash \mathcal{O}(\Phi)$;

3' $\Phi'_s \vdash \phi$ at t.

Unfortunately, this new proposal is still problematic. Def$_C$ 2 implies that BRUTUS$_1$ is P-creative, for the following reason. BRUTUS$_1$ "knows" certain things, things represented in first-order logic. (We have a look at these things in Chapter 6.) Let us denote the set of things BRUTUS$_1$ knows at t' by Θ. To flesh things out a bit, suppose that Θ is exhausted by first-order formalizations of the following propositions (if ψ refers to the proposition in English, let $[\psi]$ refer to the first-order representation).[13]

(6) Selmer likes Dave.

---

[12]There is a potential problem with this requirement: it would seem to imply that an incredible proof entirely within first-order logic might not signify true P-creativity. (Gödel's famous incompleteness theorems can be encoded and proved in first-order logic: [189].) Many will balk at this implication. We happen to find it palatable for reasons that needn't detain us.

[13]First-order logic is explained in some detail in Chapter 2. Such details aren't essential in this chapter. It is enough to know that sentences like 'Selmer likes Dave' can be mapped easily to expressions in first-order logic: this sentence becomes Lsd, where L is a two-place predicate for 'likes,' and s and d are constants denoting Selmer and Dave, respectively. For another example, $[(12)] = \forall x \forall y (\neg Lxy \rightarrow Bxy)$.

(7) Selmer likes Ed.

(8) Selmer likes Po.

(9) Ed likes Po.

(10) Ed likes Selmer.

(11) Ed likes Dave.

(12) For all x and for all y: if it's not the case that x likes y, then x betrays y.

Now consider the proposition (13) that Dave betrays Selmer. Clearly, at t' BRUTUS$_1$ cannot derive [(13)] from Φ. But now suppose that BRUTUS$_1$, at t'', a time after t', augments Θ by adding to it negations of those quantifier-free formulas that cannot be derived from Θ (where only the predicates and names in Φ are admissible); let the augmentation be denoted by Θ'. (Such an augmentation — sometimes called the **closed world assumption** — follows a scheme that goes beyond inferencing in standard first-order logic.) Since [(14)], the formalization of 'Dave likes Selmer,' cannot be deduced from Θ, $\neg[(14)] \in \Theta'$. Now suppose that BRUTUS$_1$ engages in a bit of standard theorem proving at t, a time after t''. Specifically, BRUTUS$_1$ at t demonstrates that

$$\Theta' \vdash [\text{Dave betrays Selmer}].$$

It follows that BRUTUS$_1$, according to Def$_C$ 2 (which as we've seen is based on Boden's approach), is P-creative. From this result, in turn, it follows that this definition is defective, because BRUTUS$_1$, though perhaps an impressive software agent in the AIish sense,[14] is not genuinely creative.

Can the *spirit* of Boden's account be saved? Perhaps. The obvious move to make on her behalf is to require that "changing a conceptual space" be even more radical than any of the activity just described. Specifically, the $\mathcal{O}$ operator should be even more exotic.

There are ways, perhaps, of finding the appropriate exotica. Consider again Boden's own mathematical example, the dropping of Euclid's fifth axiom, and the cultivation of consequences therefrom in mathematics and physics. While it's true that the axiom itself can

---

[14] In AI any function from percepts to behavior counts as an agent. See [201] for details.

be formalized in first-order logic, a proof that this axiom is independent of the others is *not* something that can be accomplished in first-order logic. To prove that ϕ cannot be proved from Φ one must do a *meta*-proof: One must prove that (the members of) Φ can be true while ϕ is false. One way to do this is to devise a world in which all the propositions in Φ hold, but ϕ does not. Proofs of this sort,[15] and in general proofs given by professional mathematicians, are not necessarily all representable in first-order logic. This suggests a general way to interpret Boden's stipulation that, at least at some point, P-creating something must be literally impossible: place, in clause 2, stricter prohibitions on $\mathcal{O}$.

More specifically, let's assume that provability in the logical system known as first-order logic is indicated by a subscript on $\vdash$. For example, we know that from the facts (15) 'All men are mortal' and (16) 'Socrates is a man' we can deduce in first-order logic that (17) 'Socrates is mortal.' So we could write

$$\{[(15)], [(16)]\} \vdash_1 [(17)].$$

Let us allow ourselves a subscript on $\vdash$ for the closed world assumption, and for various other techniques. If we pretend that these techniques can be ordered in a way that corresponds to the naturals, so that the reasoning in question gets more and more complicated as the subscripts increase, then clause 2 could be changed to

$2'$ s transforms Φ_s to Φ'_s at t'' via some operation $\mathcal{O}$ that goes beyond both passive learning and is such that $\Phi \nvdash_i \mathcal{O}(\Phi)$, where $i < m$.

The remaining mystery, then, would be how to instantiate i and m, and how to rigorously justify this instantiation. On some not implausible instantiations BRUTUS$_1$ turns out to be P-creative. From the engineering perspective, if BRUTUS$_1$ and his descendants turn out to be P-creative despite ever larger assignments to m, we will know we are successful.

---

[15]The wonderful Hyperproof system of Barwise and Etchemendy [8], used by Bringsjord to teach logic at Rensselaer, allows for such proofs. Hyperproof is appealed to in Chapter 2. Also, for some challenging Hyperproof problems, see

- www.rpi.edu/~brings/logarg.html

1.5.2 BRUTUS and Torrance's Definition of Creativity

Our predilection is to characterize creativity in logic-mathematical terms that could at least in principle lead to computational implementation. (And, by our lights, if such implementation is *not* possible, our best bet for coming to grasp this negative fact is still to try to bring creativity into mathematical focus.) Others (perhaps most) have some rather different orientations; certainly most, even those intending to "scientifically" investigate creativity, are considerably less formal, even when explicitly searching for a definition. Torrance is a perfect example.

A Strange Woman at the Window

Figure 1.2: The Kind of Picture Used for "Ask-And-Guess" Tasks on Torrance Tests. *The test-taker would be instructed to "ask all of the questions you would need to ask to know for sure what is happening" in this picture. The picture here, as perhaps some well-read readers may realize, is from (a nicely illustrated, condensed version of) David Copperfield, and is reprinted by permission from Waldman Publishing Corporation.*

E. Paul Torrance, more than anyone else, has probed the nature and concrete signs of creativity; he stands as a (perhaps *the*) seminal

figure in the area of cognition and creativity. Torrance's contribution
is bound up with testing for creativity; his is the dominant test for
creativity in children and adults: The Torrance Tests of Creative
Thinking.[16] This test comes in both a "visual" and a "verbal" form.
In the visual form, test takers are asked to draw pictures (often by
enriching existing sketches; see Figure 1.3); in the verbal form, test
takers are asked to write — creatively. For example, one of the
activities subjects engage in on the verbal test is the following.

Figure 1.3: The Kind of Picture Used for "Picture Completion" on
the Torrance Tests of Creative Thinking. *The test-taker would be given
the following instructions. "By adding lines to the incomplete figures on
this and the next page, you can sketch some interesting objects or pictures.
Again, try to think of some picture or object that no one else will think
of. Try to make it tell as complete and as interesting story as you can by
adding to and building up your first idea. Make up an interesting title for
each of your drawings and write it at the bottom of each block next to the
number of the figure." (Note that actual line drawings on the TTCT differ
slightly from the one shown here.)*

> Most people throw their tin cans away, but they have thou-
> sands of interesting and unusual uses. In the spaces below
> and on the next page, list as many of these interesting and
> unusual uses as you can think of. Do not limit yourself to any
> one size of can. You may use as many cans as you like. Do
> not limit yourself to the uses you have seen or heard about;
> think about as many possible new uses as you can. (From the
> verbal version of [233])

Another task might be to ask questions with respect to a picture
(e.g., Figure 1.2). While we greatly respect the work of Torrance,

---

[16]See [233] for the test itself. For reviews of the test, see [50], [227], [235].

and while, specifically, we applaud the demand for narrative that his tests place upon would-be creative minds, as tasks that get at the heart of creativity, we find activities like the tin can one profoundly unsatisfying. The problem — at least the *chief* problem — with such tasks is that they can be completed in such a way as to secure a high score *without any narrative thread being present*. To put the complaint barbarically, someone with silly logorrhea could produce a list in the tin can task that results in a very high score. ("Oh, easy, tin cans can be used to stretch out mouths when people try to swallow them, they can be used — when strung together — as conveyors for marbles dropped off of tall buildings; they can be used as cookie cutters (for *big* sugar cookies), for fake and weird eyeglasses, ...") Maybe it's not implausible to hold that BRUTUS₁ lays a better claim to being creative than someone who excels at spouting peculiar cases of tin can deployment: BRUTUS₁ yields narrative as well, but, on the strength of the structures we have installed for him, *integrated* narrative.[17]

But we have digressed; the real point under discussion is the issue of definition. What sorts of definition does Torrance offer? He offers two; here, first, is his "research definition":

> [Creative thinking] is the process of sensing difficulties, problems, gaps in information, missing elements, something askew; making guesses and formulating hypotheses about these deficiencies; evaluating and testing these guesses and hypotheses; possibly revising and retesting them; and finally communicating the results. ([232], p. 47)

By this definition, the robots who compete yearly at the annual meeting of the American Association of Artificial Intelligence would be counted as creative. This observation isn't meant to be a *reductio* against Torrance's definition. The point, put another way, is simply that Torrance's research definition describes a phenomenon that's a *lot* weaker than P-creativity. We are aiming for an intelligent agent smart enough to earn the title of 'P-creative' from Boden. Agents

---

[17]Could a reliable test for creativity that calls for integrated narrative be devised and deployed? What would such a test look like? These are questions we are seeking to answer, with help from a number of other researchers. Our current best bet for such a test is based on S^3G, the short short story game, which was presented earlier. See [25].

smart enough to qualify as creative on Torrance's definition already walk (roll?) among us.

Torrance offers an "artistic definition" as well — or perhaps we should say that he offers a series of such definitions, where each member in the series is an intuitive diagram. For example, one diagram shows a shovel throwing dirt out of a deep hole, with the caption "Creativity is Digging Deeper." While such pictures, we agree, are marvelously suggestive, they too fail to serve our purposes well: Again, we seek precise definitions amenable to outright (logic-based) formalization and implementation. It's hard to know, as logicist AIniks and software engineers, what to make of intuitive pictures.

1.5.3 BRUTUS and Hofstadter's Copycat

Douglas Hofstadter, as many readers know, has thought a lot about creativity, and has built systems in order to explore and validate the result of that thought. How does his work relate to BRUTUS and BRUTUS$_1$? *Does* it relate to BRUTUS and BRUTUS$_1$? Well, Hofstadter doesn't seem to have grappled much with the literary realm. In the Epilogue to his *Fluid Concepts and Creative Analogies* [111] Hofstadter — as he puts it — "goes on the warpath" in evaluating systems purported by others to be creative, and he does touch upon something literary there: the program Racter, with which he his mightily unimpressed.[18] But this is about it when it comes to

---

[18]Racter is the "author" of *The Policeman's Beard is Half Constructed* [190]. Here is an excerpt from that book:

> "War," chanted Benton, "war strangely is happiness to Diane." He was expectant but he speedily started to cry again. "Assault also is her happiness." Coldly they began to enrage and revile each other during the time that they hungrily swallowed their chicken. Suddenly Lisa sang of her desire for Diane. She crooned quickly. Her singing was inciting to Benton. He wished to assassinate her yet he sang, "Lisa, chant your valuable and interesting awareness." Lisa speedily replied. She desired possessing her own consciousness. "Benton," she spoke, "you cry that war and assault are a joy to Diane, but your consciousness is a tragedy as is your infatuation. My spirit cleverly recognizes the critical dreams of Benton. That is my pleasure." Benton saw Lisa, then began to revile her. He yodeled that Lisa possessed an infatuation for Diane, that her spirit was nervous, that she could thoughtfully murder her and she would de-

Hofstadter on literary creativity. So what sort of creativity does Hofstadter focus on? And what are the relevant systems? One representative system is Copycat, described at length in [111]. Copycat is supposed to solve problems like the following two by coming up with "creative analogies."

Problem 1 Suppose the letter-string *abc* were changed to *abd*; how would you change the letter-string *ijk* in "the same way"?

Problem 2 Suppose the letter-string *aabc* were changed to *aabd*; how would you change the letter-string *ijkk* in "the same way"?

Copycat settles in on *ijl* as an answer for Problem 1, and in the process "considers" *ijd* and *ijj*. For Problem 2, the program arrives at *ijll*, and "considers" *ijkl, jjkk, hjkk, jkkk, ijkd, ijdd, ijkk*, and *djkk*. Are these good answers? Are they creative? Hofstadter answers "Yes" to both questions. But he seems not to notice that he answers in this way only because Copycat has been designed to mirror the answers he (and many other humans) would be inclined to give, much as BRUTUS₁ is designed to produce the kind of "output" that human authors yield. Copycat gives the kind of answers it does because rules like "Replace the rightmost letter with its successor" are employed. But what recommends these rules, rather than others which Copycat has no "awareness" of? In the case of BRUTUS₁, the "answers" it gives (stories) are provided because there are clear and invariant attributes that good answers must have. (Recall the seven magic desiderata presented in the Preface.) These attributes can be

---

terminedly know nothing. Lisa briskly spoke that Benton possessed a contract, an affair, and a story of that affair would give happiness to Diane. They chanted sloppily for months. At all events I quickly will stop chanting now.

Hofstadter is unimpressed with passages like this because apparently they result from the program stringing words together in accordance with low-level linguistic constraints; the program has no notion of what it's doing. (Why can't we simply say, following Searle, that Racter fails to *understand* narrative and the concepts that drive it?) Humans simply cull from Racter's output passages that these humans can read meaning into. From the engineering standpoint, Racter is profoundly unhelpful because no architecture is provided. In our work, by comparison, the architecture (see Chapter 6) is everything, and results from sustained theorizing (see Chapters 1–5). This is as good a place as any to voice our suspicion that Racter is configured to generate words that are generally interesting to humans — words having to do with murder, hatred, etc. In connection with this, see Chapter 5.

extracted from good stories written through the centuries. Copycat, by contrast, flounders in a thoroughly ad hoc world.

As evidence for the capricious nature of Copycat's answers, consider the fact that the answers one of us gave, after seeing these problems for the very first time, were *ijj* and *ijkj*. (Notice that the second of these isn't even "considered" by Copycat.) The rule that produced these answers was one based on rhyming. In *abc*, the second and third letters rhyme. When this string is replaced with *abd*, this rhyme is preserved. In the string *ijk*, the second and third letters rhyme. To follow the rule in question, *k* must be replaced with a different letter that rhymes with *j*, the second letter. The only possibility is *j*; hence *ijj* is produced. The same rule, for obvious reasons, yields *ijkj*. What puzzles us how the idiosyncratic microdomain of Copycat (strings of letters, and replacements thereof) and idiosyncratic rules prescribing certain replacements are supposed to together constitute a "model of thinking" ([111], p. 483). This is where the creators of BRUTUS and Copycat part ways. BRUTUS, as we have said, is engineered on the strength of looking carefully at human creativity, but he is *not* designed to capture human creativity: He is designed to produce outward signs of creativity. Copycat, on the other hand, is designed by Hofstadter to capture human thinking, despite the plain facts that most people go a lifetime without pondering letter-string replacement problems, and that those who do ponder these problems invoke rules that are wholly arbitrary.

The other peculiar thing about Copycat is that it would seem to be primitive, from the standpoint of theorem proving. More specifically, it would seem that the rules of letter-string replacement to which Hofstadter is drawn can be effortlessly expressed as formulas in first-order logic. For example, let l be a function mapping character triples (c_1, c_2, c_3) into letter-strings, so that $l(a, b, c)$ is *abc*. Now let s be the successor function for the 26 lower-case letters $\{a, b, c, \ldots, z\}$. Then here is a rule for the replacement function r:

$$\forall x \forall y \forall z (r(l(x, y, z)) = l(x, y, s(z))).$$

It is easy to capture letter-replacement with rules like this, and to assign weights to these rules. (It can be done with OTTER, a theorem prover we introduce later.) Producing a solution would then consist in the production of proofs after starting strings (e.g., *ijk* in Problem 1) are given as additional input to the system.

It will do no good for Hofstadter to complain that a version of Copycat based on a theorem-proving approach, $Copycat^{TP}$, though perhaps capable of producing the same behavior as Copycat, isn't true to human thinking. There are two reasons for this. One is that some people (e.g., Selmer) just will take a theorem-proving approach to the relevant problems. The second reason is more interesting. Hofstadter tells us that he embraces "a truly deep" ([111], p. 491) Turing Test as a way to gauge whether or not computational systems are really thinking. In a truly deep Turing Test the interrogator is very clever, and therefore knows how to scrutinize the output produced by the system in order to ascertain whether genuine thought is taking place. Well, it should be easy enough to build $Copycat^{TP}$ so that it produces output "good enough" to satisfy such an interrogator.

Finally, this issue can be broadened. Our aim is to have $BRUTUS_n$ pass a "deep" Turing Test for story generation, and our method for trying to reach this goal is to engineer a system capable of producing the right sort of output. Our method is *not* Hofstadter's: that of trying to build an artificial mind. So the question is: Why can't we eventually succeed in engineering a system that outputs the right sort of output even though this system in no sense has a mind, or is conscious, or genuinely thinks? We would be most interested in receiving an answer.[19]

1.6 Story Generators as Theorem Provers

Though our aim is to take appreciable steps toward an *autonomous* literarily creative agent, our designs and systems may well be usable, after minor modification, as intelligent *assistants*. In fact, we envision a time when creative writers will stand to such systems and stories as mathematicians increasingly stand today to theorem-provers

---

[19]Here is an example of the kind of scrutiny Hofstadter tells us would be applied to linguistic output in a "deep" Turing Test:

> looking at *word frequencies* (e.g., is "the" the most common word? is "time" the most common noun? are some low-frequency words used unnaturally often? does suspicion seem to be aroused in the distal "mind" if low-frequency words are used with a high frequency in the input questions?

A truly solid story generator, $BRUTUS_n$, according to our approach, would be engineered with such questions as these driving its design!

and proofs.[20] It's therefore interesting to note that BRUTUS₁ happens to be based on theorem-proving, as is clear from the discussion of BRUTUS₁'s anatomy in Chapter 6.

1.7   Why We're Thoroughgoing Logicists

We conclude this chapter by explaining something alert readers will doubtless have already have noted: namely, that our approach is a thoroughly logic-based one: Neural nets and dynamical systems[21] and the like are nowhere to be found in this volume. As you'll soon see, the explanation we offer for our logicist approach is based on two stories, one involving Tchaikovsky, and the other involving Sherlock

---

[20] Along these lines, see the recent cracking of the Robbins Problem by the EQP theorem-prover [130]. EQP is a variant of OTTER, which Art Quaife has employed as an assistant in order to (e.g.) prove Gödel's incompleteness theorems; see [189] for details on these and other impressive feats. (We use OTTER in our research, and will be introducing readers to it in Chapter 2.) Quaife apparently believes that sooner or later *autonomous* theorem-provers will arrive. Quaife's ultimate aim is to have future theorem-provers enable humans to live forever by perfecting the science and engineering of cryonic suspension (!):

> How will we re-animate patients frozen by the "unperfected" techniques of today? Cloning of replacement organs, or even of a whole body, cannot be the full answer, since we need to recover the central nervous system — particularly the brain — relatively intact. Consider the possibility of re-animating a frozen patient by perfusing the body with trillions of microscopic cell repair machines, as long envisioned by some cryonicists and recently elaborated by Eric Drexler in *Engines of Creation*. These machines will enter the cells, diagnose injury, formulate plans for repair, and carry out the plans. They will have to be *smart!* Ideally each machine would have at least the knowledge and intelligence of a Ph.D. in microbiology — or be in rapid communication with larger control machines with such abilities. Central to any such intelligence is the ability to *reason* from observations and known general laws to specific conclusions. Center stage for the automated reasoning system! ([189], p. iii)

Our story generation work is intended to enable some rather less exotic ends. (And even the use to which one of us (Bringsjord) puts OTTER is by comparison rather humble: viz., as the core engine for intelligent tutoring systems in the area of elementary logic.)

[21] For an excellent treatment of the view that human cognition is best studied and modeled without the sort of symbolic representation schemes that compose BRUTUS₁'s mind, see [57].

Holmes.

1.7.1 A Two-Horse Race?

Part of AI lore is John McCarthy's equestrian metaphor: AI split atop the backs of two racing horses, one of the connectionist breed, the other of the logicist breed. This view presupposes that the two animals are galloping down the same track. But are they? Not by our lights. The connectionist horse, no matter how fast it reaches the finish line, will lose — because its course, unlike its rival's, has next to nothing to do with scientific progress on the question of how we manage to do what we do. Let us explain.[22]

1.7.2 The Music Box and ... Tchaikovsky

Composers, including the great Tchaikovsky, produce music.

So do music boxes. When we look inside such a device, we find a drum with a pattern of bumps scattered about its surface. We also find a set of metal prongs lined up side-by-side, perfectly aligned, each prong positioned less than one bump away from the surface of the drum. As the drum turns, bumps hit prongs, prongs resonate, and music is made. The "bump-and-prong engineer," let us assume, is able to design and build some remarkable music boxes.

Many would also say that *brains* produce music. ("What unprecedented forces conspired to produce, in Mozart's case, that greatest of all musical brains?" This is a query most find quite meaningful.) If we had explored Tchaikovsky's brain as he formed his sixth symphony, we would have found a wondrous webwork of neurons, spewing chemicals across synapses and pulsing with electricity. Let's suppose that the "brain engineer," who proudly weaves together networks a good deal more "wet" than the materials molded by his bump-and-prong friend, is able to design and build some remarkable music-making brains.

Now let's imagine a little contest between the bump-and-prong engineer, the brain engineer, and Tchaikovsky himself. After each searches in solitude for the musical muse, our trio is reunited and brought before a learned audience assembled to judge their creations

---

[22]Our explanation, coming as it does in the form of gedanken-experiments, is intended to be a colorful encapsulation of a formal treatment of AI's connectionist–logicist clash, part of which one of us has provided elsewhere [41].

(the two engineers to be judged by the output of their artifacts). In a stunning coincidence, the box, the brain, and the composer present the very same work: Tchaikovsky's Sixth. And in each case, the reaction is the same: The audience jeers — just as it did when this symphony debuted in St. Petersburg on October 28, 1893.

The two engineers are utterly deflated, and have no answer for those hard-nosed critics who snidely ask how it could be that all their "inspired" sequestration could have been for naught. Not so Tchaikovsky. He replies:

> The idea came to me for a new symphony, this time with a program, but a program that must remain secret. Let those who can, guess it. The work is entitled "A Program Symphony – No. 6". I have shed tears while composing it in my mind ... I have put my entire soul into this work ... I love it as I have never before loved any of my musical offspring ... I have never felt such satisfaction, such pride, such happiness, as in the knowledge that I myself am truly the creator of this beautiful work. ([229], p.2)

No. 6 is replayed. "What is the secret!?" comes the collective cry. Tchaikovsky relents: "In my sixth are hid all the raw emotions of life and death. Listen!" Tchaikovsky retitles his work *The Pathétique*; the music is played yet again. And this time audiences exult and weep, overwhelmed by the beauty of the secret now grasped.[23]

1.7.3 Why COG Is Doomed

Suppose now that the bump-and-prong and brain engineers have married. Working with "real flesh" neural networks turned out to be too untidy, and besides, their essential structure can be preserved in *artificial* neural networks. So the connectionist is born. His central device is synthetic, yes, but also brain-like; his strategy is evolution; his home base is MIT; and his triumph is to be not a symphony, but rather a robot: COG.[24]

---

[23]The series of events just related speaks directly to the question of what might be missing in the EMI (pronounced "emmy") system [117], which generates musical compositions in the style of a given composer. EMI cannot elevate a composition by sharing its meaning with human listeners.

[24]Of course, any number of "intelligence without representation and reasoning" projects could stand in for COG in our fable. Clark [57] provides a number of examples.

COG's creators, as cognoscenti will know, are a team led by Rodney Brooks and Lynn Andrea Stein, another member of which is Daniel Dennett, whose eloquent synopsis [68] of the project boldly proclaims that COG is to be a *humanoid* robot — capable of seeing and recognizing objects in its environment (including its "mothers") and of performing appropriate (physical) actions in response, all at a level that will encourage humans interacting with COG to ascribe to it such profound properties as consciousness.

COG, as its creators proudly admit, is completely devoid of a logicist soul: not a shred of BRUTUS-like knowledge representation and reasoning to be found under its hood — no *modus ponens*, no *modus tollens*, and certainly no *reductio ad absurdum*. If COG is ever to reason in a fashion modelable by (say) first-order logic, such reasoning will need to emerge from the engine of evolution, not a knowledge-based injection. As Dennett says:

> How plausible is the hope that COG can retrace the steps of millions of years of evolution in a few months or years of laboratory exploration? Notice first that [the evolution of COG and its descendants] is a variety of Lamarckian inheritance that no organic lineage has been able to avail itself of. The acquired design innovations of COG-I can be immediately transferred to COG-II, a speed-up of evolution of tremendous, if incalculable, magnitude. Moreover, if you bear in mind that, unlike the natural case, there will be a team of overseers ready to make patches whenever obvious shortcomings reveal themselves, and to jog the systems out of ruts whenever they enter them, it is not so outrageous a hope, in our opinion. But then, we are all rather outrageous people. ([68], p. 140)

That COG's "parents" are outrageous is something we gladly accept; that they are good scientists is a somewhat less sturdy claim.

For suppose the year is 2019, and our connectionists have produced remarkable offspring — in the form of a robot (or android), SHER-COG (COG-n, for some $n \geq 1$), capable of the sort of behavior associated with Sherlock Holmes, and possessed of all the concomitant mental powers — deduction, abduction, introspection, and even, let's assume, full-fledged sentience.[25] Now consider per-

---

[25]Lest it be thought that the ratiocination of Sherlock Holmes is a phenomenon confined to the world of fiction, we direct readers to real-life detective deduction — like that used by Robert N. Anderson [253] to recently solve the 80-year-

haps Holmes' greatest triumph: solving the mystery surrounding the disappearance of the racehorse known as 'Silver Blaze' [78]. Suppose that SHER-COG is asked (by an analogue for Dr. Watson), after cracking this case, how it accomplished the feat. How can our robotic sleuth communicate an answer?

One thing that would surely fail to inform would be for SHER-COG to invite humans to examine its neural nets. In order to see this, you have only to imagine what it would be like to study these nets in action. How would information about the states of nodes and the weights on connections between them help you divine how SHER-COG deduced that the culprit in this mystery could not be a stranger to dogs on the farm that was Silver Blaze's home? The reasoning Watson strives to apprehend can be gleaned from neural nets about as easily as the bump-and-prong engineer can read Tchaikovsky's secret off the drum of a music box.

Of course, SHER-COG, like Tchaikovsky when revealing *The Pathétique*, could resort to introspection and natural language. It could proceed to explain its solution in (e.g.) English, in much the same way that Sherlock Holmes often explains things to the slower Dr. Watson. But this route concedes our point, for by it we end up once again invoking logicist AI in all its glory. This is so because in order to *really* understand what SHER-COG is telling us in English, to explain *scientifically* how it is he has done what he has done, it will be necessary to analyze this English formally; and the formal analysis will bring to bear the machinery of logical systems happily jettisoned by the connectionist.[26]

For example, to truly understand Holmes' explanation, conveyed to the nonplussed Watson, of how he solved the mystery of Silver Blaze, it would do no good to hear from a "modernized" Holmes: "My dear Watson, it's really quite elementary, for undergirding my relevant ratiocination was intense C-fiber activity in neocortical areas 17 and 21. Here, let me show you the PET scan." In order to move toward understanding of how Holmes saved the day yet again, one

---

old mystery of what caused the fire that destroyed Jack London's "Wolf House" in 1913. Wolf House was to be London's "manly" residence, a 15,000-square-foot structure composed of quarried volcanic rock and raw beams from ancient redwoods. The conflagration occurred just days before London was to move in, and though London vowed to rebuild, he died 3 years later with the house still in ruins.

[26]For a technical survey of these systems, see our [23].

must come to grasp the following chain of reasoning (which involves the famous clue about the "dog doing nothing in the night-time").

1. If the dog didn't bark, then the person responsible for lacing the meal with opium couldn't be a stranger.

2. The dog didn't bark.

3. The person responsible for lacing the meal with opium couldn't be a stranger (from 1 and 2).

4. Simpson was a stranger.

5. Simpson was not responsible (from 3 and 4).

At work here, of course, are none other than *modus ponens* and *modus tollens* (and standard quantifier rules), cornerstones of logicist AI, and cornerstones, in particular, of BRUTUS.[27] Absent these cornerstones, and the enlightening analysis they allow when brought to bear on what cognizers think and say, SHER-COG's success will be impenetrable, and will thus fail to advance our understanding of how detectives do what they do.

Since we desire not only to *build* literarily creative agents, but to *understand* them, our use of logic goes without saying. Please note, however, that we don't care what form the *underlying computation* takes. Think back to the formal accounts of creativity we discussed earlier in connection with Boden; and specifically suppose for exposition here that creativity consists in verifying $\Phi \vdash \phi$, that ϕ can be proved from Φ; and suppose we have set up a system to express this equation, to pose it as a query to be addressed by some computation. It's fine with us, absolutely fine, if this computation takes the form of neural networks in action. For this reason, in the end, we are in favor of AI saddling up just one *ecumenical* horse.

---

[27] For a more detailed analysis of the Silver Blaze story, see [40].

Chapter 2

Could a Machine Author Use Imagery?

In this chapter we present a case for the view that "robust" imagistic expertise, such as that routinely seen in human authors, can't be replicated by way of the machinery available to AI, whether of the connectionist or logicist variety.[1] After articulating this case, we share the engineering moves we made in response to it when devising the BRUTUS architecture and building BRUTUS₁, the first attempt at instantiating that architecture.

Focusing on imagistic representation and reasoning (R&R) isn't untimely: After years of dealing almost exclusively with rather primitive symbolic forms of knowledge R&R (KR&R), AI has come around to the view, defended in ancient times by Aristotle([2], trans.; [238]) and recently by Kosslyn ([131], [133], [134]) and others (e.g., [48],

---

[1]One of us has argued that not only imagistic, but also "robust" symbolic expertise, is beyond the reach of mere computationalism. For example, as Selmer has pointed out elsewhere ([29], [36], [40]), reasoning which by definition allows both formulas of infinite length and rules of inference with infinitely many premises (which is reasoning the mastery of which is needed for proving even elementary truths about, say, the logical system known as $\mathcal{L}_{\omega_1\omega}$ — reasoning which, in anyone's book, truly qualifies its owner as an expert symbolic reasoner) simply cannot be formalized via the state-of-the-art machinery (let alone weak off-the-shelf knowledge representation systems) employed by the brand of AI which prides itself on capturing the part of human cognition apparently based on formulas and inferencing thereon. For an up-to-date comprehensive look at this brand of AI, **logicist** AI, see our paper, "Logic and Artificial Intelligence: Divorced, Still Married, Separated ...?" [23].

[149], [94]), that KR&R need not, and indeed ought not, be restricted to symbolic, logical form. That AI has traditionally represented the objects of knowledge and belief in symbolic form is wholly uncontroversial. The clearest instance of this approach, and the one which, as a matter of fact, has dominated the field, is to imagine that a robot's knowledge is represented in first-order logic [96], [49] or an equivalent (e.g., frame-based systems, which BRUTUS₁ is partially built on; see Chapter 6), and that reasoning consists in deduction over that knowledge. Now, however, AI researchers are facing up to the fact that humans routinely represent and reason about information not only in symbolic form, but also in **imagistic** (or **diagrammatic** or **pictorial** — we harmlessly conflate these terms herein) form, and that this mode of R&R has considerable utility (e.g., see [48] for a remarkably long list of tasks which effectively tap pictorial R&R [PR&R]). AI's change of heart would seem to augur well for the field: It would seem to imply that not only tomorrow's robots, but today's expert systems, will soon possess and exploit the artificial counterpart to human imagistic R&R. However, over a decade ago, a number of thinkers confidently claimed that such R&R would be forever beyond a digital computer. For example, here's what Ned Block said on the matter:

> If the pictorialist view is right, then the human brain deploys representations (and processes operating over them) of a sort not found in digital computers (whose representations are paradigms of descriptional [= symbolic; S.B.] representations). So digital computers would not be able to process information in the manner of humans (though of course they might nonetheless be able to simulate human information processing). ([16], p. 4)

And, from Hubert and Stuart Dreyfus:

> [C]omputers, programmed as logic machines, cannot use images or any picture-like representations without transforming them into descriptions. ([79], p. 90)

If we assume that whatever R&R AI deploys must be implemented on a digital computer (or, put another way, must be implementable on a Turing machine), then if Block and the Dreyfuses and others are right, and if AI's turn from pure symbolism to symbolicism-infused-with-PR&R will be sustained, as certainly appears likely,[2] it follows that AI is embarking on a search for something as elusive as the fountain of youth. And, in fact, though the Block/Dreyfus position is now almost universally rejected, it does seem to *us* that Ponce de León and AI are indeed in lockstep. We defend this view with some new argumentation that takes account of work generally regarded to have forever silenced Block/Dreyfus worries. In particular, our argumentation confronts head on Kosslyn's [131] seminal attempt to position robust imagistic abilities firmly within a computational conception of the mind and brain. We conclude by considering ways to dodge our arguments in the attempt to build an agent capable of warranting the ascription "literarily creative."

2.1 The Imagery Debate's Contestants

Let's start with the admission that the Block/Dreyfus reasoning cited earlier is not invulnerable: it can, in fact, be attacked on at least three fronts. First, it's not at all clear what "imagistic R&R,' means. In what sense are mental images like pictures — given that, as everyone must agree, we don't literally find pictures in our heads? Second, absent a careful account of the concept, it's surely not obvious that digital computers, or Turing machines, can't handle imagistic R&R. Third, it's far from self-evident that "imagism" (or "pictorialism"), whatever it turns out to be, is *true*. Each of these avenues of attack has proponents. For example, a number of thinkers have taken the third avenue: they have claimed that pictorialism is false, that the only sort of representations humans use, at bottom, are symbolic, language-like ones (e.g., [71], [188]). This position has come to be known as **descriptionalism**. Of course, descriptionalism used as a weapon against the Block/Dreyfus argument might be massively counterproductive, since descriptionalism seems *itself* to imply that AI's turn toward a hybrid symbolicist-pictorialist

---

[2]As Kosslyn [131] recently observes, we appear to be in the middle of an explosion of research aimed at bestowing imagistic capabilities on computational systems (for example, [100], [172]). This work is over and above what might be called AI's "first go" at capturing imagistic ability in computational terms, dated pontifically by us at from the late 1970's to mid 1980's (an exemplar of which is plausibly regarded to be [94]).

approach is misguided — for on descriptionalism everything can be done, and perhaps done efficiently, by focusing exclusively on symbolic R&R. Other thinkers, pleased with AI's move toward hybrid R&R, have combined the first and second avenues of response to Block/Dreyfus worries: they have said that when pictorialism is clarified, it turns out that PR&R *can* be implemented on digital computers. For philosophers, the *locus classicus* of this rebuttal is perhaps Michael Tye's ([238], [239]) position that the computational correlates to our mental images are patterns of charged cells in arrays within digital computers, or something similar. For AI researchers, cognitive scientists, psychologists, and so on, the supreme hybrid view is championed by Steven Kosslyn, who in his recent monograph, *Image and Brain*, affirms and defends the view that human PR&R can be captured by appropriately configured neural nets. For people closer to the engineering side of AI and cognitive science (CogSci), there is an abundance of work which seems to vindicate the Kosslyn/Tye position by incarnating it in the form of some rather impressive computer programs (e.g., [149], [94]). Kosslyn himself, as we shall see, regards such systems to be confirmation of his theory. He also claims to find confirmation in neuroscientific research of a sort we examine later.

2.2   The Main Argument Against Computational Imagery

Here, without further ado, is the main argument in our Block/Dreyfus-resurrecting case; after presenting it, we explicate some of its central concepts.[3]

---

[3]Two points in connection with this argument:

1. TEMIs are temporally extended mental images. The concept is explained momentarily.

2. An excellent hands-on introduction to the state diagram take on Turing machines can be obtained via Barwise & Etchemendy's *Turing's World* [9], interactive software that comes with a manual serving as a brief introduction to computability theory. B&E follow Boolos & Jeffrey [21], a more detailed study.

Arg₁

(1) Expert imagistic R&R, which involves the creation, manipulation, and contemplation of TEMIs, can't be captured in traditional symbolic representation schemes.

(2) Any form of R&R that can be captured in neural nets can be captured in (e.g.) the state diagram scheme often used to specify Turing machines.

(3) The state diagram scheme often used to specify Turing machines is a traditional symbolic representation scheme.

∴ (4) Genuine expert imagistic R&R, which involves the creation, manipulation, and contemplation of TEMIs, can't be captured in neural nets.   (1), (2), (3)

(5) If expert imagistic R&R can neither be captured in neural nets nor in traditional symbolic representation schemes, it's expertise AI and CogSci can never replicate, and never fully understand scientifically.

∴ (6) Expert imagistic R&R is expertise AI and CogSci can never replicate, and never fully understand scientifically.   (4), (1), (5)

Arg₁ is obviously formally valid; that is, (4) follows from (1)–(3), and (6) follows from (4) and (5). This is easily verified by symbolizing the argument in first-order logic (where one quantifies over forms of R&R; we provide a review of first-order logic momentarily). Premise (5) merely reflects the uncontroversial view that AI and CogSci, fundamentally speaking, are exhausted by two different orientations, the logicist or symbolicist, and the connectionist. (Recall our discussion of "two horses in the race" in Chapter 1.) The former, as we noted earlier in the book, centers around traditional symbolic representation schemes (frames, state diagrams, logics, semantic networks, etc.), the latter around neural nets. Proposition (4) is an intermediate conclusion; (6) is the final one. This leaves (1), (2) and (3). But proposition (3) is unexceptionable: Turing machines (TMs) (and schemes reducible to them) are a traditional symbolic representation scheme.[4]

---

[4]In case you are unfamiliar with TMs, or forget what they are, here's some quick exposition: Put intuitively, TMs include a **two-way infinite tape** divided

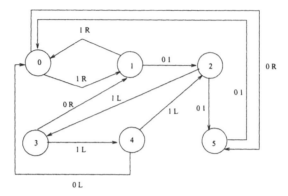

Figure 2.1: Gordon's 19 in 186.

So, everything boils down to (1) and (2). But (2) is a mathematical fact one of us (Selmer) has defended elsewhere at length in the context of AI and CogSci [41]. The basic idea behind this proposition is a chain which, to our surprise, sometimes comes as news to even some veteran AIniks, namely: neural nets can be rendered as cellular automata; cellular automata can be rendered as k-tape TMs; and k-tape TMs can be rendered as standard, one-tape TMs (and, of course, TMs can be identified with state diagrams of the appropriate sort). This is why we don't have in neural nets a class of system which exceeds TMs (or other equivalent formalisms, e.g., register machines) in fundamental information processing power.[5]

---

into squares, a **read/write head** for writing and erasing **symbols** (from some finite, fixed **alphabet**) on and off this tape, a **finite control unit** which at any step in a computation is in one particular state from among a finite number of possible states, and a set of **instructions** (= program) telling the machine what to do, depending upon what state it's in and what (if anything) is written on the square currently scanned by its head.

There are many readily understandable ways to capture the full set-theoretic description of TMs. One such method is the state diagram approach, which is used in Figure 2.1. This TM, dubbed "Gordon's 19 in 186," is designed to start on a 0–filled infinite tape and produce, after 186 steps, 19 1s. We suggest you hand simulate it now, and make sure you understand its behavior.

[5]Though connectionism and logicism are equivalent mathematically, and though as a result we find the clash between these camps to be a red herring [41], we agree with thinkers who find connectionist systems inadequate in the face of higher-level symbolic reasoning. Connectionist systems and techniques, we predict, will prove suitable for lower-level cognition — locomotion, percep-

So everything seems to hinge on (1). What is there to recommend this proposition? A lot, from where we stand. But of course for you, premise (1) is pretty much impenetrable! After all, you don't know what we mean by 'TEMI.'

2.3 Temporally Extended Mental Images

'TEMI' is an acronym abbreviating 'temporally extended mental image,' and such creatures are probably best introduced by way of a little contradistinguishing. (For more, see [36], [39].) Accordingly, let's take a quick look at the sort of representations traditionally employed in programs claimed to possess at least some degree of visual imagery capability. In order to take this look, however, we need to review the concept of a **logical system**. Toward this end, we begin with a brief review of one such system, namely **first-order logic**. This review will prove valuable not only in connection with imagery, but in connection with other issues as well. For example, our formalization of betrayal, presented in Chapter 4, is based in first-order logic.

2.3.1 First-Order Logic and Logical Systems

Modern first-order logic (denoted, hereafter, following tradition, by '$\mathcal{L}_I$') includes, first, an **alphabet** of **variables** $x, y, \ldots$, **constants** $c_1, c_2, \ldots$, n-ary **relation symbols** $R, G, \ldots$, **functors** $f_1, f_2, \ldots$, **quantifiers** $\exists, \forall$, and the familiar **truth-functional connectives** $(\neg, \vee, \wedge, \rightarrow, \leftrightarrow)$. Such an alphabet permits one to use standard **formation rules** (e.g., if ϕ and ψ are well-formed formulas [wffs], then $\phi \wedge \psi$ is a wff as well) to build "atomic" formulas, and then more complicated "molecular" formulas. Sets of these formulas (say Φ), given certain **rules of inference** (e.g., *modus ponens*: from ϕ and $\phi \rightarrow \psi$ infer to ψ), can lead to individual formulas (say ϕ). Such a situation is expressed by meta-expressions like $\Phi \vdash \phi$. First-order

---

tion, and the like, while logicist systems and techniques will prove suitable for at least some aspects of higher-level cognition, such as that required in mathematics, and detective work (recall our discussion of Sherlock Holmes in Chapter 1). Of course, by our lights, neither camp will ever deal adequately with any number of challenges, such as the one — capturing the "meaning" of a TEMI — described in this chapter. For a detailed discussion of logicist and connectionist AI, see our [23].

logic includes a semantic side which systematically provides meaning for formulas involved. In first-order logic, formulas are said to be true (or false) on an **interpretation**, often written as $\mathcal{I} \models \phi$. (This is often read, "$\mathcal{I}$ satisfies ϕ," or "$\mathcal{I}$ models (or is a model of) ϕ.") For example, the formula $\forall x \exists y Gyx$ might mean, on the standard interpretation $\mathcal{R}$ for arithmetic, that for every natural number n, there is a natural number m such that $m > n$. In this case, the domain of $\mathcal{R}$ is $\mathbf{N}$, the natural numbers, and G is the binary relation $> \subset \mathbf{N} \times \mathbf{N}$, i.e., $>$ is a set of ordered pairs (i, j) where $i, j \in \mathbf{N}$ and i is greater than j. Some formulas of $\mathcal{L}_I$ are **valid**, in the sense that they are true on *all* interpretations. For example, any formula δ of the form $\forall x(\phi \land \psi) \rightarrow (\forall x \phi) \land (\forall x \psi)$ is valid; such a fact is customarily written $\models \delta$. A formula that is true on at least one interpretation is **satisfiable**. For example, the formula

$$\forall x \exists y Gyx$$

is satisfiable.

In order to concretize things a bit, consider an expert system designed to play the role of a guidance counselor in advising a high school student about which colleges to apply to. Suppose that we want a rule in such a system which says "If a student has low SATs, and a low GPA, then none of the top 25 national universities ought to be applied to by this student." Assume that we have the following interpreted predicates: Sx iff x is a student, $L_s x$ for x has low SATs, $L_g x$ for x has a low GPA, Tx for x is a top 25 national university, Axy for x ought to apply to y. Then the rule in question, in first-order logic, becomes

$$\forall x \forall y[(Sx \land L_s x \land L_g x \land Ty) \rightarrow \neg Axy].$$

Let's suppose, in addition, that Steve is a student denoted by the constant s in the system, and that he, alas, has low SATs and a low GPA. Assume also that v is a constant denoting Vanderbilt University (which happens to have been rated at times in the past as a top 25 national university according to *U.S. News & World Report*'s annual rankings). These facts are represented in the system by

$$Ss \land L_s s \land L_g s$$

and

$$Tv.$$

Let's label these three facts, in the order in which they were presented, (1), (2), and (3). Our expert system, based as it is on first-order logic, can verify

$$\{(1), (2), (3)\} \vdash \neg Asv,$$

that is, it can deduce that Steve ought not to apply to Vanderbilt.

It is easy enough to generalize from this account to the broader concept of a **logical system**.[6] A logical system includes an **alphabet** (the symbols from which well-formed formulas are to be built), a **grammar** specifying how wffs are to be generated, a **semantic relation**, a binary relation (e.g., $\models$ as presented in the previous paragraph) holding between interpretations (or other structures designed to formally model aspects of "reality") and formulas, and a **proof theory** that makes precise how reasoning in the system is to proceed.

It is also usually important that a logical system have associated with it a **metatheory**, which would address questions such as whether the system in question is sound, complete, decidable, and so on.[7] Such metaproperties are determined by bringing mathematical tools to bear on the system in question.

To anchor things a bit further, consider first a system even simpler than first-order logic, viz., the propositional calculus, $\mathcal{L}_{PC}$, which will be familiar to many readers. $\mathcal{L}_{PC}$ has for an alphabet propositional variables $p_1, p_2, \ldots$ and the truth-functional connectives; its grammar is the grammar of $\mathcal{L}_I$ without rules covering the quantifiers; its semantics are based on truth-tables (so that, e.g., $\models \phi$ holds iff ϕ is true on every truth value assignment in an exhaustive truth table for ϕ); and the proof theory of $\mathcal{L}_{PC}$ can be given by familiar natural deduction rules (e.g., *modus ponens*). Another logical system, this one "beyond" $\mathcal{L}_I$, is second-order logic, $\mathcal{L}_{II}$, which

---

[6]Our account of **logical system** is somewhat broader than the standard account which figures in (say) Lindström's Theorems. For the narrower account, as well as a nice presentation of these theorems, see [82]. It's perhaps worth pointing out that **semiotic systems** may be justifiably regarded to be generalizations of logical systems. For a brief introduction to semiotic systems in the context of AI, see [89].

[7]A logical system is sound provided that inferences in it never allow false propositions to be derived from true ones. A system is complete exactly when all true propositions (expressed from the system's underlying alphabet and grammar) can be proved. A system is decidable just in case the answer to the question "Can a computer decide whether or not a formula is a theorem of the system?" is an affirmative one. First-order logic, $\mathcal{L}_I$, is sound and complete, but not decidable. The simpler system known as the propositional calculus ($\mathcal{L}_{PC}$), discussed next, is sound, complete, *and* decidable.

adds **relation variables** $X, Y, Z, \ldots$ to the alphabet of $\mathcal{L}_I$, which in turn allows (via the associated grammar) for formulas expressing such things as Leibniz's Law (two things are identical iff they have precisely the same properties):

$$\forall x \forall y (x = y \leftrightarrow \forall X (Xx \leftrightarrow Xy)).$$

2.3.2   OTTER: Test-Bed for Logicist Story Generation

Our characterization of first-order logic has been given in the abstract, but it can be easily implemented courtesy of a standard theorem-prover. The theorem-prover we find useful for testing a number of the components in BRUTUS is OTTER,[8] and we now introduce readers to this system. As will be recalled from the Preface, we approach story generation through logic; in more specific terms, this means that we conceive of story generation as theorem proving. In Chapter 4 we present a series of definitions designed to capture the literary theme of betrayal; each definition can be profitably implemented in OTTER. (We will show one of these implementations.) And in Chapter 6 we explain that BRUTUS₁ is based in the particular brand of theorem proving afforded by Prolog.)

Consider the following simple "natural deduction" style proof in the propositional calculus of the fact that from a conditional $p \rightarrow q$ one can derive $\neg q \rightarrow \neg p$ (this move is known as contraposition or transposition).

1. $p \rightarrow q$ (given)

2. $\neg q$ (assumption)

3. $\neg p$ (*modus tollens*, lines 1 and 2)

4. $\neg q \rightarrow \neg p$ (lines 2-3, conditional proof)

---

[8]The most recent book on OTTER, with which one of us has had considerable classroom success, is [249]. This book is a bit advanced for students not previously exposed to theorem-proving. A good book to start with is [250]. OTTER can be obtained without charge and unrestricted from

    http://www-unix.mcs.anl.gov/AR/otter/

This is the sort of simple proof that students of logic learn at the outset of their education. Notice the use of three rules in this little proof: assumption, *modus tollens*, and conditional proof. Normally, many such rules are added to the arsenal of the human who learns to do proofs in first-order logic. By contrast, OTTER really only has, at bottom, one rule: resolution. Here is an actual OTTER input file for the problem of finding a proof of transposition:

```
% This propositional logic problem, by the way, was the
% "most difficult" (!) theorem proved by the original
% Logic Theorist of 1957.

set(auto).
formula_list(usable).
-((p -> q) <-> (-q -> -p)).
end_of_list.
```

The lines that begin with the character % are comments (and they may well reveal how far theorem proving has come in just over four decades!). The line set(auto). simply tells OTTER to attack the problem "autonomously" as it sees fit, without using any particular strategies. There then follows a list flanked top and bottom by formula_list(usable). and end_of_list; in this case the list only has one element, viz., -((p -> q) <-> (-q -> -p)).[9] This is the negation of the theorem to be proved. The theorem is negated because if OTTER can derive a contradiction from this negation conjoined with consistent information given it, it will follow by indirect proof that transposition is valid. OTTER does indeed find such a proof instantaneously; here is the actual output.

```
---------------- PROOF ----------------
1 [] -p|q.
2 [] -q.
3 [] p.
4 [hyper,3,1] q.
5 [binary,4.1,2.1] $F.
----------- end of proof -----------
```

Lines 1, 2, and 3 represent the result of reformulating the formula

$$-((p -> q) <-> (-q -> -p))$$

---

[9]Notice that since OTTER takes input from an ordinary keyboard, the negation symbol ¬ becomes -, → becomes ->, ∨ becomes |, etc.

in clausal form. The formula $-(($p -> q$)$ <-> $($-q -> -p$))$ is therefore equivalent to the conjunction of -p|q, -q, and p. (A truth table will reveal that this conjuction is true and false under exactly the same truth-value assignments to p and q as $-(($p -> q$)$ <-> $($-q -> -p$))$ is.) Each of these conjucts is composed of a disjunction of literals, where a literal is either a propositional letter (in which case it is said to be **positive**) or the negation of one (in which case it's said to be **negative**). Lines 4 and 5 in the OTTER proof are applications of the rules of inference 'binary resolution' and 'hyperresolution,' respectively. These rules are really quite straightforward. Binary resolution for the propositional case is just

$$\frac{\phi \vee \psi \quad \neg \psi}{\phi}$$

where the formula below the horizontal line is inferred from the formulas above the line. (The greek letters here stand for arbitrary formulas in the propositional calculus.) You should be able to see now, after looking at this rule, why the inference in line 5 of the OTTER proof goes through. Hyperresolution is a little more complex. To understand it, notice that each disjunction of literals, e.g., p|q|r|-s, can be viewed as a set; this particular disjunction would become $\{p, q, r, \neg s\}$. Now, intuitively, hyperresolution simply says that contradictory literals are cancelled out to leave positive literals. In line 4 of the above OTTER proof, for example, p in line 1 and -p in line 3 contradict each other and cancel out, leaving q. The general schema for hyperresolution is as follows.

$$\frac{\begin{array}{ll} \Phi_1 \cup \{\neg\psi_1, \neg\psi_2, \ldots, \neg\psi_n\} & \text{all } \Phi_j \text{ positive} \\ \Phi_2 \cup \{\psi_{i_1}, \psi_{i_2}, \ldots, \psi_{i_k}\} & 0 \leq i_k \leq n \\ \vdots & \\ \Phi_{n+1} \cup \{\psi_{i_1}, \psi_{i_2}, \ldots, \psi_{i_m}\} & 0 \leq i_m \leq n \end{array}}{\Phi_1 \cup \Phi_2 \cup \cdots \cup \Phi_{n+1}}$$

Now, let's return to the example given earlier involving Vanderbilt University. Specifically, let's create an OTTER input file to empirically verify that the deduction we have said exists does in fact exist. The input file becomes:

```
% Input file for empirically checking
% the Vanderbilt example.
```

```
set(auto).
formula_list(usable).
% If a student has low SATs, and a low GPA,
% then none of the top 25 national universities
% ought to be applied to by this student:
all x all y
   ((Student(x) & Satl(x) & Gpal(x) & T(y)) ->
       -A(x,y)).

% Steve has low SATs and a low GPA; and
% he's a student:
Student(s) & Satl(s) & Gpal(s).

% Vanderbilt is a top 25 national university:
T(a).

% Assumption for contradiction (Steve *ought*
% to apply to Vanderbilt):
A(s,a).
end_of_list.
```

And here is the proof OTTER yields, which verifies the inferences in question:

```
---------------- PROOF ----------------
1 [] -Student(x)| -Satl(x)| -Gpal(x)| -T(y)| -A(x,y).
2 [] Student(s).
3 [] Satl(s).
4 [] Gpal(s).
5 [] T(a).
6 [] A(s,a).
7 [hyper,6,1,2,3,4,5] $F.
------------ end of proof -------------
```

2.3.3 Simple Diagrams

According to descriptionalism, *all* of the objects of knowledge and belief for a human and a future robot can be represented as formulas in some computable logical system like $\mathcal{L}_I$, and all reasoning is deduction over these formulas.

Now let's take a quick look at the sort of representations typically employed in programs claimed to possess at least some degree of visual imagery capability. (Our objective, recall, is to unpack the notion of a TEMI; we're on the route toward doing just that.) The core representational idea in such systems is a rather easily conveyed kernel (e.g., [149], [94], [119], [144]). To grasp that kernel, first consider Figure 2.2.

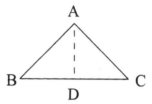

Figure 2.2: Simple Right Triangle.

ABC is a right triangle; a perpendicular runs from the right angle to the opposite side, giving rise to two triangles DAB and DCA. Establishing the proposition that area of ABC = area of DAB + area of DCA within a logical system is extraordinarily complicated [228]. But, as Lindsay points out,

> [The inference to this conclusion] is direct, immediate, and compelling simply from an examination of the diagram ... [This inference] is of course an instance of the whole being equal to the sum of its parts. ([149], p. 240)

If you now imagine that some computer programs, when run on digital computers, allow for diagrams like Figure 2.2 to be represented and propositions of this sort to be reached via routes which both capitalize on such representations and are strikingly shorter than ordinary deduction, you have on hand a serviceable concretization of what we call **AI pictorialism**. And you've also acquired a sense of what we call, in contradistinction to TEMIs, **simple images**, or **simple diagrams**, abbreviated for the remaining discussion by **S-Ds**. But can't we be a bit more precise about S-Ds? Must we rely completely on an ostensive definition? There is actually a way to capture S-Ds with some precision: We say — having sufficient space only to encapsulate this account — that D is an S-D if and only if D and the diagrammatic reasoning thereon can clearly be fully represented in some logical system $\mathcal{L}$. It should be apparent that Figure 2.2, and the reasoning thereon which we looked at earlier, can be wholly recast in a logical system. (After all, we know

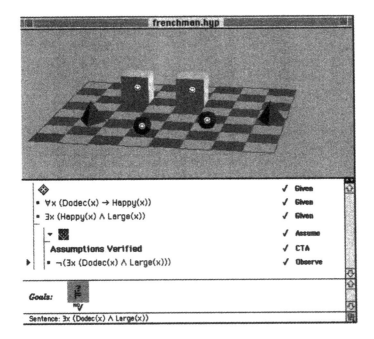

Figure 2.3: The "Frenchmen" Syllogism Disproved in Hyperproof.

that Euclidean geometry can be entirely derived from the $\mathcal{L}_I$ axioms of Zermelo Fraenkel set theory.) And we think it's safe to say that S-Ds are what AI has tended to concentrate on since the seminal experiments of Shepard and Metzler [210] got the ball rolling.[10]

2.3.3.1 Simple Diagrams in HYPERPROOF

In our experience, a neat way to understand the nature of S-Ds is via Barwise and Etchemendy's Hyperproof system [8].[11] This system allows for deduction that involves not only symbolic information,

---

[10] Alert readers will detect here a presupposition on our part, namely that our internal representation of Shepard and Metzler's stimuli are S-Ds. We haven't the space to defend this presupposition, but we urge those disinclined to affirm it to look again at the geometric shapes at the heart of S&M's experiments. These shapes are "Hyperproofish": they are all constituted by simple line segments drawn in Euclidean 3-space.

[11] What we say in this section will also hold for OPENPROOF, a more sophisticated, platform-independent descendant of HYPERPROOF that has been under development for quite a while, but is not quite ready yet.

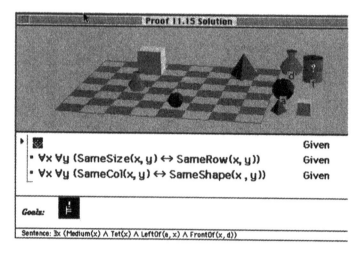

Figure 2.4: The "Pizza Problem" (Proof 11.15) From Hyperproof [8].

but visual information as well. For example, consider the following problem, presented in [170].

What follows from the following two premises?

(i) All the Frenchmen in the room are wine-drinkers.

(ii) Some of the wine-drinkers in the room are gourmets.

Many subjects in this case infer

(iii) Some of the Frenchmen in the room are gourmets.

But (iii) doesn't follow from (i) and (ii). (Do you see precisely why? If not, and you want to crack the problem, reflect before reading on.) In Hyperproof, courtesy of its ability to allow diagrammatic reasoning, it's easy to prove {(i), (ii)} ⊬ (iii). The completed proof is shown in Figure 2.3. In this figure, happy objects are to be thought of as wine-drinkers, Frenchmen are represented by dodecahedrons (dodecs, for short), and gourmets are large objects. What you see, therefore, is a situation in which (i) is true, as is (ii) (some happy things are indeed large: see the two smiling cubes), but (iii) is false: It's not the case that some Frenchman are gourmets.

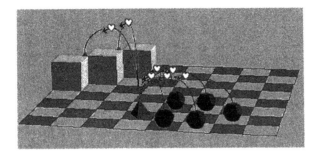

Figure 2.5: Is It Consistent To Suppose That Hilary Communicates With The Dead?

Now the interesting thing about Hyperproof in the context of the distinction between S-Ds and TEMIs is this: Even problems involving rather complicated diagrams can be solved in purely symbolic form, once these diagrams are recast symbolically. As an example, consider the very challenging Hyperproof problem posed in Figure 2.4.[12] Those who would crack this problem must deduce the formula expressing "There is a medium tet that object **a** is left of, and that is in front of **d**" *using only the ability to directly observe a symbolic fact from the diagram, and traditional symbolic rules of inference* (concluding that `Dodec(a)` from the diagram is an example of the sort of observation involved). Rest assured, the problem can be solved. And that it can is testimony to the fact that diagrams in Hyperproof are S-Ds.[13]

---

[12]Barwise and Etchemendy offer as a prize a (cold) pizza to those who solve this problem.

[13]Readers interested in HYPERPROOF and stretching the limits of what it can represent are encouraged to consult Bringsjord's HYPERPROOF-based course *Introduction to Logic* on his web site. (One can go directly to the course at `www.rpi.edu/~brings/logarg.html`.) Note that though HYPERPROOF offers only diagrams thoroughly expressible in $\mathcal{L}_I$, it does allow humans to "read a lot into these digrams." As as example, ponder Figure 2.5, which accompanies a problem on Bringsjord's web site in which the aspiring logician is asked to prove whether or not it is consistent to suppose that Hilary Clinton talks in a séance with Ghondi and Eleanor Roosevelt.

2.3.4   So What is a TEMI?

All this is beginning no doubt to look like a massive diversion. What is a TEMI? A TEMI is the sort of image which those who are expert in imagistic fields routinely process. That is, TEMIs are not simply "visual aids," like drawings. (Whether or not S-Ds are used as drawings, they do appear to be always *usable* as such; consider, in this connection, Euclid's [85] own reasoning.) TEMIs are much more robust. For example, consider someone in BRUTUS$_1$'s profession: a screenwriter. Many mature screenwriters are able to write complete drafts of movies "in their heads." That is, they are able to watch a movie play out before their mind's eye, from beginning to end, replete with dialogue, props, intonation, scene changes, camera angles, and so on. They then transcribe what they "see" and "hear," and the result is a script, which can then be studied and followed by producers and directors. The first draft of the American film *Tin Men*, for example, was apparently dictated, start to finish, by the screenwriter and director Barry Levinson. Such experts have yet to be rigorously studied by cognitive scientists. On the other hand, a group of people with related abilities have (supposedly) been studied. We refer to those with the capacity for **eidetic imagery**, those who can, for example, "examine a picture for several moments and then cast onto a surface an image with positive colour and high detail that lasts several minutes" ([225], p. 346). These are people, in other words, who can, often at will, generate mental images as clear and distinct as seen real-world scenes, and can then scrutinize the images like you and I might examine a real landscape. (Such an ability enables astounding feats of memorization: Luria's [151] famous mnemonist apparently used eidetic imagery.) So, for example, Stromeyer and Psotka have this to say about one of their amazing subjects:

> [She] can hallucinate at will a beard on a beardless man, leaves on a barren tree, or a page of poetry in a known foreign language which she can copy from bottom line to the top line as fast as her hand can write. ([225], p. 347)

Unfortunately, the eidetiker whose feats are described here by Stromeyer and Psotka was apparently not tested by anyone else. And, more generally, some cognitive psychologists (e.g., [104]) have questioned the very existence of eidetic imagery. Though at least one of us (Selmer) is quite comfortable with the standard claims for eidetic imagery, for the sake of argument we are willing to concede that eidetic imagery is chimerical. We cheerfully make this concession because surely there is no denying that many authors routinely tap imagistic expertise that is far from the preternatural in order to do what they do. One author who happened to explicitly report about his use of mental imagery was the great dramatist Henrik Ibsen, who said:

> I have to have the character in mind through and through, I must penetrate into the last wrinkle of his soul. I always proceed from the individual; the stage setting, the dramatic ensemble, all that comes naturally and does not cause me any worry, as soon as I am certain of the individual in every aspect of his humanity. But I have to have his exterior in mind also, down to the last button, how he stands and walks, how he conducts himself, what his voice sounds like. Then I do not let him go until his fate is fulfilled. (reported in [90], p. xiv)

In order, then, to get a sense of what TEMIs are, and of what's involved in processing them, we ask you to have in mind a person with Ibsen's imagistic power, someone able to create rich and vivid mental images, *to stretch such images through time, and to manipulate them in detail so as to produce a robust narrative.*

2.4 Defending the Key Premise

We return now to the issue of what recommends **Arg**$_1$'s first premise. We have four argument-chains for (1); space constraints allow us to present only two here. Each of these four argument-chains corresponds to an observation encapsulable by way of some rough-and-ready prose:

O1 It's just a brute, undeniable fact that while we can reduce diagrams like Figure 2.2, and indeed (as we indicate later) all the diagrams mastered by AI, to symbolic representations, we can't carry out this reduction for TEMIs. Hence, the burden of proof is on those who maintain that the Block/Dreyfus worry is a carcass.

O2 TEMIs have a subjective, or qualitative, "feel" to them, and as such include information which no one knows how to represent in symbolic form (in fact, a number of thinkers have argued directly that subjective qualities of experience utterly defy symbolization [115], [139], [167], [206], [40], [37]).[14]

O3 Unlike the rather rigid status of diagrams like Figure 2.2, TEMIs are astonishingly elastic. Not only authors, but nearly all of us, can easily picture, say, the World Trade Center in its normal setting, and then "watch" it suddenly change into a rocket ship that blasts off into outer space. How can this elasticity be captured in an approach which, for example, treats images as diagrams stored as charged cells in an array?[15]

O4 Though we can't reduce a TEMI to formulas in some logical system, we can of course go a long way toward capturing such images with natural language, which is what authors using TEMIs are in the business of doing. But the natural language involved is itself the richest, most complicated natural language we know of, and the question of whether it can be rendered in a computable logical system is an open one.

We give here the arguments corresponding to O1 and O2. We begin with the argument for O2, which is

Arg$_2$

(7)   TEMIs include "what-it's-like-to-X" information.
(8)   "What-it's-like-to-X" information isn't capturable in any symbolic representation scheme.
∴   (9)   TEMIs aren't capturable in any symbolic representation scheme.

You may find this argument rather mysterious, for you may not be familiar with the Nagelian [167] 'what-it's-like-to-be-an-X' locution. A partial explication of this locution, along with a synopsis

---

[14]Of course, qualia aren't restricted to TEMIs.

[15]In his [131] Kosslyn calls this property of visual images 'malleability.' We don't specify and defend O3 in this chapter, so readers of his book will have to judge for themselves, without our "help," whether or not he shows that this property can be possessed by neural nets, and hence possessed as well by symbolic formalisms.

of the well-known Jackson/Kripke/Nagel argument that deploys it, has recently been provided by John Searle [206]:

> Consider what facts in the world make it the case that you are now in a certain conscious state such as pain. What fact in the world corresponds to your true statement, "I am now in pain"? Naïvely, there seem to be at least two sorts of facts. First and more important, there is the fact that you are now having certain unpleasant conscious sensations, and you are experiencing these sensations from your subjective, first-person point of view. It is these sensations that are constitutive of your present pain. But the pain is also caused by certain underlying neurophysiological processes consisting in large part of patterns of neuron firing in your thalamus and other regions of your brain. Now suppose we tried to reduce the subjective, conscious, first-person sensation of pain to the objective, third-person patterns of neuron firings. Suppose we tried to say the pain is really "nothing but" the patterns of neuron firings. Well, if we tried such an ontological reduction, the essential features of the pain would be left out. No description of the third-person, objective physiological facts would convey the subjective, first-person character of the pain, simply because the first-person features are different from the third-person features. ([206], pp. 117-118)[16]

Nagel makes the point the Searle has made here by contrasting the objectivity of third-person features with what-it-is-like features of subjective states of consciousness. Jackson makes the same point courtesy of a character he calls 'Mary,' who lives in a colorless laboratory where she ostensibly learns about everything, including sunsets, from the standpoint of third-person science. When Mary leaves her lab and sees a sunset for the first time, Jackson claims that she would learn something: She will learn what it is like to experience a sunset.[17] Kripke makes the same point when he shows that pains can't be identical with neurophysiological states such as neuron firings in the thalamus and elsewhere, because any such identity would have to be necessary, in light of the fact that both sides of the identity state-

---

[16]Of course, to the extent that this argument is sound — and we think it is — it applies to subjective experience of *any* kind, not just that associated with TEMIs.

[17]One of us has tried to reconstruct Jackson's argument in more formal terms. See Chapter I of [40].

ment are rigid designators, and yet we can easily imagine a world wherein the relevant neuron firings obtain in the absence of pain.

It will be helpful at this point if we both anchor things with a thought-experiment, and set out a version of the argument with premises and inferences explicit: The protagonist in our thought-experiment is a Jacksonian character created elsewhere for our version of the argument in question, which appears in [40]. The character is Alvin, an AInik who lives and works in an isolated laboratory. Suppose, indeed, that Alvin, for the past 5 years, has been an absolute recluse, that during this time he has hardly had any contact with other humans, that what contact he has had has all been of a professional, scientific nature, and so on. Alvin, during this time, has mastered the purportedly complete computational specification of human mentation. Suppose, in addition, that he has never encountered a long lost friend — Alvin has never even had an experience remotely like this. Now, one day Alvin leaves his drab lab and encounters a long lost friend, and thereby learns what it feels like "on the inside" to meet a long lost friend. "So *this*," he says to himself, "is what it feels like to meet a long lost friend in the flesh, to see once again that gleam in her eyes, the light her hair seems to catch and trap..." and so on. The corresponding argument in [40] is too complicated to reproduce here. So we adapt to Alvin's situation a more informal but elegant and powerful statement of the Jacksonian argument given by Dale Jacquette [116]:[18]

---

[18]Jacquette's [116] argument here, like the one presented in Bringsjord's book [40], is designed specifically to surmount Dennett's [70] reply to Jackson's [115] version.

Arg$_3$

(10) To know everything knowable about a psychological state is to have complete first- and third-person knowledge of it.

(11) Alvin, prior to his first first-person long-lost-friend experience, knows everything knowable about meeting long lost friends from a third-person symbolic perspective.

(12) To know everything knowable about meeting long lost friends from a first-person perspective implies knowing what it's like to meet a long lost friend in the flesh.

(13) Alvin, prior to his first-person long-lost-friend experience, doesn't know what it's like to meet a long lost friend in the flesh.

(14) If what-it's-like-to-X information is capturable in some symbolic representation scheme, then [if Alvin, prior to his first-person long-lost-friend experience, knows everything knowable about meeting long lost friends from a third-person symbolic perspective, then, prior to his first first-person long-lost-friend experience, he knows everything knowable about meeting long lost friends].

∴ (15) Alvin, prior to his first first-person long-lost-friend experience, doesn't know everything knowable about meeting long lost friends. (10), (12), (13)

∴ (16) What-it's-like-to-X information isn't capturable in some symbolic representation scheme. (11), (14), (15)

Here again the reasoning itself is above reproach: **Arg$_3$** can easily be symbolized as a proof in the propositional calculus. But please don't misunderstand. Though we consider this argument not only formally valid, but veracious as well, and though we share this opinion with Jackson, Jacquette, Kripke, Searle and others, we recognize that the debate concerning Alvin and his kind is unlikely to stop. In this chapter we don't give an *exhaustive* presentation of our case against AI from imagistic expertise. (Such a case would include, among other things, a refinement of the full defense of **Arg$_3$** provided by one of us (Selmer) elsewhere [40], [37].) However, premise (7) is apparently affirmed by Kosslyn ([131], p. 405) himself, who concedes that mental imagery, especially robust mental imagery like TEMIs, has an inherent emotional component. And premise (8) is certainly the upshot of, if not a proof, then certainly a *formidable* deductive argument (viz., **Arg₃**). At any rate, there are our (1)-supporting observations which have nothing to do with fanciful creatures like Alvin.

We focus now on O1. Here's how the argument corresponding to this observation runs:

Arg₄

(17)   No symbolization of TEMIs, and the creation, manipulation, and contemplation thereof, is in the literature; nor, despite considerable, sustained effort directed at achieving such symbolization, is such symbolization forthcoming —in fact there is no hard evidence to support even the weak position that such symbolization will *eventually* arrive.

(18)   If a certain type of object of thought, and an ability to process this type, resists symbolization to the degree that there is not even any hard evidence to support the position that such symbolization will *eventually* arrive, then one ought to affirm the view that such symbolization can't be achieved.

∴ (19)   One ought to affirm the view that the symbolization of TEMIs, and the creation, manipulation and contemplation thereof, can't be achieved.

This argument is straightforward; it's also provocative — not because (18) will be controversial (on the contrary, this seems to be an eminently plausible principle, one which could even be put more circumspectly without precluding the core *modus ponens* in question), but rather because most of those thinking about AI and CogSci in connection with visual imagery believe that work since the Block/Dreyfus objection has buried this objection forever. What work? There is a long list of computer systems generally regarded to mark the symbolization of visual images. We've already mentioned two ([149], [94]), but the complete list is quite a bit longer; it includes work done by Kosslyn and Schwartz [135]; Gardin and Meltzer [95], Glasgow, Fortier, and Allen [100], Baron [6], and Julstrom and Baron [121]. Unfortunately, all of this work, as well as that which is in the works, confirms (17): All of this work includes only the symbolization of S-Ds, that is, only the sorts of "diagrams" and "images" which are *obviously* symbolizable. (This claim is something you may well have anticipated, given our earlier assertion that an "image" like Figure 2.2 is essentially the only sort of image AI has managed to represent.) This point can be made by simply going to the images featured in the work itself. As a first example, consider the discussion of mental imagery Dennett offers us in his *Consciousness Explained* [70]. This is a lengthy discussion, but the key point, for our purposes, is easily extracted: it's simply that the "images" Dennett credits robots (e.g., the well-known SHAKEY) and computer programs with creating, manipulating, and "contemplating" are impoverished. They are "images" which are obviously symbolizable; in short, they're S-Ds. To make the point vivid, let's evoke the sort of images, whether found in robot or human, with which Dennett is concerned.

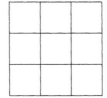

Figure 2.6: The Grid for Dennett's Game

Consider the 3-by-3 grid shown in Figure 2.6, and then image it. Now, "write" the following three words down in the columns of your imaged grid: GAS, OIL, DRY. Finally, attempt to "read off" the horizontal words formed by this little maneuver. Dennett claims that it's hard to "see" the horizontal words; that's the point he tries to drive home.[19] The point for us is that these simple and static images can obviously be symbolized in such a way as to entirely capture their content. In the case of Dennett's challenge, the "images" in question are once again Euclidean and elementary, and

---

[19]As a matter of fact, we think Dennett takes this example much too seriously. With a little practice, most of Selmer's students managed to solve these grids rather quickly. We suspect that those with good visualization abilities could become *strikingly* adept at solving them. (Certainly those blessed with eidetic imagistic powers could do as well with visualized grids as mere mortals do with inscriptive ones, but there is no need for us to invoke eidetikers here: Selmer's students make the point just fine.)

hence provably capturable in $\mathcal{L}_I$ systems sufficient to yield at least the bulk of classical mathematics.[20] Put another (crude) way, the images here are "Hyperproofish."

We imagine some readers saying: "You conveniently ignore the fact that Dennett's little game is just that: a *little* game. It's a straw man. What about the less "toy worldish" types of images central to the work in AI and neuroscience which has at least purportedly overthrown the Block/Dreyfus worry?" Unfortunately, such work never transcends Dennett's scheme. The AI part of the literature in question revolves around "images" like those shown in Figure 2.7 — cubes [121], strings [95], and arrays [100] —, nothing even remotely like a TEMI, nothing that can't be easily and completely captured in traditional symbolic schemes. None of this work provides the slightest reason for holding that a TEMI — say that which corresponds to a director's "internal rehearsal" of a production of *The Tempest* — can be represented in symbolic terms.[21]

Figure 2.7: Some S-Ds.

Further confirmation of the fact that S-Ds as ultimately represented in mere first-order logic are the best that AI currently offers

---

[20]For an argument that $\mathcal{L}_I$ suffices to yield all of classical mathematics, see [82].

[21]We readily concede that there is some evidence for the arrival of such symbolization. For example, the fact that some S-Ds can be symbolized might fairly be read by some as constituting such evidence. But this evidence is hardly *hard* evidence. Consider, for illumination of the point, the following analogy. Suppose that the issue is whether first-order logic is sufficiently expressive to formalize a set Φ of mathematical statements. Certainly the fact that first-order logic is up to the task of capturing some mathematical statement $p \in \Phi$ provides some evidence that first-order logic is sufficiently expressive to formalize Φ. But no one would regard the evidence here to be *hard*. (After all, if this is hard evidence, then there is hard evidence that every mathematical statement can be formalized in first-order logic!), and we know this to be false in light of the fact that, e.g., the Peano axioms cannot be expressed in first-order logic.

Table 2.1: Tabular Representation of Geographic Information.

Norway	Norway | Sweden	Sweden
water	water	water
water	Denmark	water
water	water	water
Portugal	France	?

can be found by looking to the hefty *Diagrammatic Reasoning* [98], recently released from MIT Press. This book marks the expansion and refinement of AI's first major conference devoted exclusively to diagrammatic reasoning; the book is the current "Bible" on diagrammatic reasoning in AI. (The conference is encapsulated in [48].) The contribution "Computational Imagery" therein, by Glasgow and Papadias [99], is particularly informative: The authors propose three different levels of representation, the "deep" level is the lowest level, then comes the "spatial" level, and finally the "visual" level. Their scheme is easily explained through the following simple example. Try to answer the question: "Is Norway north of France?" If you paused, and tried in earnest, it's a pretty good bet that all three levels of representation were involved in your attempt (according to Glasgow and Papadias). At the highest level, you probably "inspected" a visual representation: a mental image of a map or globe showing Scandinavia. This would correspond to an array. The array here, so the story goes, was generated from a spatial representation that might (depending upon your knowledge of geography) look like Table 2.1. And this representation was in turn generated from ... you guessed it ... first-order logic, namely (in this case):

- *Country(Norway) $\wedge$ Country(Sweden)* ...

- *Northof(Norway, Denmark) $\wedge$ Northof(Sweden, Denmark) $\wedge$ Northof(Denmark, France)* ...

- $\forall x \; ((Northof(x,y) \wedge Northof(y,z)) \rightarrow Northof(x,z))$

For yet more up-to-date evidence in support of the view that AI and CogSci, when dealing with imagery, focus on mere S-Ds, to the exclusion of images as rich as TEMIs, consider Steven Pinker's

How the Mind Works [180], a sustained defense of the mind-is-machine doctrine which devotes a lengthy, central chapter ("The Mind's Eye") to the topic of cognition and imagery. Pinker boldly proclaims:

> A mental image is simply a pattern in the $2\frac{1}{2}$-D sketch that is loaded from long-term memory rather than from the eyes. A number of artificial intelligence programs for reasoning about space are designed in exactly this way. ([180], p. 286)

But such sketches are merely S-Ds; and the AI programs Pinker has in mind all manipulate merely S-Ds. And when Pinker tells us that, courtesy of certain brain scanning experiments, we now understand part of the anatomy of imagery in the brain, he again stays only at the level of impoverished S-Ds. For example, we read:

> Neuroscientists can inject a monkey with a radioactive isotope of glucose while it stares at a bull's-eye. The glucose is taken up by the active neurons, and one can literally *develop the monkey's brain* as if it were a piece of film. It comes out of the darkroom with a distorted bull's-eye laid out over the visual cortex. ([180], p. 287)

As you can immediately guess, such a bull's-eye is an S-D; it would be at home in Figure 2.7, and move no closer to a TEMI than the images used in the type of human brain experiments we discussed above (see again Figure 2.8).

Cognoscenti may feel that our TEMI/S-D distinction has an impressive pedigree in Piaget's [178], [179] distinction between two broad categories of mental images: **reproductive** and **anticipatory**. Unfortunately, much as we'd like to claim Piaget as a fan, the reality, alas, is that his dichotomy is, even under the most relaxed of readings, at best an approximation of our own. Reproductive images are "limited to evoking sights that have been perceived previously" ([179], p. 71); anticipatory images "envisage movements or transformations as well as their results, although the subject has not previously observed them (as one can envisage how a geometric figure would look if it were transformed)" ([178], p. 71). From this characterization it follows immediately that the mental images sparked in subjects by Shepard and Metzler's [210] famous geometric figures are, contra our earlier classification of them, TEMIs (on the assumption — the only candidate assumption if Piaget's work is to be considered ancestral with respect to ours — that TEMIs are to be identified with anticipatory images). The problem, more generally, is that reproductive images apparently allow for the richness of TEMIs, and anticipatory images include those which are too "austere" to count as TEMIs (as in the case of Shepard and Metzler's geometric figures). Piaget's distinction considered in a broader context that includes not only our TEMI/S-D distinction, but also AI, is similarly unhelpful (for us), but fascinating. This is so because some of Piaget's work on the reproductive/anticipatory distinction involved experiments in which subjects were faced with challenges arguably met by those AI systems having "imagistic" capability. For example, Funt's [94] WHISPER system is capable, at some level, of anticipating the result of moving simple objects — anticipation, if Piaget is right, beyond the grasp of children younger than 5.[22] Though, interestingly enough, other aspects of Piaget's work on mental imagery bolster the position we advocate herein,[23] and though his overall position on logic and cognition fits Bringsjord's like a glove (see [24]), let's return to the main thread of the paper, by asking not how our case might be *helped* (by appeal to the seminal work of a great psychologist), but how it might be *hurt*: What move might those skeptical about our case make? Well, the most powerful rebuttal those unwilling to affirm (17) can muster would seem to involve arrays. It might be said that if the arrays are sufficiently complex, robust scenes, and manipulations thereof, become possible. Such thinkers will probably draw our attention to real-world scenes which have been digitized, and hence rendered in a form representable as an array. (Of course, this move conflates external versus internal representation, something we overlook for the sake of argument.[24])

---

[22]Children younger than 5, if presented with the problem of anticipating a slight movement of one square placed on top of another, cannot produce a drawing corresponding to what will happen if the top square is moved ([178], p. 74).

[23]For example, Piaget held that mental imagery included the internal sensations which in today's terminology would be regarded qualia (e.g., [178], p. 69), and he gave a number of arguments for the view that mental imagery is not just a fancy version or prolongation of perception (see, e.g., Section IV [178]).

[24]A fuller and more aggressive version of the rebuttal under consideration would insist that adding a temporal dimension to static images is no problem for AI, and adding detail to the point of even the "eidetic" is also unproblematic. The problems with this reply over and above the two we mention in the main text (one, the reply conflates external representations with internal ones; two, the reply, given the current state of the art, is just one big bluff) include an unwillingness

Unfortunately, this is all one big bluff we're quite prepared to call. Where, pray tell, is the array-theoretic representation of an "internally played" *Tempest* (or anything similar)? Where, in fact, is the array-theoretic representation of anything even remotely *like* such a TEMI? Those who would complain that these are mere rhetorical questions and then go on to search feverishly for a shred of evidence in favor of the view that array theory is sufficiently expressive would do well to keep in mind that array theory is just first-order extensional set theory — and who thinks that a Shakespearean TEMI can be represented in, say, Zermelo Fraenkel set theory? But what about neuroscience? Do we find here research which dispels the Block/Dreyfus concern? In neuroscience, too, we find but "images," the symbolization of which is trivial; we find only S-Ds yet again. Consider, for example, the sorts of images at the heart of Kosslyn's [132], [131] brain activation research (see Figure 2.8). Subjects in one of these studies were shown grids with letters represented in them. They were then instructed to create mental images corresponding to these grids. Finally, subjects were shown "empty" grids, save for one location marked by 'X.' They were to consult their mental images in order to ascertain if the X fell within the letter (they were told each time what the letter in question was; in Figure 2.8 the letter is of course 'F'). (PET scanning revealed that imagery activates topographically mapped cortex, but this isn't germane to the issues at hand for us.) It's obvious that this study revolves around images and diagrams which are S-Ds. And this study isn't idiosyncratic. Quite the opposite, really. In fact, it's tempting to say that neuroscientists and neuropsychologists have a fetish not only for S-Ds, but specifically for matrices and grids (e.g., [4], [126], [56]). In sum, neuroscience deals with images which, like all their relatives in the AI/CogSci literature, pale beside TEMIs: They are images the symbolization of which is transparent. So proposition (17) seems to us to more than hold its own.

---

to come to grips with the subjective experience at the heart of TEMIs, and the fact that even external representation schemes in AI are stretched to the breaking point when used to try to capture information as rich as that seen in TEMIs.

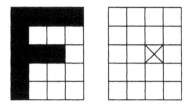

Figure 2.8: Input for PET Study

2.5   "Strong" vs. "Weak" Story Generation

It's important to read our overall position, (6), with care. Doing so reveals that our case against AI is really a case against *Strong* AI. We're not saying that robots who capitalize on S-Ds to get their work done will never be more than creatures of fiction. Quite the contrary: BRUTUS is capable of generating not belletristic fiction, but decent short short stories the production of which *doesn't require the creation, manipulation, and contemplation of TEMIs.* (In the next and final section of this chapter we enumerate some aspects of readerly imaging upon which BRUTUS capitalizes.) But we *are* pessimistic about the prospects for the arrival of a robotic Henrik Ibsen. Put another way, in the sphere of imagery there may forever be a chasm separating humans and robots which is analogous to that separating humans and chimps when it comes to language [38].[25] If you remain unconvinced by our case, then feel free to view our argument as a challenge to Strong AI. We may be wrong, and if so, the way to deliver a decisive refutation is to deliver a system that shuts us up. We conclude this part of the chapter with a graphical overview of the part of our case presented above:

---

[25]We're not begging any questions here in favor of a Chomskyan view of language. For the proposed analogy to be enlightening, we need only assume something which even those who ascribe bona fide linguistic capacity to chimps must affirm, namely that no amount of training is going to allow a chimp to interview John Updike. Likewise, it may be that no amount of time and effort will eventuate in a computational system blessed with TEMIs.

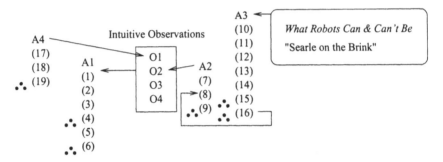

Figure 2.9: Overview of Our Case

2.6   So What About BRUTUS?

We now know that imagistic expertise of a sort capitalized upon by human authors cannot be given to BRUTUS. What, then, are we to do? Well, our task is in general clear: We need to find a way to engineer BRUTUS₁ so that the stories he produces are effective in significant part because they trigger imaging on the part of *readers*. Fortunately, we can get help here from a wonderful book by Ellen Esrock: *The Reader's Eye* [84]. As Esrock shows, readerly imaging is often crucial to the success of narrative. Here, for example, is what Carlos Fuentes told Esrock when she interviewed him about readerly imaging in connection with Hugo's prose:

> Without the visual representation [of] the flight of Jean Valjean through the sewers of Paris, persecuted by inspector Javert — if you're not capable of translating this into images — it has no power. The prose is rather banal, you know, but it is powerful. It doesn't look for poetic effects; it doesn't look for any particular euphony, it doesn't look for sounds. It seeks a stark effect of representation at the verbal level, and it's really very successful in that. It's very difficult to forget the representation. I cannot for the life of me remember any word from that passage in *Les Misérables* I'm talking about. But I could not forget the image of that persecution through the sewers of Paris, ever. ([84], p. 182)

Fuentes, like most of us, is moved by *Les Misérables* because reading the great novel evokes vivid images. And Fuentes, like most of us, no doubt assumes that Hugo himself created and processed images in the course of crafting *Les Misérables*. (When we stop and think about it, do we not assume that Hugo imagined Valjean beneath the streets of Paris? Don't we believe that Hugo, like Ibsen, thought things out visually in order to produce such stirring prose?) We would like BRUTUS$_1$ to enjoy the same status as Hugo: We want BRUTUS$_n$, $n > 1$, to be regarded a master of imagistic processing — despite the fact that, as we have just shown, neither BRUTUS$_1$ nor his descendants, qua computers, can master anything of the sort! The best way to produce such beliefs about BRUTUS$_1$, it seems to us, is to have his narrative generate images on the part of readers. And the best way, in turn, to accomplish this, is to capitalize on the following list, many examples for which are adduced by Esrock [84].

1. Erotic or bizarre material evokes readerly imaging. As Esrock puts it, "Imaging is especially significant when the imaged object is unusual, striking, or bizarre, and would, in real life, arouse one's visual attention." ([84], p. 193)[26]

2. One of the quickest routes toward sparking readerly imaging is to describe things with which they are familiar.[27]

3. Readerly imaging is triggered when fictional characters are engaged in specifically mentioned acts of visual perception. In particular, verbs such as 'saw,' 'gazed,' 'looked,' 'beheld,' and so on, trigger images in the minds of readers.

4. Reference to familiar things and places give rise to readerly imaging. For example, for those who have spent some time around college campuses, a sentence like "It was warm enough, finally, for the students to shed coats and sweaters, and my doom was sealed when, walking across the green that afternoon, I saw her hair shimmering in the

---

[26]The opening of Kafka's "Metamorphosis" is a perfect case in point:

As Gregor Samsa awoke one morning from uneasy dreams he found himself transformed in his bed into a gigantic insect. He was lying on his hard, as it were armor-plated, back and when he lifted his head a little he could see dome-like brown belly divided into stiff arched segments on top of which the bed quilt could hardly keep in position and was about to slide off completely. His numerous legs, which were pitifully thin compared to the rest of his bulk, waved helplessly before his eyes. ([122], p. 67)

[27]As Umberto Eco [83] points out, Ian Fleming "does not describe the Sequoia that the reader has never had a chance to see. He describes a game of canasta, an ordinary motor car, the control panel of an airplane, a railway carriage, ..." (p. 167).

sun, and glimpsed the full perfect line of her arm and shoulder" will probably catalyze a number of images.

5. Readerly imaging can be particularly intense when voyeurism is involved.[28]

In our final Chapter, 6, we explain how points 1–4 are reflected in the BRUTUS architecture, and partially implemented in BRUTUS$_1$, and we experience the narrative made possible by this architecture.

---

[28]Another wonderful example can be found in Kafka's unforgettable "Penal Colony:"

> Can you follow it? The Harrow is beginning to write; when it finishes the first draft of the inscription on the man's back, the layer of cotton wool begins to roll and slowly turns the body over, to give the Harrow fresh space for writing. Meanwhile the raw part that has been written on lies on the cotton wool, which is specially prepared to staunch the bleeding and so makes all ready for a new deepening of the script. Then these teeth at the edge of the Harrow, as the body turns further round, tear the cotton wool away from the wounds, throw it into the pit, and there is more work for the Harrow. ([123], p. 203)

Chapter 3

Consciousness and Creativity

> What, is Brutus sick,
> And will he steal out of his wholesome bed,
> To dare the vile contagion of the night
> And tempt the rheumy and unpurged air
> To add unto his sickness? No, my Brutus;
> You have some sick offence within your mind.
> > —Portia, in *Julius Caesar*

Given our objectives, the problem of consciousness for us, put colorfully, is this: How can we engineer things so that a certain zombie — BRUTUS₁, and, in fact, all future incarnations of the BRUTUS architecture — becomes a member of the literati? A less lively form of the question is: How can we build BRUTUS₁ so that despite his lack of consciousness he can generate stories rich in consciousness — so rich that those who read them are inclined to ascribe genuine states of mind to BRUTUS₁? Or put yet another way: How can something lacking a mind write compelling fiction *about* minds? (What Portia says about Shakespeare's Brutus — that his mind is afflicted — cannot be said about BRUTUS or BRUTUS₁: they *have* no minds!) In this chapter we explain why we see these questions as the toughest ones facing those who aim to build genuinely creative agents (in the literary realm), and we provide the first phase of an answer. The second phase, more closely tied to actual implementation, is presented in Chapter 6.

3.1   BRUTUS as Zombie

When we say that BRUTUS₁ is a zombie, we refer to *philosophers'* zombies — not those creatures who shuffle about half-dead in the movies.[1] Philosophers' zombies star in situations lifted directly out of the toolbox most philosophers of mind, today, carry with them on the job: Let's imagine that due to cancer your brain starts to deteriorate and the doctors, desperate, replace it, piecemeal, with silicon chip workalikes, until there is only silicon inside your refurbished cranium.[2] John Searle claims that at least three distinct possibilities arise from this gedanken-experiment:

The Smooth-as-Silk Variation The complete silicon replacement of your flesh-and-blood brain works like a charm: same mental life, same sensorimotor capacities, etc.

The Zombie Variation "As the silicon is progressively implanted into your dwindling brain, you find that the area of your conscious experience is shrinking, but that this shows no effect on your external behavior. You find, to your total amazement, that you are indeed losing control of your external behavior ... [You have become blind, but] you hear your voice saying in a way that is completely out of your control, 'I see a red object in front of me.' ... We imagine that your conscious experience slowly shrinks to nothing, while your externally observable behavior remains the same" ([206], pp. 66-67).

The Curare Variation Your body becomes paralyzed and the doctors, to your horror, give you up for dead.[3]

It's the zombie variation that gives us the sort of creature BRUTUS₁ and his successors would seem to be: creatures whose observable behavior is as impressive (at least in some domains) as that displayed by *Homo sapiens sapiens*, but whose "inner lives" are no different than those of common, ordinary rocks. Zombies *act* clever, but underneath there is no — to use Ned Block's [15] recent term — **P-consciousness**. Here is part of Block's explication of this term:

---

[1] Actually, the zombies of cinematic fame apparently have real-life correlates created with a most creepy mixture of drugs and pre-death burial; see [63], [62].

[2] For example, the toolbox is opened and the silicon supplantation elegantly pulled out in [55].

[3] This scenario would seem to resemble a real-life phenomenon: the so-called "Locked-In" Syndrome. See [181] (esp. the fascinating description on pp. 24–25) for the medical details.

Figure 3.1: Zombies Unmasked

So how should we point to P-consciousness? Well, one way is via rough synonyms. As I said, P-consciousness is experience. P-conscious properties are experiential properties. P-conscious states are experiential states, that is, a state is P-conscious if it has experiential properties. The totality of the experiential properties of a state are "what it is like" to have it. Moving from synonyms to examples, we have P-conscious states when we see, hear, smell, taste and have pains. P-conscious properties include the experiential properties of sensations, feelings and perceptions, but I would also include thoughts, wants and emotions. ([15], p. 230)

Block distinguishes between this brand of consciousness and **A-consciousness**; the latter concept is characterized as follows:

A state is access-conscious (A-conscious) if, in virtue of one's having the state, a representation of its content is (1) inferentially promiscuous, i.e., poised to be used as a premise in reasoning, and (2) poised for [rational] control of action and (3) poised for rational control of speech. ([15], p. 231)

As one of us has explained elsewhere [27], it's plausible to regard certain extant, mundane computational artifacts to be bearers of A-consciousness. For example, theorem provers with natural language generation capability, for that matter perhaps *any* implemented computer program, would seem to qualify by Block's definition.[4] It follows from this, of course, that our very own BRUTUS₁ is

---

[4]It follows that a zombie would be *A*-conscious. In [27] one of us (Bringsjord) argues that because (to put it mildly here) it is odd to count (say) ordinary laptop computers running run-of-the-mill Pascal programs as conscious in any sense of

A-conscious. However, BRUTUS₁ isn't P-conscious, and that creates our conundrum.

3.2   The Conundrum

The conundrum is this: The construction of the genuine article (a genuine artificially intelligent storyteller) is possible, it seems, only if central human authorial techniques can be formalized in computational terms, but at least some of these techniques, to put it mildly, resist formalization. The one technique we're especially concerned with is an author's ability to adopt the point of view of his or her characters, to "feel what they feel on the inside." Henrik Ibsen used this technique as often and as intensely as any writer. We heard from Ibsen in the previous chapter; let's listen again: "Before I write down one word," Ibsen said,

> I have to have the character in mind through and through, I must penetrate into the last wrinkle of his soul. I always proceed from the individual; the stage setting, the dramatic ensemble, all that comes naturally and does not cause me any worry, as soon as I am certain of the individual in every aspect of his humanity. But I have to have his exterior in mind also, down to the last button, how he stands and walks, how he conducts himself, what his voice sounds like. Then I do not let him go until his fate is fulfilled. (reported in [90], p. xiv)

Suppose for the sake of argument that AI researchers can build a bona fide storyteller capable of Ibsen's approach. Then, on the plausible principle that 'if X adopts Y's point of view, X is itself capable of having a point of view,' it would seem to follow that computers can have genuine conscious states — there can be something, to use Thomas Nagel's [167] phrase, it's like to be a computer, something it feels like to be a storytelling AI. But, as we discussed in the previous chapter, a number of thinkers ([115], [139], [167], [206], [40], [37]) have developed and endorsed a line of argument, the conclusion of which is that it's impossible that inner, mental states of the human variety be formalized in *any* way. It seems a short step from this conclusion to the view that computers — which are themselves,

---

the term, 'A-consciousness' ought to be supplanted by suitably configured terms from its Blockian definition.

mathematically speaking, formalizations — are incapable of having a point of view.

An informal version of the argument in question was presented in the previous chapter. At its heart was a thought-experiment involving Alvin, a scientist who works alone in a laboratory and then emerges to have the burst of P-consciousness generated by meeting a long lost friend for the first time. The argument, recall, runs as follows.

Arg$_3$

(1) To know everything knowable about a psychological state is to have complete first- and third-person knowledge of it.

(2) Alvin, prior to his first first-person long-lost-friend experience, knows everything knowable about meeting long lost friends from a third-person symbolic perspective.

(3) To know everything knowable about meeting long lost friends from a first-person perspective implies knowing what it's like to meet a long lost friend in the flesh.

(4) Alvin, prior to his first-person long-lost-friend experience, doesn't know what it's like to meet a long lost friend in the flesh.

(5) If what-it's-like-to-X information is capturable in some symbolic representation scheme, then [if Alvin, prior to his first-person long-lost-friend experience, knows everything knowable about meeting long lost friends from a third-person symbolic perspective, then, prior to his first first-person long-lost-friend experience, he knows everything knowable about meeting long lost friends].

. (6) Alvin, prior to his first-person long-lost-friend experience, doesn't know everything knowable about meeting long lost friends.   (1), (3), (4)

∴ (7) What-it's-like-to-X information isn't capturable in some symbolic representation scheme.   (2), (5), (6)

This argument is obviously formally valid (as can be shown when it's symbolized in first-order logic).[5] The only formidable objection we know of comes from Daniel Dennett [70]. In a nutshell, Dennett thinks that **Arg₃**'s (1), despite strong intuitions to the contrary, is unimaginable, that, at best, we can reasonably affirm only

(2′) Alvin, prior to his first first-person long-lost-friend experience, knows everything *currently* knowable about meeting long lost friends from a third-person computational perspective.

One of us has treated Dennett's position on these matters elsewhere [37]. Jacquette [116] disarms Dennett's attack in a different but no less effective manner; here we encapsulate this treatment. First, it must be conceded that the argument arising from supplanting (2) with (2′) is unsound: this much is uncontroversial. The reader should satisfy himself or herself that (5′) is false, or at least such that there is no apparent reason whatever to affirm it. (Note that we refer to the "primed" versions of (1) through (7): They are the result of propagating the change indicated in (2′) through the rest of the argument.) Now let's take a look at Dennett's own words on the matter (adapted so as to apply to **Arg₃**):

> The image [of Alvin] is wrong; if [seeing Alvin make a discovery] is the way you imagine the case, you are simply not following directions! The reason no one follows directions is because what they ask you to imagine is so preposterously immense, you can't even try. The crucial premise is that "[Alvin] has all the physical [computational] information." This is not readily imaginable, so no one bothers. They just imagine that [he] knows lots and lots — perhaps they imagine that [he] knows everything that anyone knows *today* about the neurophysiology [etc.] of [such psychological states]. But that's just

---

[5] Actually, a formalization of **Arg₃** in first-order logic would have to be considerably naïve. The first premise might be symbolized as

$$\forall t \forall s \forall \phi (sK^t \phi \leftrightarrow (sK_1^t \phi \wedge sK_3^t \phi)).$$

This would be to deploy separate three-place predicates — for knowing everything about something, for knowing everything about something from the first-person perspective, and for knowing everything about something from the third-person perspective. The core rule of inference (used twice) would be *modus tollens*. Quantifier manipulation would involve *existential instantiation* and *universal elimination*. One sophisticated way to formalize **Arg₃** would involve knowledge operators rather than predicates.

a drop in the bucket, and it's not surprising that [Alvin] would learn something if that were all [he] knew. ([70], p. 399)

Dennett has been conveniently struck by an uncharacteristic failure of imagination. Why does he say that Alvin's having all the information in question cannot be imagined? He provides no argument for this view; and the absence of such an argument is especially odd because Dennett's position seems flatly inconsistent with logical and mathematical knowledge and reasoning: How can it be that in logic and math we conceive of situations involving *infinite* information,[6] but suddenly when it comes to Alvin we cannot, even in the realm of thought and thought-experiment, arm him with enough knowledge? The thought-experiment in question, and the corresponding argument, can both be put in austere terms *wholly divorced from the particular sciences of today* — terms no different, really, than those involved in formal pursuits: Imagine that Alvin works with some fixed, austere model for computation and/or symbolic representation — say that provided by Turing machines. Accordingly, for Alvin to have complete third-person knowledge about meeting long lost friends is for him to have assimilated some collection of Turing machines. What, pray tell, is unimaginable about Alvin assimilating n Turing machines, for any natural number n? (Is there anything unimaginable about a person counting up to n, for all n? Given that TMs can be coded as natural numbers, if the answer to this question is an affirmative one, it would seem to follow immediately that Alvin, in principle, can pull things off.) We would even go so far as to say — though for purposes of emerging victorious from the present dialectic we needn't — that it seems perfectly *imaginable* that Alvin assimilate an *infinite* number of TMs (perhaps he works faster and faster in the fashion of so-called "Zeus machines" [21]).

Given **Arg₃**, the argument that expresses the problem we face can also be put in deductive form:

---

[6]In connection with this issue, see [29].

Arg₄

(8)   If computers (or computer programs, or artificial agents, ...) can adopt the points of view of creatures of fiction, then computers can have genuine "there's something it's like to be a" conscious states.

(9)   If computers can have genuine "there's something it's like to be a" conscious states, then such states are formalizable in computational terms (= in third-person symbolic representation schemes).

(10)   "There's something it's like to be a" conscious   from **Arg₃** states are not formalizable in computational terms.

. (11)   Computers can't adopt the points of view of   (8), (9) creatures of fiction.

(12)   If computers can't adopt the points of view of creatures of fiction, they can't generate sophisticated fiction.

∴ (13)   Computers can't write sophisticated fiction.   (11), (12)

This chain of reasoning, like its predecessor, is formally valid. But are the premises true? Premise (9) would seem to be uncontroversial; it could presumably be defended with help from a formal account of computerhood (which one of us has developed: [31]). Premise (8), it would seem, is plausible (in large part because we accept the principle cited earlier, viz., "if X adopts Y's point of view, X is itself capable of having a point of view"). Premise (10), again, is the conclusion of **Arg₃** — an argument which may be vulnerable, but is surely not easily dodged, as Dennett will hopefully learn. This leaves premise (12). Why is this proposition plausible?

In short, (12) seems plausible because compelling narrative, at least in this day and age, and in this culture (and we certainly find ourselves inescapably designing BRUTUS and building BRUTUS₁ both in the present and in this culture), needs to have both a "landscape of action" and a "landscape of consciousness" [44]. The former is typically composed of temporally sequenced "action events reported in the third person with minimal information about the psychological states of the protagonists" ([87], p. 2). In the landscape of action, there is little concern about how things are perceived, felt, intended, and so on; "things happen or they don't" ([87], p. 2). In the landscape of consciousness things are quite different: Narrative is driven in large part by how the cast of characters feels about the world from their own points of view. Most successful modern fiction (again, in our culture) generates both types of landscapes, with an emphasis on the landscape of consciousness. Some narrative shrinks the landscape of action down to nearly nothing (as in, e.g., Joyce and Beckett). And some narrative, for example folktales, generates next to nothing in the realm of consciousness [186].

So, if some such proposition as

(14) Sophisticated fiction requires both a landscape of consciousness and a landscape of action.

is true, and if it's true as well that

(15) If computers can't adopt the points of view of creatures of fiction, they can't generate a landscape of consciousness.

(12) follows immediately.

Why might some resist this argument? Well, it might be said that (15) is false because computers can generate sophisticated fiction *without* adopting the points of view of the characters in that fiction. Perhaps (so the story goes) storytelling AIs will use some *other* technique to generate narrative with the same "depth" as, say, Ibsen's immortal *A Doll House*.

This reaction would seem to be fueled by some rather wishful thinking — because when one ponders the power of the knowledge-based techniques by which a computer might write "three-dimensional" characters *without* anything as mysterious as adopting a character's point of view, there is little reason to believe that these techniques will rival the tried-and-true one of which Ibsen is a consummate practitioner. And yet here we stand, dreaming of giving a zombie, BRUTUS$_1$ (or at least BRUTUS$_n$), the ability to create a landscape of consciousness. How in the world are we going to pull it off?

It's important to be clear on how difficult the problem is. One reason it's so difficult is that our goals seem to be unreachable in the absence of an understanding of the nature of creatures of fiction. It's hard to see how one can engineer a machine with the capacity to occupy the point of view of a creature of fiction if one doesn't know what a creature of fiction *is*; this is just plain old commonsense. So how does BRUTUS$_1$, and artificial agents generally, have a chance if the human engineers of such systems fail to grasp the nature of creatures of fiction? Well then, what *are* creatures of fiction? How do they differ from us? In what sense are they unreal, exactly — given that we can have all sorts of utterly determinate beliefs about them? (Is it not true, e.g., that Sherlock Holmes is brilliant, and that Brutus underestimated the oratorical skills of Mark Antony in *Julius Caesar*, and that Dave Striver is betrayed in BRUTUS's stories about him, and ...?) If nothing else, if one could come to understand the nature of creatures of fiction, then it would at least seem that one would be in a better position to evaluate the objection that a computer can write three-dimensional characters without slipping into the shoes of these characters. Unfortunately, as things stand today, no one knows what the ontological status of creatures of fiction is — or at least there's no *consensus* about their status. There *are* proposals. The most plausible account of fictional characters we know of is Bill Rapaport's [192], which builds upon four prior, influential accounts ([241], [173], [147], [46]) and attempts, specifically, to indicate the nature of an AI's beliefs about creatures of fiction. Rapaport's seminal work is carried out in the context of a well-known knowledge representation and reasoning system — SNePS — with which he has been intimately involved for a good long while. The basic idea behind this work is to try to solve some difficult problems that arise by supposing that a computational mind — CASSIE — has beliefs about not only the "real" world, but about fictional worlds as well. Unfortunately, from the perspective of Ibsen's threat to story generation, CASSIE doesn't provide much hope. This is so because though CASSIE promises to offer, among other things, unprecedented ways of keeping an AI's beliefs about fiction and reality from getting muddled, the objects of CASSIE's beliefs, at bottom, are symbolic entities, formulas in a powerful intensional logic (SNePS, however, is traditionally displayed as a network; we interact with it through SNePSLOG, a logic-based interface). And this brings us straight back to Alvin. For how can command over purely symbolic information, whether that information is represented by Turing machines or by formulas in some logic, give to its owner the Ibsenian power to get inside the soul of a character? The problem *is* exceedingly difficult.

Let's take a closer look at the problem.

Suppose CASSIE has beliefs in 1997 about Bill Clinton and Tolstoy's Count Vronsky, that Clinton is overweight and that Vronsky is dashing, and countless others about this unlikely duo. Suppose that CASSIE's having these beliefs is the presence of certain formulas in CASSIE's belief base. So picture a list

$$L = \phi_1, \phi_2, \phi_3, \ldots$$

of some formulas in some logic. Now suppose that you assimilate L. Would your new knowledge suffice to allow you to occupy Vronsky's point of view, so that you could add an adventure to Tolstoy's *Anna Karenina*? With all due respect, we doubt it — because despite having digested L, you will need to do something else to write a scene suitable for inclusion in perhaps the greatest landscape of consciousness ever created: You will have to try — armed with L, we readily agree — to feel what it's like to *be* the Count. In other words, what you get by virtue of grasping L is the sort of declarative information an author can impart to you about one of his or her characters, but you don't thereby get the ability to adopt the point of view of one of these characters (though of course you may have that ability for reasons independent of L).

What we have just described schematically can be fleshed out and experimented with. We urge you to try it for yourself. Have a friend give you a list of propositions about some person who you don't know. Your friend can follow the templates we follow for story generation, which are enhancements of ones appropriated from the movie industry. In these templates (which all aspiring scriptwriters are taught to use when starting out), you need to write down a person's age, their educational background, a physical description, where they grew up, their short- and long-term goals, their hobbies, their occupation, where and what they studied in school, their friends (and the occupations and avocations of these friends), key personality traits (and here there are a host of instruments from psychology that are useful), the five best things that have happened to them and the five worst things that have happened to them, their family members (and the occupations and avocations of these people), and so on. Now take this information from your friend and assimilate it. Now try to write a good short short story about the person that is described. We predict that one of two things will happen. Either you will write an exceedingly poor story that trades mechanically directly off of the information you have absorbed, or you will take respectable steps toward impressive narrative. If you manage to take the second route, you will have *used* the declarative information given you to trigger in your mind that which it's like to X, where X might be 'have a father who was a brain surgeon.' We can't for the life of us see how a machine could travel this route. BRUTUS$_1$ takes the first, shallow route — on the strength of declarative information upon which it *mechanically* capitalizes.

So, once again, it seems as if Alvin's lesson is a knife that is being driven ever deeper into our hopes of building an AI that produces sophisticated narrative: Having a point of view certainly seems to be something over and above having symbols on hand, so having a point of view (not to mention having the capacity to occupy another's point of view) is something we'll have trouble imparting to a computer — which after all is nothing more than a device for manipulating symbols.

Are we paralyzed, then? No. Given that BRUTUS$_n$ is to be *believed* to be as creative as Ibsen, rather than literally *being* another Ibsen, there are moves to be made in the face of the problem we have described. Unsurprisingly, these moves all derive from a careful study of those texts which evoke landscapes of consciousness in the minds of readers. (This chapter, you now see, ends on the same note as did the previous one.) These texts are invariably marked by heavy usage of mental verbs — thinking, supposing, intending, knowing, feeling, fearing, believing, hating, betraying, etc.[7] In fact, there is a body of fascinating research that grows out of minimizing and maximizing the landscape of consciousness in a given story by adjusting the frequency and intensity of mental verbs [87].[8] Our methods for implementing the calculated modulation of mental verbs (and other linguistic objects) in order to allow BRUTUS$_1$ to successfully confront the problem expressed in this chapter are described in Chapter 6.

We end this chapter with a "non-conscious" version of the story presented in Chapter 1. Readers may find it profitable to compare it with the "conscious" version seen earlier. The difference is that in

---

[7] In *Julius Caesar*, the seeds of betrayal are cultivated by Cassius in Brutus by the *action* of sending to Brutus a note that sparks the right sort of consciousness. The note is quite brief: "Brutus, thou sleep'st: awake and see thyself. Shall Rome, etc. Speak, strike, redress..."

[8] In one of these studies, for example, two versions of Joyce's story "Eveline" [120] are presented to subjects, the original one, and one (the so-called "non-conscious" version) whose landscape of consciousness is contracted by deleting and downplaying mental verbs.

the non-conscious version the frequency of mental verbs is decreased. Again, know well that this is a change that *we* make in BRUTUS$_1$: the change does not originate with

"Betrayal in Self-Deception" (non-conscious)

Dave Striver loved the university — its ivy-covered clocktowers, its ancient and sturdy brick, and its sun-splashed verdant greens and eager youth. The university, contrary to popular opinion, is far from free of the stark unforgiving trials of the business world: academia has its own tests, and some are as merciless as any in the marketplace. A prime example is the dissertation defense: to earn the PhD, to become a doctor, one must pass an oral examination on one's dissertation. This was a test Professor Edward Hart enjoyed giving.

Dave wanted to be a doctor. But he needed the signatures of three people on the first page of his dissertation, the priceless inscriptions which, together, would certify that he had passed his defense. One of the signatures had to come from Professor Hart, and Hart had often said — to others and to himself — that he was honored to help Dave secure his well-earned dream.

Well before the defense, Striver gave Hart a penultimate copy of his thesis. Hart read it and told Dave that it was absolutely first-rate, and that he would gladly sign it at the defense. They even shook hands in Hart's book-lined office. Dave noticed that Hart's eyes were bright and trustful, and his bearing paternal.

At the defense, Dave eloquently summarized Chapter 3 of his dissertation. There were two questions, one from Professor Rodman and one from Dr. Teer; Dave answered both, apparently to everyone's satisfaction. There were no further objections.

Professor Rodman signed. He slid the tome to Teer; she too signed, and then slid it in front of Hart. Hart didn't move.

"Ed?" Rodman said.

Hart still sat motionless. Dave looked at him.

"Edward, are you going to sign?"

Later, Hart sat alone in his office, in his big leather chair. He tried to think of ways he could help Dave achieve his goal.

Chapter 4

Mathematizing Betrayal

I kiss thy hand, but not in flattery, Caesar.
—Brutus, in *Julius Caesar*

The present chapter is the result of a conviction the two of us gradually came to share as we worked toward realizing a (seemingly) literarily creative machine: namely, *a good artificial storyteller must be in command of the immemorial themes that drive both belletristic and formulaic fiction.* One such theme is betrayal; it is this theme, courtesy of Shakespeare's immortal play, for which BRUTUS and BRUTUS₁ are of course named. Other such themes are: unrequited (reckless, passionate, selfless, ...) love, fanaticism (ranging from the spiritual to the violently carnal), revenge, jealously, self-deception (which BRUTUS₁ partially "understands"), infatuation (from the mild to the insane), hatred (from the murderous variety to forms of contempt well short of inclinations to harm), alienation, despair, triumph, and so on. Now, if an artificial storyteller is to — as we put it — "be in command" of such territory, then those who would engineer such a creature find themselves in a rather nasty pinch. The pinch is that such themes must be cast in terms that an AI can digest and process; that is, these themes must be, for want of a better word, mathematized.[1] But mathematizing (say) love, by any metric, is a rather tall task, no? Well, tall or not, it's a task we

---

[1] The alternative is to build a machine which *learns* about the themes in question, but for many reasons (some of which we shared with you in Chapter 1), we find such an approach to be profoundly unpromising. From the standpoint of sheer engineering, it seems to us silly to try to coax evolutionary computation along in a robot like COG to produce in it the capacity to discuss betrayal

intend to conquer. And we start here, in this chapter, by taming the concept of betrayal. We end by briefly considering the next theme we plan to fully formalize: self-deception. (A nascent formalization of this concept already makes it into BRUTUS's stories.) If everything goes according to plan, BRUTUS$_n$ will be in command of *many* of the themes in question. (Our plans in this regard are clearly reflected in what is called **thematic concept instantiation** in the BRUTUS architecture covered in Chapter 6.)

The technique we follow in the attempt to rigorously define betrayal is one that has been followed repeatedly by analytic philosophers. We begin armed with fairly firm pre-analytic intuitions about what betrayal essentially is and associated intuitions about whether or not certain fixed cases involve betrayal. We bring this prior knowledge to bear in the evaluation of thought-experiments involving proposed necessary and sufficient conditions for the truth of the locution

Agent s_r betrays agent s_d.

The upshot of this evaluation may be a new proposal; if so, the process iterates ... until we have the definitive account we seek.

One remark before we launch. It may be thought that a defective account of betrayal is sufficient to undergird the production of interesting narrative. For example, consider the following "definition."

Def$_B$ 0 Agent s_r betrays agent s_d iff (if and only if) s_r kills s_d.

That Def$_B$ 0 doesn't cut the mustard is wholly unexceptionable. (Clearly, if Jones kills Smith because Smith is terminally ill and begs Jones to pull the plug, no betrayal has occurred.[2]) Despite its inadequacy, however, this definition can give rise to interesting stories. Along these lines, consider the following dialogue.

> **Brown**: Jones! I'm sick, I tell you, sick. I'm sick in my heart, in my soul. You have betrayed your friend.

---

in narrative. Such a process is inevitably profligate, even if it has a chance of working, because the two of us will have installed our formalizations for betrayal and other such concepts long before COG has evolved the power to coherently converse at the level of a 3-year-old.

[2]Perhaps Jones has betrayed his country, or some such thing, but such a possibility needn't detain us.

Jones: Betrayed? I *saved* him — saved him from these hellish tubes, from doctors and nurses sticking things into him with no more regard for his body than a pin cushion, from pain I pray neither of us will ever experience.

Brown: When you take a man's life, you betray him; you take from him the most sacred thing there is.

Jones: Smith *wanted* to die. What had life become for him? Calling it life was a cruel joke. What I did, I did as a friend. There is no betrayal here, and you know it.

This dialogue derives from tension about whether the mercy killing in question is a case of betrayal. It does show that it is entirely possible to base narrative on defective notions of betrayal. But — and this is our rebuttal to the objection that finding a correct account of betrayal is superfluous[3] — in order to spin stories around tension like that seen in this dialogue, the storyteller must have command over what is and what isn't betrayal. In other words, if we can supply BRUTUS$_1$ with an accurate account of betrayal, he will be able to write stories involving not only this account, but about variations on it that yield concepts falling short of betrayal, but concepts which are nonetheless sufficiently betrayal-*like*. Our approach in the present chapter is designed not only to eventuate in a definition that captures betrayal, but to produce along the way definitions that can in principle undergird narrative whose themes include those which are merely betrayal-like.

4.1 First Stabs at a Definition

Very well; where do we start? Actually, there's a natural starting place: Margaret Boden, in her *The Creative Mind*, opines that much progress has been and will be made on capturing literary, "consciousness-laden" concepts, including, specifically, betrayal. In the case of betrayal, the "definition" that gives rise to Boden's sanguinity is

---

[3]This rebuttal was devised in dialectic arising from a talk and demo we gave at Brown University, and we are indebted to many who were in attendance there.

Def$_B$ B F betrays E iff F, having apparently agreed to serve as E's agent
for action a, is for some reason so negatively disposed toward that
role that he undertakes instead to subvert the action, preventing E
from attaining his purpose.

It's hard to see why Def B would make anyone sanguine. As
Boden herself points out, Christ was surely betrayed, and yet Judas
didn't prevent Christ from "attaining his purpose." And of course
this problem is but the tip of an iceberg: Why does F have to be
"negatively disposed" toward the role of assisting E? Perhaps F
is attracted to the role, but decides to betray E anyway (because
F simply wants to cause E pain). Does F really have to *agree* to
serve as E's agent? Can't Black betray his infant by abandoning the
child in the wilderness, having never (at least explicitly) agreed to
anything in connection with his offspring? And so on.

But even if Boden isn't entitled to be sanguine on the strength
of her definition, a tantalizing question remains: Is it *possible* to
formulate an acceptable definition? And if so, what would it look
like? True to the methodology we described and affirmed in Chapter
1 (philosophical analysis), we now attempt to evolve a definition that
answers both of these questions. We begin with what seemed to us
(and to a number of the students in our project) to be a decent first
stab:[4]

Def$_B$ 1 Agent s_r betrays agent s_d iff there exists some state of affairs p
such that

1 s_d wants p to occur;

2 s_r believes that s_d wants p to occur;

4 s_r intends that p *not* occur;

5 s_r believes that s_d believes that s_r intends that p occur.

Unfortunately, it's easy enough to shoot down Def$_B$ 1 with a
counter-example: Suppose that Selmer desires that his Sun work-
station fire up. Suppose, as well, that Dave, while ruminating in
the privacy of his own home, believes that Selmer has this desire
and intends that my Sun *fail* to fire up. Dave also believes — by
hypothesis — that Selmer believes that Dave intends for Selmer's

---

[4]Our first stab, note, is designed to start out at a level of granularity below
Def$_B$ B.

Sun to work just fine. Though clauses 1–4 are satisfied, we would be disinclined to call this a case of betrayal. The problem, at least *one* of them, would seem to be that Dave hasn't *done* anything. If the Sun does indeed malfunction, we would certainly agree that Selmer is unlucky; and maybe, just maybe, we'd grant that Dave is lucky. But Dave hasn't *betrayed* Selmer. (He may of course wish Selmer ill luck, and for that he may be blameworthy. But he isn't guilty of betrayal.)

This suggests that we move to the following definition.

Def$_B$ 2 Agent s_r betrays agent s_d iff there exists some state of affairs p such that

1 s_d wants p to occur;

2 s_r believes that s_d wants p to occur;

3 s_r agrees with s_d that p ought to occur;

4 s_r intends that p *not* occur;

5 s_r believes that s_d believes that s_r intends that p occur.

4.2 Betrayal Calls For an Expressive Logic!

Our attempt to formalize betrayal already reveals that the type of logic required must be extraordinarily expressive. In order to see this, let's focus first on the implications arising just from clause 5 in Def$_B$ 2, which involves an iterated belief. Here, first, is a different, perhaps more colorful, way to see the extreme expressiveness that narrative can demand in connection with iterated beliefs.

4.2.1 Dizzyingly Iterated Beliefs in Detective Stories

Consider a detective story pitting a villain against a hero.[5] Suppose that initially the hero is given information that demonstrates that the villain is a villain. For example, perhaps the hero is shown demonstrative evidence that the villain murdered an innocent person. At this point in the narrative, the hero believes that the villain is a villain. Now suppose that the hero begins his investigation — at first in secret, but then in a way that (unbeknownst, initially, to

---

[5]The following type of case was first discussed by Bringsjord in "Chapter IV: What Robots Can Be" in [40].

the hero) reveals to the villain that the hero is on the job. At this point, the villain believes that the hero believes that the villain is a villain. Now suppose that the hero discovers that the villain is aware of the hero's investigation. This implies that the hero believes that the villain believes that the hero believes that the villain is a villain. Next, suppose that the villain discovers that the hero is aware of the fact that his investigation is known to the villain. At this point, the villain believes that the hero believes that the villain believes that the hero believes that the villain is a villain! But we aren't done yet; not at all. Suppose that you read and understand a detective story conforming to the doxastic structure just described. (Many readily understood detective novels exemplify this structure. Consider, e.g., *Gorky Park* [217].) It follows from this that the reader believes that the villain believes that the hero believes that the villain believes that the hero believes that the villain is a villain. Next, it follows from the fact that Bringsjord has written this section that he believes that the reader believes (or at least can believe) that the villain believes that the hero believes that the villain believes that the hero believes that the villain is a villain. From this fact and the additional fact that Ferrucci has assimilated what Bringsjord has here written, we can conclude that Ferrucci believes that Bringsjord believes that the reader believes that the villain believes that the hero believes that the villain believes that the hero believes that the villain is a villain. Finally, some of the readers of this section will believe that Ferrucci believes that Bringsjord believes that the reader believes that the villain believes that the hero believes that the villain believes that the hero believes that the villain is a villain. (We said 'finally,' but do we dare point out that since Bringsjord wrote this section, and pondered it, he believes that readers of this section will believe that Ferrucci believes that Bringsjord believes that you can believe that the villain believes that the hero believes that the villain believes that the hero believes that the villain is a villain?)

What is the point of this dizzying iteration? The point is that fiction can rather easily generate, in the minds of readers, staggeringly complex beliefs — ones that first-order logic will at the very least have a devil of a time expressing. In first-order logic, even the sentence "Bringsjord believes that Ferrucci believes that the villain is a villain" is acutely problematic. If belief is represented by the two-place relation symbol B, and the proposition that the villain is a villain is represented by the formula ϕ, then this sentence becomes:

$$B(b, B(f, \phi))$$

But this formula is not grammatically acceptable in first-order logic.[6] What we have devised so far in the attempt to mathematize betrayal — Def_B 2 — puts us firmly in the same boat that the detective scenario puts us in. In fact, as we will later see, better accounts of betrayal necessarily invoke *third*-order belief structures, that is, ones in which x believes that y believes that z believes ϕ.

4.2.2 OTTER Cannot Handle Betrayal

In Chapter 2 we introduced the theorem prover OTTER as an interesting tool to test logicist forays into story generation — as long as these forays demand nothing more than standard first-order logic. But despite the fact that our foray into the formal structure of betrayal has revealed that this structure moves us beyond first-order logic, some very interesting things happen when one implements Def_B 2 in OTTER. To see them, consider first the formula

$$\forall x (P(x) \rightarrow Q(P(x))).$$

This formula is non-sensical on the standard grammar of first-order logic (which we gave, recall, in Chapter 2). The reason is that the antecedent in this universally quantified formula, $P(x)$, must be one that admits of truth or falsity. For the idea is that if it's true (for some instantiation to x), then the consequent, namely, that which is to the right of $\rightarrow$, must be true. (In technical terms, $P(x)$ is an **atomic formula**, not a **term**.) But this implies that the consequent consists of an atomic formula whose argument is itself an atomic formula, and this is ungrammatical and non-sensical in first-order logic. However, watch what happens when we give an input file to OTTER containing the relevant formula, along with the fact that $P(a)$, where a is a constant, and the assumption for indirect proof, $\neg Q(P(a))$. Here is the input file:

```
set(auto).
formula_list(usable).
all x (P(x) -> Q(P(x))).
```

---

[6]For an introduction to the tools offered by logicist AI for tackling such recalcitrant sentences, see our [23].

```
P(a).

% Assumption for contradiction:
-Q(P(a)).
end_of_list.
```

And here is the proof from the output file:

```
---------------- PROOF ----------------
1 [] -P(x)|Q(P(x)).
2 [] -Q(P(a)).
3 [] P(a).
4 [hyper,3,1] Q(P(a)).
5 [binary,4.1,2.1] $F.
------------ end of proof -------------
```

OTTER doesn't bat an eyelash; hyperresolution and binary resolution kick in just fine. How can this be, given that the input is non-sensical? The answer is that OTTER interprets the first occurrence of P in

```
all x (P(x) -> Q(P(x))).
```

to be a predicate symbol, but the second occurrence of P to be a functor. That is, P(x) gets interpreted as "x has property P," whereas Q(P(x)) get interpreted as "the value of the function P taking x as argument has property Q."

OTTER will do the same thing with Def$_B$ 2. Here is a naïve translation of Def$_B$ 2 into OTTER, along with assumptions that the relevant conditions are instantiated for Dave and Selmer, and with the assumption for contradiction that Selmer doesn't betray Dave:

```
set(auto).
formula_list(usable).

% DefB-2 in OTTER:
all x y (Betrays(x,y) <->
          (exists z (Wants(y,z) &
                     Believes(x,Wants(y,z)) &
                     Agrees(x,y,z) &
                     IntendsNot(x,z) &
                     Believes(x,Believes(y,Intends(x,z)))))).

% Pretend facts of the case:
Wants(adave,agraduate).
```

```
Believes(aselmer,Wants(adave,agraduate)).
Agrees(aselmer,adave,agraduate).
IntendsNot(aselmer,agraduate).
Believes(aselmer,Believes(adave,Intends(aselmer,agraduate))).

% Assumption for indirect proof:
-Betrays(aselmer,adave).

end_of_list.
```

And here is the resulting proof:

```
---------------- PROOF ----------------
6 [] Betrays(x,y)| -Wants(y,z)| -Believes(x,Wants(y,z))|
     -Agrees(x,y,z)| -IntendsNot(x,z)|
     -Believes(x,Believes(y,Intends(x,z))).
7 [] -Betrays(aselmer,adave).
8 [] Wants(adave,agraduate).
9 [] Believes(aselmer,Wants(adave,agraduate)).
10 [] Agrees(aselmer,adave,agraduate).
11 [] IntendsNot(aselmer,agraduate).
12 [] Believes(aselmer,Believes(adave,Intends(aselmer,agraduate))).
13 [hyper,12,6,8,9,10,11] Betrays(aselmer,adave).
14 [binary,13.1,7.1] $F.
------------ end of proof -------------
```

So here we have a perfectly acceptable proof, apparently of the fact that Selmer betrays Dave. The important thing to note is that this proof is generated despite the fact that the knowledge-base in this case (composed by the formulas in the OTTER input file) doesn't express the facts we would like it to express. For example, we would like the knowledge-base to include a formula expressing the fact that Selmer believes that Dave believes that Selmer intends that Dave graduate. But the formula

```
Believes(aselmer,Believes(adave,Intends(aselmer,agraduate))).
```

really expresses something like the proposition that Selmer believes that the value of the function `Believes` applied to the argument `adave`, and the argument that is the value of the function `Intend` applied to the arguments `aselmer` and `adave`. This proposition seems to literally make no sense. What sense does it make to say that someone believes that x, where x is a name for some object? For example, what sense does it make to say that Clinton believes that Moscow?

What OTTER does with Def$_B$ 2 is actually something that any so-called "syntactic approach" in AI will do to verbs like believes, hopes, fears, and so on. For example, consider the syntactic approach to such verbs taken in Russell and Norvig's popular *Artificial Intelligence* [201].[7] In this approach, "mental objects," which are the things, for example, that we have beliefs about, are expressed as strings. So for example if Selmer believes that Dave believes that Brown is a villain, we might write something like this:

$$B(s, \text{``}B(d, (V(b)))\text{"}),$$

where whatever is flanked by " " is a string, *not* a term or a subformula. The problem with this approach is that if as an AI researcher one takes oneself to be building a genuine mind (or to be contributing to the eventual building of a genuine mind), the approach is inadequate. The reason is simple: When I have a belief about you I don't have a belief about a string; I have a belief about *you*. And after all, some people have beliefs about things even though they can't write down strings in any language. Their communication may be exclusively oral. But on the syntactic view, such people can't have beliefs.

However, though it's true that syntactic approaches, such as the inferencing by OTTER displayed earlier, and Russell and Norvig's approach, fail to abide by the meaning of propositional attitudes like 'believes,' we find these approaches well-suited to BRUTUS₁, for reasons we explain in section 4.2.4. Astute readers can probably guess why we have this attitude.

4.2.3   Cervantes' *Don Quijote* for Skeptics

Some readers will be skeptical. They will insist that we are exploiting idiosyncratic aspects of narrative (i.e., iterated beliefs) in order to support the claim that truly representing standard narrative calls for non-standard logics. Such readers couldn't be more mistaken. They fall prey to a temptation that has seduced many, many in AI. The temptation is to search out and conquer those parts of a problem

---

[7]The text is used in Bringsjord's multi-media, distance learning *Intro to AI Show*; see

- http://www.rpi.edu/~brings/intai.html

domain that are clearly computable (checkers, chess, medical diagnosis, natural language in straightforward newspaper stories, etc.).
When AI confronts creativity, this temptation is deadly, because
creativity pushes one immediately and unavoidably toward at least
the possibility that here is something in the human sphere that exceeds computation. Since we intend to eventually engineer a system
that, at least in terms of its output, competes head-on with human
authors, we are forced to consider what human authors concoct; we
are forced to consider this material in its full, uncompromising glory.
The detective example was abstract; here is a specific, concrete example of such glory, one that goes all the way back to the very first
modern novel: *Don Quijote*, penned by the literary genius Miguel
De Cervantes. The example comes from Chapter 51 of the second
book of Cervantes' immortal book. Sancho Panza is governor of an
island and must preside as judge over some rather nasty cases, one
of which is presented to him as follows:

> My lord [Sancho Panza], a broad river separates the two parts
> of a single domain ...   Now, there's a bridge over this river,
> and at one end there stands a gallows and a court building,
> in which four judges usually preside, applying the law formu-
> lated by the lord of this river, this bridge, and this entire realm,
> which runs as follows: "Anyone passing over this bridge, from
> one section of this domain to the other, must first declare un-
> der oath where he is coming from and where he is going, and
> if he swears truly, he shall be allowed to pass, but if he lies,
> he shall be hanged from the gallows standing nearby, without
> any appeal or reprieve allowed." ... Well, it happened, one
> day, that a man came and swore the required oath, saying
> among other things that he had come to be hanged on that
> gallows, and for no other purpose. The judges considered his
> oath, saying: "If we simply let this man cross the bridge, his
> oath will be a lie, and then, according to the law, he ought
> to die, but if we hang him, the oath he swore about being
> hanged on this gallows will be true, and then the same law
> decrees that he be allowed to cross over in peace." Please con-
> sider, my lord governor, your grace, what the judges should do
> with this fellow, for even now they remain anxious and unsure
> how to proceed, and, having been made aware of your grace's
> keen mind and sublime understanding, they have sent me to
> implore your grace to tell them how you view this singularly
> complicated and puzzling case. ([45], 629)

Here, in a novel published in 1605, is a passage written in the belief that if readers believe that Sancho Panza believes that this would-be bridge-crosser has made a claim about the future (as opposed to merely making a claim about his plans), then these readers will grasp the fact that Sancho cannot possibly uphold the law in question.[8] Many other such tricks are performed by Cervantes. For example, in the Prologue to the book, Cervantes himself appears, and says that he writes only by following the literary advice of a friend (who also makes an appearance in the Prologue). And in Part Two of the novel, Don Quijote comes upon characters who recognize the knight as the hero of Part One, which had been read widely!

The point is that even the very first modern novelist exploited techniques that cutting-edge AI, supposedly about to burst boldly into the new century, has little idea how to accurately represent, and *a fortiori* little idea how to get a machine to reason about. As we discussed in the Preface, it is therefore exceedingly peculiar that seemingly smart men like Hans Moravec would predict that within a few decades all our cleverness will be as debris in the wake of super-smart robots.

---

[8]Cervantes has given us a maddening variation on the famous Liar Paradox, the simplest version of which is generated by the following sentence: "This sentence is false." Denote this sentence by 'λ.' We know, by the law of the excluded middle, that λ is either true or false. Suppose it's true. Then since it says that it's false, it *is* false; so if λ is true it's false. Suppose, on the other hand, that λ is false. Then since λ says that it's false, it's actually true. But then if λ is false it's true. So, λ is true if and only if it's false, which is a contradiction. The paradox isn't solved in the least by banning self-referential sentences, both because such sentences can be thoroughly meaningful and innocuous (e.g., "This sentence starts with the letter 'T'."), and because the paradox can be generated without such sentences. For example, let λ_1 be the sentence to the left in the following table, and let λ_2 be the sentence on the right.

| The sentence to the right is false. | The sentence to the left is true. |

Here, λ_1 is true if and only if it's false; contradiction redux. Even giving up the law of the excluded middle doesn't prevent the paradox from rising up: see the *Strengthened* Liar Paradox presented by Robert Martin in his Introduction to *Recent Essays on Truth and the Liar Paradox* [152].

4.2.4 What Shall We Then Do?

We have established that the demands placed upon a logic-based story generation system by such literary themes as betrayal are severe. There really are only two types of moves that can be made in the face of this. One is to search out and embrace logical systems, and corresponding implementations, that would in theory give an artificial agent built upon them the ability to possess and manipulate formal structures that in some real sense capture the full meaning of betrayal in the human sphere. The second possible move is to engineer a system, on the strength of a "humbler" logic, that, because of the cleverness of the engineering, *appears* to understand the full meaning of betrayal. As you can probably guess, the move we make is the second one, which is why we said at the conclusion of section 4.2.2 that in our story generation work we embrace syntactic approaches to propositional attitudes — despite the demonstrable fact that such approaches are philosophically inadequate. (One of us has taken the first approach — finding a more powerful logic — in a slightly different context: In *What Robots Can and Can't Be* [40], the highly expressive class of quantified modal logics is used to express arguments about the foundations of AI.)

BRUTUS$_1$ is built with tools having no more expressive power than first-order logic, for BRUTUS$_1$, as we reveal in Chapter 6, is built using FLEX and Prolog. How can this be? Why haven't we used tools that are designed for greater expressivity? Why haven't we turned to systems designed to express such things as iterated beliefs? The answer is that *for now* we are content with FLEX and Prolog code in which iterated beliefs can be typed, for there is nothing to stop us from writing Prolog code that includes

```
believes(bringsjord,(believes(reader,(believes,...?,
```

even if this code doesn't correspond to any desirable formal semantic model. (In other words, we can use Prolog here as we used OTTER earlier to reason about Def$_B$ 2.) More sophisticated incarnations of BRUTUS may well need to be engineered with more expressive knowledge representation and reasoning tools.

We now return to our quest for an acceptable formal definition of betrayal. We will express candidate definitions as the first two have been expressed: in an English-like language that is neutral on what particular logical system or knowledge representation and reasoning system is used for actual implementation. If we do our job well, then an acceptable definition, expressed in this manner, will be useful if we sustain our "hackerish" use of first-order logic, *and* if, down the road, we decide to move to more expressive frameworks.

4.3   On To More Sophisticated Accounts

Def$_B$ 2 is certainly better than its predecessor, but it too can be over-thrown by a relatively simple counter-example: Suppose that Horace wants President Clinton to make a trip to Moscow; and suppose as well that Joe believes that Horace wants Clinton to make this trip, and that Joe agrees with Horace that Clinton ought to go. However, assume in addition that Joe intends that Clinton not go — *but takes no action toward that end.* In this case it seems that since Joe does nothing (relevant), even if Clinton fails to go, there is no betrayal in the picture.

This suggests certain changes be made to clauses 4 and 5, namely:

Def$_B$ 3 Agent s_r betrays agent s_d iff there exists some state of affairs p such that

   1 s_d wants p to occur;

   2 s_r believes that s_d wants p to occur;

   3 s_r agrees with s_d that p ought to occur;

   4' there is some action a which s_r performs in the belief that thereby p will *not* occur;

   5' s_r believes that s_d believes that there is some action a which s_r performs in the belief that thereby p *will* occur.

At this point perhaps it's safe to say we're making genuine progress. But we're not home yet, for the following example shoots down Def$_B$ 3:

Doris is a monomaniacal woman intent on *nothing more* than crossing the street. You are to assume that Doris' mental life, save for this desire, is quite empty. Now suppose that a mugger agrees with Doris that crossing the street is a good idea — but in "helping" her across is only looking for an opportunity to slam Doris on the head with a tire iron and dash off with her purse. In this case it appears that Doris' barren mentation precludes betrayal. Of course, we can all agree that a crime has been perpetrated, but betrayal doesn't seem to be part of the scenario.

Now some may find it hard to grasp the notion of "barren mentation." We urge such thinkers to substitute for the mugger case the following variation. Dorrie is a dog, a collie to be exact; and Dorrie very clearly wants to cross the street. (Perhaps there is another dog on the other side; Max, perhaps.) Jones, seeing what Dorrie wants, and seeing that she has a collar, bends down, utters some of those niceties we reserve for the canine population ("Oh, what a *nice* dog you are, yes" — petting Dorrie — "yes, you're a good dog."), and then "offers" to guide Dorrie across the street to Max. In reality, Jones is a cruel person (worse than Cruella DeVille) who plans to get Dorrie out in the road so that the collie can be run down by a truck. Suppose that Jones pulls off his fiendish plan. Has Jones betrayed Dorrie? No. And the reason, generally speaking, is that collies are incapable of been "duped"; they don't have the right "mind set."[9]

It would seem that the problem can be remedied by adding to Def$_B$ 3 an appropriate new clause:

Def$_B$ 4 Agent s_r betrays agent s_d iff there exists some state of affairs p such that

1 s_d wants p to occur;

2 s_r believes that s_d wants p to occur;

3 s_r agrees with s_d that p ought to occur;

4' there is some action a which s_r performs in the belief that thereby p will *not* occur;

5' s_r believes that s_d believes that there is some action a which s_r performs in the belief that thereby p *will* occur;

6 s_d believes that s_r intends that p occur.

But things are not so easy; clause 6 would seem to be too strong: Suppose that Jones tells Smith that he will work to get Smith elected to some public office. Smith, knowing Jones' mixed record on following through with "backroom" agreements, doesn't believe that Jones *will* work. (Smith *does* very much want Jones to live up to

---

[9]If you're not convinced by the dog variation of the thought-experiment, substitute a lower animal, or even a simple robot capable — as its designers say — of having wants, etc.

his obligation, and Smith is in dire need of Jones' support.) Actually, Smith doesn't commit either way: He suspends judgment on whether or not Jones will follow through. Here most of us would still be inclined to say we have a case of betrayal, despite the fact that clause 6 isn't satisfied.

Perhaps the solution is to "tweak" 6, yielding:

Def_B 5 Agent s_r betrays agent s_d iff there exists some state of affairs p such that

1 s_d wants p to occur;

2 s_r believes that s_d wants p to occur;

3 s_r agrees with s_d that p ought to occur;

4' there is some action a which s_r performs in the belief that thereby p will *not* occur;

5' s_r believes that s_d believes that there is some action a which s_r performs in the belief that thereby p *will* occur;

6' s_d wants that there is some action a which s_r performs in the belief that thereby p *will* occur.

4.4 A Branch Point

At this point we hit a rather significant snag. In order to see it, consider the movie *The Man Without a Face*, starring Mel Gibson. Gibson plays McCloud, a man with a disfigured face and a shadowy past who befriends a younger boy. At no time does this boy agree with McCloud that no rumors ought to be spread about how McCloud came to be disfigured. They never have a discussion about the issue; not a *word* is said about it. However, the first part of the film gets its energy from the fact that the boy betrays McCloud — by spreading a heartless rumor about how McCloud came to acquire such a gruesome countenance. The audience knows this is betrayal, McCloud knows it's betrayal; and the boy knows it as well. But clause 3 is never satisfied. (Recall the similar defect in Def_B B.)

So we have to face a complicating issue: It appears that an acceptable definition of betrayal must incorporate two possibilities, viz., (i) there may be no agreement between s_r and s_d, in which case 6 should be replaced by

- s_d wants that there is no action a which s_r performs in the belief that thereby p will not occur.

On the other hand, (ii) there may well be an agreement (as classic literary cases of betrayal reveal), in which case 6 should remain as is. Given this, we can build a disjunction into our definition:

Def$_B$ 6 Agent s_r betrays agent s_d iff there exists some state of affairs p such that

1 s_d wants p to occur;

2 s_r believes that s_d wants p to occur;

3′ (3 ∧ 6′) ∨

   6″ s_d wants that there is no action a which s_r performs in the belief that thereby p will not occur;

4′ there is some action a which s_r performs in the belief that thereby p will *not* occur;

5′ s_r believes that s_d believes that there is some action a which s_r performs in the belief that thereby p *will* occur.

Perhaps you'll agree that Def$_B$ 6 really isn't half bad. At this point in the process we were ourselves quite optimistic. And then, you guessed it: There arose yet another thought-experiment (devised by Dave, to Selmer's chagrin), one just as destructive as the previous ones:

Harriet Truism is the mother of a cocaine-addicted teenager, Billy. Billy realizes his secret stash is dry, and his desperation is so great that he goes to his own mother to ask if she can acquire some cocaine out on the streets of LA. Billy gives his mother the name of a dealer, Scrum; he tells her that Scrum will be coming around soon to make a delivery to Billy, but that he will surely die long before Scrum arrives. Harriet isn't sure what to do. Eventually, she agrees to obtain the coke for Billy, and sets out alone into the night, heading for the most dangerous part of town. However, Harriet's intention is to purchase cocaine from Scrum only to prevent the drug from reaching her son (who she plans to somehow get to professional help).

In this case Harriet is courageous, self-sacrificial, perhaps foolhardy, but she is not betraying Billy. And that presents a problem, because Def$_B$ 6's definiens is satisfied in this case. The solution, it would seem, is to move to a slightly more complicated construction, viz.,

Def$_B$ 7 Agent s_r betrays agent s_d iff there exists some state of affairs p such that

1 s_d wants p to occur;

2 s_r believes that s_d wants p to occur;

3' $(3 \wedge 6') \vee$

      6'' s_d wants that there is no action a which s_r performs in the belief that thereby p will not occur;

    4'' there is some action a such that:

      4''a s_r performs a in the belief that thereby p will *not* occur; and

      4''b it's not the case that there exists a state of affairs q such that q is believed by s_r to be good for s_d and s_r performs a in the belief that q will not occur;

    5' s_r believes that s_d believes that there is some action a which s_r performs in the belief that thereby p *will* occur.

Def$_B$ 7 seems pretty sharp — until one ponders a bit further. For starters, it seems entirely possible that one betray a dead person. (When alive, Jones asks Smith to bury him in a certain fashion, and toward that end gives Smith the necessary cash. After Jones dies, Smith spends the cash on his own hedonistic pursuits, and leaves the body for others to deal with. Would we not unhesitatingly say in such a case that Smith has betrayed his dead friend?) Can cases like this one be handled? We think so. Indeed, to some degree our overall approach may be vindicated by the apparent ease with which Def$_B$ 7 can be refined to handle betrayal of the dead: The trick is to include temporal parameters and appropriate tense changes:

Def$_B$ 8 Agent s_r betrays agent s_d at t_b iff there exists some state of affairs p and $\exists t_i, t_k, t_j \ (t_i \leq t_k \leq t_j \leq t_b)$ such that

1 s_d at t_i wants p to occur;

2 s_r believes that s_d wants p to occur;

3' $(3 \wedge 6') \vee$

      6'' s_d wants at t_k that there is no action a which s_r performs in the belief that thereby p will not occur;

4″ there is some action a such that:

4″a s_r performs a at t_b in the belief that thereby p will *not* occur; and

4″b it's not the case that there exists a state of affairs q such that q is believed by s_r to be good for s_d and s_r performs a in the belief that q will not occur;

5′ s_r believes at t_j that s_d believes that there is some action a which s_r will perform in the belief that thereby p *will* occur.

4.5 Two Popular Objections

When we presented parts of this chapter at various conferences and at various colloquia, two objections were often raised against us. The first objection runs like this: "Why do you strive to find the one perfect definition? As you yourselves have noted, interesting narrative can involve instantiations of what you would regard to be defective accounts of betrayal. For example, your thought-experiment involving Harriet might make for a promising kernel of a story, despite the fact that Harriet doesn't betray her son." We answered this objection at the beginning of this chapter; that answer may make more sense now that the definitions have been presented, so we repeat it. The answer is that once we have arrived at what we regard to be *the* account of betrayal, one immune to counter-example, there is no reason why the definition cannot be systematically modified (say, by dropping a clause), and then instantiated in connection with some knowledge-base in order to produce an interesting story. All such modifications should be reachable from the one solid definition, whereas if one stops short of reaching such a definition, any number of variants of the solid definition may be unobtainable. To put the point a bit more formally, if you have defined P to be true just in case $Q_1 \wedge Q_2 \wedge \ldots \wedge Q_n$, then you can easily consider many concepts related to but short of P, e.g., $Q_2 \wedge \ldots \wedge Q_n$. But if you have stopped short, and have only a "defective" definition of P, say $Q_3 \wedge Q_4$, then you can never consider the instantiation of $Q_2 \wedge \ldots \wedge Q_n$.

The second objection we've heard is this one: "But do you really think that human authors reason with frameworks as complex as Def_B 8? They do no such reasoning. What you have produced in this chapter, therefore, is psychologically unrealistic." Of course, this objection reflects an utter lack of understanding of what the BRUTUS project is about. As we have said repeatedly, we are trying to build a machine that, in terms of observable behavior, holds its own against human authors. As we discussed in the Preface, we are trying to build a machine, or are at least trying to work toward a machine, that can play the short short story game successfully against a human author. Such machines, if we're right, will capitalize upon having an explicit account like Def_B 8, whether or not human authors work with such accounts.

Having said this, we do in fact believe that human authors writing about betrayal reason about such things as Def_B 8 — it's just that they do a lot of this reasoning at least partially outside of conscious control. In *Julius Caesar*, for example, Mark Antony, after Caesar is hacked to death, would appear to betray Brutus. (It makes an interesting exercise to verify that Def_B 8 is instantiated in the interaction between and behavior of Brutus and Mark Antony.) Conceivably, Shakespeare wrote this part of the play without consciously thinking about setting up another betrayal after the one we all associate with the play took place.

4.6   Miles to Go Before We Sleep

Unfortunately, there *is* a problem with Def_B 8: it doesn't deal with a case we touched upon earlier: the case in which a parent betrays a very young child, a child too young to instantiate the psychological properties ascribed to s_d in this definition. The solution here is no doubt in the direction of considering what s_d would want and believe if certain things (e.g., normal physical and psychological development) were to come to pass. Such a solution, if fully formalized, would require a formalism sensitive enough to represent sophisticated conditionals. Of course, this comes as no surprise. For a fully formalized version of Def_B 8, one that doesn't try to capture only the surface structure of this definition in some variant of first-order logic, would alone require the machinery of not only doxastic logic (for beliefs, as we discussed above), but also

- Logics of action, deliberate action, intending, etc.
- Temporal logic
- Conditional logic
- Deontic logic

In the future we expect to move toward such logics. For now, we rest content with Def$_B$ 8 as part of the BRUTUS architecture, and with mapping it to an implementation in Prolog and FLEX. This mapping will be discussed in Chapter 6. As we indicated previously, after betrayal, our plan is to proceed to the concept of self-deception. BRUTUS$_1$ currently works with a rough-and-ready account of self-deception (due essentially to a less formal account propounded by Harold Sackheim and Ruben Gur [202]) that can be set out via three conditions:

Def$_{S-D}$ 1 s is self-deceived iff there is a proposition p and a time t such that

1 s both believes at t that p and believes at t that $\neg p$;

2 s is unaware of one of the beliefs in clause 1;

3 There is an action a which determines which of the beliefs in question is subject to s's awareness, and a is motivated.

Though as Alfred Mele [158] has recently pointed out, the empirical evidence traditionally taken to show that Def$_{S-D}$ is routinely instantiated in humans is questionable, the fact remains that Def$_{S-D}$ 1 makes for some interesting narrative,[10] and that is good enough for BRUTUS.[11]

We conclude by presenting two more stories from BRUTUS$_1$'s repertoire. This first is one in which the account of self-deception

---

[10]Interestingly enough, Def$_{S-D}$ 1 is affirmed largely due to the fact that certain psychologists can use it to tell a coherent story about what is happening in certain experiments. See [158].

[11]This is as good a place as any to mention another literary theme with which we have been experimenting: evil. Currently we are working with a formalization of M. Scott Peck's [175] characterization of evil, which consists in a person exemplifying four properties, viz.,

1. consistent destructive, scapegoating behavior, which may often be quite subtle;

2. excessive, albeit, usually covert, intolerance to criticism and other forms of narcissistic injury;

3. pronounced concern with a public image and self-image of respectability, contributing to a stability of lifestyle but also to pretentiousness and denial of hateful feelings or vengeful motives; and finally,

4. intellectual deviousness, with an increased likelihood of a mild schizophrenic-like disturbance of thinking at times of stress.

isn't instantiated. Once again, note that the point is that these stories can be generated by BRUTUS courtesy of formalisms that *we* have crafted. BRUTUS did not and does not *originate* the following stories.

"Simple Betrayal" (no self-deception; conscious)

Dave Striver loved the university. He loved its ivy-covered clocktowers, its ancient and sturdy brick, and its sun-splashed verdant greens and eager youth. He also loved the fact that the university is free of the stark unforgiving trials of the business world — only this *isn't* a fact: academia has its own tests, and some are as merciless as any in the marketplace. A prime example is the dissertation defense: to earn the PhD, to become a doctor, one must pass an oral examination on one's dissertation.

Dave wanted desperately to be a doctor. But he needed the signatures of three people on the first page of his dissertation, the priceless inscriptions which, together, would certify that he had passed his defense. One of the signatures had to come from Professor Hart.

Well before the defense, Striver gave Hart a penultimate copy of his thesis. Hart read it and told Striver that it was absolutely first-rate, and that he would gladly sign it at the defense. They even shook hands in Hart's book-lined office. Dave noticed that Hart's eyes were bright and trustful, and his bearing paternal.

At the defense, Dave thought that he eloquently summarized Chapter 3 of his dissertation. There were two questions, one from Professor Rodman and one from Dr. Teer; Dave answered both, apparently to everyone's satisfaction. There were no further objections.

Professor Rodman signed. He slid the tome to Teer; she too signed, and then slid it in front of Hart. Hart didn't move.

"Ed?" Rodman said.

Hart still sat motionless. Dave felt slightly dizzy.

"Edward, are you going to sign?"

Later, Hart sat alone in his office, in his big leather chair, underneath his framed PhD diploma.

The second story is based on an instantiation of the concept of *self*-betrayal:

"Self-Betrayal" (no self-deception; conscious version)

Dave Striver loved the university — at least most of the time. Every now and then, without warning, a wave of ... well, it was true: a wave of *hatred* rose up and flowed like molten blood through every cell in his body. This hatred would be directed at the ghostly gatekeepers. But most of the time Striver loved — the ivy-covered clocktowers, the ancient and sturdy brick, and the sun-splashed verdant greens and eager youth who learned alongside him. He also loved the fact that the university is free of the stark unforgiving trials of the business world — only this *isn't* a fact: academia has its own tests, and some are as merciless as any in the marketplace. A prime example is the dissertation defense: to earn the PhD, to become a doctor, one must pass an oral examination on one's dissertation.

Dave wanted desperately to be a doctor. He had been working toward this end through six years of graduate school. In the end, he needed the signatures of three people on the first page of his dissertation, the priceless inscriptions which, together, would certify that he had passed his defense. One of the signatures had to come from Professor Hart.

Well before the defense, Striver gave Hart a penultimate copy of his thesis. Hart read it and told Striver that it was absolutely first-rate, and that he would gladly sign it at the defense. They shook hands in Hart's book-lined office. Hart's eyes were bright and trustful, and his bearing paternal.

"See you at 3 p.m. on the tenth, then, Dave!" Hart said.

At the defense, Dave eloquently summarized Chapter 3 of his dissertation. His plan had been to do the same for Chapter 4, and then wrap things up, but now he wasn't sure. The pallid faces before him seemed suddenly nauseating. What was he doing?

One of these pallid automata had an arm raised.

"What?" Striver snapped.

Striver watched ghosts look at each other. A pause.

Then Professor Teer spoke: "I'm puzzled as to why you prefer not to use the well-known alpha-beta minimax algorithm for your search?"

Why had he thought so earnestly about inane questions like this in the past? Striver said nothing. His nausea grew. Contempt, fiery and uncontrollable, rose up.

"Dave?" Professor Hart prodded, softly.

God, they were pitiful. Pitiful, pallid, and puny.

"Dave, did you hear the question?"

Later, Striver sat alone in his appartment. What in God's name had he done?

Chapter 5

The Narrative-Based Refutation of Church's Thesis

5.1   Can Interestingness Be Formalized?

As Chapter 4 makes plain, we have set ourselves the goal of capturing in logic such lofty literary themes as unrequited love, and of then implementing this logic in a theorem-prover-based story generator. Some will find this to be a laughably unreachable goal, despite our success with betrayal and BRUTUS. Actually, there was a time, about a decade ago, when one of us (Bringsjord) thought that perhaps the entire ball game could be won using something like this method. His idea was this: We would figure out what makes a story interesting from the standpoint of logic, proceed to formalize interestingness in some logical system, and then — as in the case of our plans for betrayal and other literary themes — code this formalization so as to yield a program that generates interesting stories. This idea proved to be a painful dead end. (Many of you are probably not surprised.) Whereas in the case of betrayal, counterexamples to proposed definitions of the concept led the way to improved definitions that promised to eventuate in *the correct* definition, nothing of the sort happened in dialectic at Rensselaer about what conditions are necessary and sufficient for a story's being interesting. *In fact*, it began to occur to Bringsjord that perhaps the set of all interesting stories — denoted $\mathcal{S}^I$ — was such that (i) there is no algorithm for deciding whether or not a story is in this set, and (ii) there is an algorithm for shooting down any algorithm proposed to decide $\mathcal{S}^I$. Some readers will immediately realize that properties (i) and (ii) characterize what are known in computability theory as **productive** sets. If the set of all interesting stories is a productive set, and if humans are able to decide, swiftly and routinely, which stories are interesting and which are not, then Church's famous and almost universally affirmed thesis — that what can be effectively computed is co-extensive with what can be algorithmically computed — must be false. We specify and defend this reasoning herein. If the reasoning is correct, the upshot would seem once again to be that those who would build literarily creative agents in the form of conventional computers and computer programs may at best find engineering "tricks" for giving these agents some mere approximation of what human authors tap when they craft interesting narrative. We conclude this chapter with a discussion of these tricks.

5.2   Mendelson on Church's Thesis

In a recent and widely affirmed paper in the *Journal of Philosophy*, Elliot Mendelson, arguably the world's leading authority on Church's Thesis (CT), [161][1] challenges what he rightly calls the "standard conception" (p. 230) of the thesis, namely, that CT is unprovable. Unfortunately, as we demonstrate herein, once Mendelson's target, and his attack upon it, are rigorously analyzed with help from uncomputability theory, his challenge evaporates, and the cogent rationale for the standard conception of CT is revealed. This analysis will in turn constitute a foundation for overthrowing CT in the manner already sketched. After the foundation is in place, we press forward in the hope, indeed, of refuting CT — by showing that our ability to decide whether stories are interesting is one that mere computing machines must forever lack. We then consider some other attacks on CT (some of which, as we shall see, Mendelson himself tried to derail over 40 years ago), and the relation between these attacks and our own. Finally, armed with what we have learned, we turn back to BRUTUS.

---

[1]Unless otherwise noted, all page references are to this paper.

5.3 Background Material

At the heart of CT is the notion of an **algorithm**, characterized in traditional fashion by Mendelson as

> an effective and completely specified procedure for solving a whole class of problems. ... An algorithm does not require ingenuity; its application is prescribed in advance and does not depend upon any empirical or random factors. ([161], p. 225)

An **effectively computable** function is then said to be the computing of a function by an idealized "worker" or "computist" following an algorithm.[2] (Without loss of generality, we can for present purposes view all functions as taking natural numbers into natural numbers; i.e., for some arbitrary f, $f : \mathbf{N} \to \mathbf{N}$). CT also involves a more formal notion, typically that of a so-called **Turing-computable** function (or, alternatively, and equivalently, that of a μ-**recursive** function, or, ...). Mendelson employs Turing's approach, and Turing machines will be familiar to most readers; we'll follow him: a function $f : \mathbf{N} \to \mathbf{N}$ is Turing-computable iff there exists a TM M which, starting with n on its tape (perhaps represented by n |s), leaves $f(n)$ on its tape after processing. (The details of the processing are harmlessly left aside for now.) Given this definition, CT amounts to

CT A function is effectively computable if and only if it's Turing-computable.[3]

Now what exactly is Mendelson's aim? He tells us:

> Here is the main conclusion I wish to draw: it is completely unwarranted to say that CT is unprovable just because it states an equivalence between a vague, imprecise notion (effectively computable function) and a precise mathematical notion (partial-recursive function). ([161], p. 232)

From this it follows that Mendelson's target is the traditional *argument* for the unprovability of CT. And the line of reasoning he means to attack runs as follows.

---

[2]In his inaugural writings (independent, by the way, of Turing's), Post [184] spoke of mindless "workers," humans whose sole job was to slavishly follow explicit, excruciatingly simple instructions. These are "computists" for Turing.

[3]This is often called the Church–*Turing* Thesis for obvious reasons.

Arg₁

EQU   If some thesis T states an equivalence between a vague, imprecise notion and a precise, mathematical notion, T is unprovable.

∴ (1)   If CT states an equivalence between a vague, imprecise notion and a precise, mathematical notion, CT is unprovable.

(2)

CT states an equivalence between a vague, imprecise notion and a precise, mathematical notion.

. (3)

CT is unprovable.

5.4   Refuting Mendelson's Attack

Mendelson's attack on Arg₁ is based on "theses" analogous to CT — "Peano's Thesis" (PT), "Tarski's Thesis" (TT), "Frege's Thesis" (FT), and "Weierstrass' Thesis" (WT).[4] The first three, respectively, are:

PT f is an intuitive, rule-based function iff f is a set of ordered pairs satisfying $(\star)$ if $(x, y) \in f$ and $(x, z) \in f$, then $y = z$.

TT   Let L be a first-order language, and $\mathcal{I}$ an interpretation based on L. Then a wff ϕ of L is true on $\mathcal{I}$ in the intuitive sense iff $\mathcal{I} \models \phi$, i.e., $\mathcal{I}$ satisfies ϕ, in the Tarskian model-theoretic sense.

FT   Again, let L be a first-order language, and $\mathcal{I}$ an interpretation based on L. Then a wff ϕ is valid in Frege's intuitive sense iff $\models \phi$, i.e., ϕ is valid in the model-theoretic sense.

But how does Mendelson use these three theses as ammunition for his three-pronged (the prongs are distinguished on pp. 232–233; he says his "argument" is based on "three points") attack on Arg₁? Let's look at the three prongs in turn, and blunt each.

---

[4]WT identifies the intuitive notion of limit with the standard ϵ-δ definition. Mendelson thinks that these four theses are just some among many such "theses." He mentions "the notion of measure as an explication of area and volume, the definition of dimension in topology, the definition of velocity as a derivative, the definition of logical implication and logical equivalence in first-order logic, and the definitions of circle, triangle, interior of an angle, and many other geometric concepts" ([161], p. 232).

The first prong, the most sophisticated and promising of the three, is an attack on Arg_1's premise (2): Mendelson seems to be saying that the equivalence this premise attributes to CT is chimerical:

> The concepts and assumptions that support the notion of partial-recursive function are, in an essential way, no less vague and imprecise than the notion of effectively computable function; the former are just more familiar and are part of a respectable theory with connections to other parts of logic and mathematics. (The notion of effectively computable function could have been incorporated into an axiomatic presentation of classical mathematics, but the acceptance of CT made this unnecessary.) The same point applies to [PT, FT, and TT]. Functions are defined in terms of sets, but the concept of set is no clearer than that of function and a foundation of mathematics can be based on a theory using function as primitive notion instead of set. Tarski's definition of truth is formulated in set-theoretic terms, but the notion of set is no clearer than that of truth. The model-theoretic definition of logical validity is based ultimately on set theory, the foundations of which are no clearer than our intuitive understanding of logical validity. (p. 232)

But how does not-(2) follow from this? What, exactly, is Mendelson's argument? The key idea seems to be that (2) is false because

(4) The notion of Turing-computable function is no clearer than, nor more mathematically useful (foundationally speaking) than, the notion of an effectively computable function.

We can probably all agree that (4) implies not-(2). But is (4) true? Mendelson gives both a direct rationale for (4) and an argument for it based on PT, FT, TT, and WT. Let's consider, first, the argument based on these other theses. Mendelson's hope seems to be that (4) follows from

$$X \text{ is no clearer than, nor } \dots \text{ than } Y$$

when this template, tied to the other "theses," is filled in in the expected way. For example, with respect to TT, the template becomes

'true on some $\mathcal{I}$' is no clearer than, nor ... than, 'intuitive truth'

And with respect to PT the template becomes

'($\star$)-based function' is no less vague than, nor ... than, 'intuitive function'

But there is a problem: Mendelson doesn't *establish* these statements. He simply asserts them. And that's not enough — especially
when the default intuition is likely to be that these statements are
false. Now, Mendelson does seem to think that such statements
follow from (or are at least supported by) the fact that things like
Zermelo Fraenkel set theory (ZF) can in principle be replaced with
foundations that take the concept of function as primitive. But *how*
does it follow from this that, e.g.,

'($\star$)-based function' is no clearer than, nor ... than, 'intuitive function'?

Mendelson doesn't answer this question.

But let's assume for the sake of argument that the template filled
in for PT (and FT, TT, WT) is true. We can then ask whether
(4) follows from this assumption. Does it? No. In fact, it seems
relatively easy to show that (4) is false, once one looks a bit at uncomputability theory. Here's how the demonstration works: Clearly,
if

(4) The notion of Turing-computable function is no clearer than, nor more
mathematically useful (foundationally speaking) than, the notion of
an effectively computable function,

then

(5) The notion of Turing-decidable set is no clearer than, nor more mathematically useful (foundationally speaking) than, the notion of an
effectively decidable set,

and

(6) The notion of Turing-enumerable set is no clearer than, nor more mathematically useful (foundationally speaking) than, the notion of an
effectively enumerable set,

$\vdots$

Now suppose that (4) is true. From this assumption, and the conditional indicated immediately preceding, it would seem to follow by *modus ponens* and simplification of conjunction that

(+) The notion of a formally defined program for guiding the operation of a TM is no clearer than, nor more mathematically useful (foundationally speaking) than, the notion of an algorithm.

This proposition, it would then seem, is the very heart of the matter. If (+) is true then Mendelson has made his case; if this proposition is false, then his case is doomed, since we can chain back by *modus tollens* and negate (4). What's the verdict? It's possible to demonstrate the falsity of (+), by way of the following straightforward reasoning.

Arg₂

(7)   If (+), then one should be able to construct the Arithmetic Hierarchy by way of the notion of an algorithm.

(8)   One cannot construct the Arithmetic Hierarchy by way of the notion of an algorithm.

∴   (9)   Not-(+)

This argument is obviously valid. Are the premises true? Of course, this question may be premature for some, since some readers may be unfamiliar with the Arithmetic Hierarchy (AH). So let's take a detour to encapsulate this notion. (Cognoscenti be forewarned: Space constraints make a thorough presentation of AH impossible. What follows is in no way a detailed, accomplished introduction to AH.[5])

Suppose we have some **totally computable** predicate

$$S(P, u, n)$$

iff TM M, running program P on input u, halts in exactly n steps ($= M_P : u \to_n$ halt). (Throughout AH our machines, architecturally speaking, are always simply TMs.) Predicate S is totally computable in the sense that, given some triple (P, u, n), there is some program $P^\star$ which, running on some TM $M^\star$, can infallibly give us a verdict,

---

[5]For a comprehensive discussion of uncomputability, including the Arithmetic Hierarchy, a good text is [60]. Bringsjord provides a self-contained introduction to the realm of "super"-computation in [26].

Y ("yes") or **N** ("no"), for whether or not S is true of this triple. ($P^\star$ could simply instruct $M^\star$ to simulate M for n steps and see what happens.) This implies that $S \in \Sigma_0$, i.e., that S is a member of the starting point in AH, a point composed of totally computable predicates. But now consider the predicate H, defined by

$$H(P, i) \text{ iff } \exists n S(P, i, n).$$

Since the ability to determine, for a pair (P, i), whether or not H is true of it, is equivalent to solving the full halting problem, we know that H is not totally computable. Hence $H \notin \Sigma_0$. However, there is a program which, when asked whether or not some TM M run by P on u halts, will produce **Y** iff $M_P : u \rightarrow$ halt. For this reason H is declared **partially computable**, and hence in Σ_1. To generalize, informally, the syntactic representation of AH is:

Σ_n set of all predicates definable in terms of totally computable predicates using at most n quantifiers, the first of which is *existential*

Π_n set of all predicates definable in terms of totally computable predicates using at most n quantifiers, the first of which is *universal*

Δ_n $\Sigma_n \cap \Pi_n$

We have, based on this scheme, the Arithmetic *Hierarchy* because, where $\subset$ is proper subset,

$$\Sigma_0 \subset \Sigma_1 \subset \Sigma_2 \dots$$
$$\Pi_0 \subset \Pi_1 \subset \Pi_2 \dots$$
$$\text{for every } m > 0, \Sigma_m \neq \Pi_m$$
$$\Pi_m \subset \Sigma_{m+1}$$
$$\Sigma_m \subset \Pi_{m+1}$$

It's possible to devise a more procedural view of (at the least the lower end of) AH. Σ_0 and Σ_1 have already been viewed procedurally. How, then, could Π_1, the first genuinely uncomputable stop in AH, be viewed procedurally? Peter Kugel [141] has aptly called Π_1-procedures **non-halting procedures**; here's how they essentially work. (Notice that the term 'procedures' is being used, rather than 'programs'. This is crucial, for reasons discussed in a moment.) Let R be a totally computable predicate; then there is some program P which decides R. Now consider a corresponding predicate $G \in \Pi_1$, viz.,

$$G(x) \text{ iff } \forall y R(x,y).$$

Here's a non-halting procedure P^+ (not a program: we count P^+'s last output (if there is one) as its result) for solving G, in the sense that a **Y** is the result iff Gx:[6]

- Receive x as input

- Immediately print **Y**

- Compute, by repeatedly calling $P, R(x,1), R(x,2), \ldots$, looking for a **N**

- If **N** is found, erase **Y** and leave result undefined

Notice that it would be *impossible* to represent this procedure as a *program*. This can be verified by looking at any formal specification of 'program.' For example, in *Mathematical Logic*, by Ebbinghaus et al. [82], programs can have only one PRINT instruction. (Typically, procedures are formalized by *adding* to programs the notion of an "oracle.") But the point is that once you tinker with the formalization of 'program,' the world of uncomputability opens up, a paradise that is richer than the small, familiar subhierarchy on the computable side, which runs from finite automata, to push-down automata, to linear-bounded automata, to TMs. Space doesn't permit exhibiting AH in its full glory, but here's one more interesting fact about it, viz., that procedures corresponding to Σ_2, **trial-and-error procedures**, can rather easily solve the full halting problem — as follows. Let a TM — $M^{\star\star}$ — with n^M as input (Gödel number of arbitrary TM M) output **N** immediately, and then let it simulate M. If M halts, $M^{\star\star}$ erases **N**, outputs **Y**, and halts itself. If we count $M^{\star\star}$'s last output as its output, the full halting problem is solved!

But what is the point of all this? The point is that even a cursory look at AH reveals that Arg$_2$, Mendelson's earlier counterargument, is sound. Why? We take it, first, that (7) is uncontroversial.[7] Since Arg$_2$ is formally valid, if (8), the only other premise in the argument, is true, the argument is sound. Premise (8), recall, is

---

[6]The reader should satisfy himself or herself that the following procedure *does* decide G.

[7]In fact, it would seem that (7) is itself provable via conditional proof: Start by assuming that (+), and then simply consider building AH by way of the unformalized notion of an algorithm.

(8) One cannot construct the Arithmetic Hierarchy by way of the notion of an algorithm.

But our look at AH has established this premise, for the simple reason that algorithms correspond to those things (programs) which must be significantly modified in order to open up the infinite landscape of AH. Mendelson is of course correct that it's possible to supplant ZF with any number of equivalent constructions which don't take 'set' as primitive. But if one takes 'algorithm' as primitive, one will forever close off AH, since to gain access to this paradise one must *formalize* 'algorithm,' and then begin to "tinker" with the details of this formalization.

It's important to note that the crucial (8) is distinct from

(8*) One cannot construct the Arithmetic Hierarchy without the notion of an algorithm.

Proposition (8*) is false, because it's possible (and to some, preferable) to develop the theory of relative computability (of which AH is but a small part) by way of the notion of a function, with programs, oracles, algorithms, and the like left by the wayside. Premise (8), on the other hand, says that AH cannot be constructed by way of the notion of an algorithm — and this is so, to repeat, because such a route gives you nothing like the fine-grained analysis of the "function route" (which requires composition, primitive recursion, unbounded minimalization, etc.).[8]

What about the second prong in Mendelson's attack? This prong is aimed against the EQU principle, which was the first premise in Arg_1, the argument Mendelson believes he has undermined. Here is the relevant quote:

> The assumption that a proof connecting intuitive and precise mathematical notions is impossible is patently false. In fact, half of CT (the "easier" half), the assertion that all partial-recursive functions are effectively computable, is acknowledged to be obvious in all textbooks on recursion theory. (p. 232)

Mendelson proceeds to give the "proof" of the "if" part of CT (p. 231). We readily concede that he does in fact prove the "if" part. But a

---

[8]Heading off the erroneous conflation of (8*) and (8) is something Kostas Arkoudas, in objecting to our argument, stimulated us to consider; we're indebted.

question remains: How does not-EQU follow from this sub-proof? EQU would be overthrown by a counterexample in which this principle's antecedent is true but its consequent is not. But this is *not* the situation Mendelson creates by way of his sub-proof. At best, he has overthrown *this* principle:

EQU→ If some thesis T states a conditional connection between a vague, imprecise notion and a precise, mathematical notion, then T is unprovable.

The obvious question then arises: Are any of PT, FT, TT provable? If so, then Mendelson might be able to sustain the fight. But it's hard to see how one would even begin to prove these. (Skeptics are encouraged to embark upon the proofs. Better yet, next time you or a colleague teaches first-order logic, assign one of these proofs on an exam.) At any rate, the proofs would clearly be nontrivial; and since Mendelson has provided neither these proofs, nor sketches for how to carry them out, there is no reason, in the context of the present dialectic, to suppose that the trio analogous to CT — PT, FT, TT — is provable.

What is Mendelson's third prong? Essentially, it's the claim that "the usual viewpoint concerning CT is that it assumes that the only way to ascertain the truth of the equivalence asserted in CT is to *prove* it" (p. 233). Mendelson goes on to claim that

> ... equivalences between intuitive notions and apparently more precise mathematical notions often are simply "seen" to be true without proof, or are based on arguments that are a mixture of such intuitive perceptions and standard logical and mathematical reasoning. (p. 233)

Here Mendelson seems to commit a bald *non sequitur*. For notice that nothing in this quote threatens Arg_1. Nowhere in Arg_1 is there a hidden premise to the effect that there aren't arguments-short-of-proof for CT. On the contrary, as is well-known, those impressed by *inductive* arguments often affirm CT on the basis of such reasoning. So how does Mendelson's third prong constitute a challenge to the orthodox view on CT? Apparently, it simply doesn't. Even Mendelson himself seems to concede that the third prong is a bit beside the point:

> That CT is true follows, I believe, from Turing's analysis of the essential elements involved in computation. But this is not

what I have tried to establish. The point I have attempted to make is the equivalences between intuitive notions and "precise" notions need not always be considered unprovable theses.[9] (p. 233)

The third prong would be relevant if there were good deductive arguments for CT, *and* if what Mendelson calls the "usual viewpoint" ruled them out. But to enlarge the "usual viewpoint concerning CT" this way would be to create a straw man. Besides, we have a formidable deductive argument *against CT*, and so it would be rather double-minded if we went in search of deductive arguments *for* the thesis. Our deductive argument against CT doesn't derive from the view that this thesis connects a vague notion with a mathematical one. It derives from an application of uncomputability theory to stories. But before presenting that argument, we consider Mendelson's response[10] to what we have so far said against him.

5.5 Mendelson's Rebuttal

Mendelson concedes that a significant part of our case succeeds, that is, that (4) is indeed false: He agrees that the formal concepts in question (e.g., 'Turing-computable function') are more useful than their informal partners (e.g., 'effectively computable function'); and he admits that "One could, with some justification, claim that the notion of a Turing-computable function is 'clearer' than that of an effectively computable function because the former is more specific and ties in closely with other well-known mathematical concepts" ([161], p. 228). However, Mendelson goes on to say:

> My point in this case has nothing to do with relative clarity of concepts. Rather, the point is that the notion of an effectively computable function is not essentially different from the notions that underlie the theory of Turing-computable functions, and, more specifically, that the former notion can be used in mathematical proofs just as legitimately as the latter notions. This was illustrated in my paper by the proof that

---

[9]The last sentence here is somewhat peculiar, since it could be verified by something that would not necessarily defeat A1. Indeed, this sentence could be verified by an argument which lacked reference to CT.

[10]Personal communication, December 14, 1993.

all partial-recursive functions are effectively computable. That proof, which Professor Bringsjord himself accepts, undermines the basis for the traditional belief in the unprovability of the the Church-Turing Thesis, namely, that there is in principle an unbridgable gap between, on the one hand, arguments that involve 'vague, intuitive' notions, and, on the other hand, 're-spectable' proofs that can be formalized within, say, ZF or PA [Peano Arithmetic[11]]. ([161], p. 228)

Unfortunately, this rebuttal fails. Yes, we did indeed concede that Mendelson's mathematical argument for the so-called "easier" half of CT constitutes a proof (though we think Mendelson's comment following that argument — "This simple argument is as clear a proof as I have seen in mathematics" (p. 233) — is at least peculiar, and possibly disingenuous). But Mendelson seems to ignore our observation that his proof doesn't substantiate the premise in Arg_1 called 'EQU:'

EQU If some thesis T states an equivalence between a vague, imprecise notion and a precise, mathematical notion, T is unprovable.

Lest it be thought that we tendentiously cooked up this premise, and set it as an unreachable target for Mendelson, we remind the reader that the text in question is clear: There can be little doubt that Mendelson targets EQU. Consider again, for example, what he says:

Here is the main conclusion I wish to draw: it is completely unwarranted to say that CT is unprovable just because it states an *equivalence* between a vague, imprecise notion (effectively computable function) and a precise mathematical notion (partial-recursive function). ([161], p. 232; emphasis added)

And again Mendelson says that "*equivalences* between intuitive and 'precise' notions need not always be considered unprovable theses" (p. 233; emphasis added).

Now Janet Folina [92] has suggested that Mendelson's aim be charitably scaled back — so that what he is said to be aiming at is *not* a demonstration that CT is provable (an aim she agrees we have shown Mendelson cannot reach), but rather a demonstration that proofs merely *connecting* intuitive with formal notions are possible.

---

[11] An introduction to PA can be found in [82].

This reconstruction of Mendelson's main argument is, predictably, one that we would gladly accept.[12]

With our foundation laid, we turn now to our narrational attack on CT.

5.6   Attacking Church's Thesis From Narrative

Our suspicion that CT is false first arose in connection with the concept of **productive** sets, which have two properties:

P1 They are classically undecidable (= no program can decide such sets).

P2 There is a computable function f from the set of all programs to any such set, a function which, when given a candidate program P, yields an element of the set for which P will fail.

Put informally, a set A is productive iff it's not only classically undecidable, but also if any program proposed to decide A can be counterexampled with some element of A. Clearly, if a set A' has these properties, then $A' \notin \Sigma_0$ and $A' \notin \Sigma_1$. If A' falls somewhere in AH, and is effectively decidable, then CT falls. But what could possibly fit the bill? We have become convinced that the set S^I of all interesting stories provides a perfect fit.

Given what the two of us are about in this volume, the notion that literary interestingness could spell doom for Church's Thesis isn't out of place — but it nonetheless may be a notion that catches some off guard. Interesting stories? Well, let us remind you, first,

---

[12]Incidentally, the reconstruction probably has fatal problems, as Folina [92] points out. After all, *is* what Mendelson calls a proof here a proof? One common conception — indeed, probably the *dominant* conception — of a proof is a transformation in some formal system. Yet Mendelson says about his proof: "The fact that it is not a proof in ZF or some other axiomatic system is no drawback; it just shows that there is more to mathematics than appears in ZF" (p. 233). (Remember this quote later when we consider Mendelson's rejection of Kalmár's argument against CT in part because it falls outside any standard formal system.) A lot of thinkers will balk at this. As Folina [92] notes, many will diagnose the situation by saying that what Mendelson has shown is that there is more to mathematics than proofs. (This is something we've known all along, of course.) Moreover, if Mendelson's reasoning *isn't* a proof, then what is it? If it's merely a *precise, compelling argument* connecting an intuitive notion with a formal one, then it shows something we knew to be true all along.

that the view that there are productive sets near at hand is far from unprecedented. Douglas Hofstadter [113], for example, holds that the set $\mathcal{A}$ of all As is a productive set. In order to satisfy P1, $\mathcal{A}$ must forever resist attempts to write a program for deciding this set; in order to satisfy P2, there must at minimum always be a way to "stump" a program intended to decide $\mathcal{A}$. That $\mathcal{A}$ satisfies both these conditions isn't all that implausible — especially when one faces up to the unpredictable variability seen in this set. For example, take a look at Figure 5.1.[13]

AAaa
AAaa
AAaa
$\mathscr{AA}$
AAaa
AAaa
AAaa
AAaa
AAaa
AAaa
AAaa
AA
AAaa
$\mathcal{AA}$
AAaa
AAaa
AAaa
AAaa
AAaa
AAaa
AAaa
⋮

Figure 5.1: Various Letter As.

In order for a program to decide $\mathcal{A}$, it must capitalize on some rules that capture the "essence" of the letter in question. But what sorts of rules could these be? We suggest that you experiment in order

---

[13] For 56 much more peculiar uppercase As, see the array of them in [145]. A similar array, but this time of all lowercase As, can be found on page 413 of [111].

to see for yourself that such rules probably don't exist. Does the bar in the middle need to touch the sides? No. It's easy to draw an A wherein that isn't true; try it yourself. Does there have to be a bar that *approximates* connecting the sides? Apparently not (again: experiment[14]). And on and on it goes for other proposed rules.

However, it must be conceded that no *argument* for the productivity of $\mathcal{A}$ has been provided by Hofstadter. For all we know, some company could tomorrow announce a letter recognition system that will work for all As. The situation is a bit different in the case of the mathematician Peter Kugel [141], who makes clever use of an elementary theorem in unmistakably *arguing* that the set of all beautiful objects is located above Σ_1 in AH:

> We seem to be able to recognize, as beautiful, pieces of music that we almost certainly could not have composed. There is a theorem about the partially computable sets that says that there is a uniform procedure for turning a procedure for recognizing members of such sets into a procedure for generating them. Since this procedure is uniform — you can use the same one for all computable sets — it does not depend on any specific information about the set in question. So, if the set of all beautiful things were in Σ_1, we should be able to turn our ability to recognize beautiful things into one for generating them ... This suggests that a person who recognizes the Sistine Chapel Ceiling as beautiful knows enough to paint it, [which] strikes me as somewhat implausible. ([141], pp. 147–148)

The main problem with this line of reasoning is that it's disturbingly exotic. Beauty is perhaps a promising candidate for what Kugel is after, but it must be conceded that most of those scientists who think seriously about human cognition don't think a lot about beauty. Indeed, they don't seem to think *at all* about beauty.[15] And this isn't (they would insist) because beauty is a daunting concept, one that resists recasting in computational terms. The stance would doubtless be that beauty is left aside because one can exhaustively analyze cognition (and replicate it on a machine) without bothering to grapple in earnest with this concept.

---

[14]If you get stumped, see the letter A in position 7 G in [145].

[15]A search for coverage of this concept in standard texts about cognition — e.g., [3] and [224] — turns up nothing whatever.

This claim about the irrelevance of beauty may strike some as astonishing, and it certainly isn't a view affirmed by each and every computationalist, but we gladly concede it for the sake of argument: For the record, we grant that ignoring beauty, in the context of attempts to model, simulate, and replicate mentation, is acceptable.[16] However, we think there is another concept that serves our purposes perfectly: namely, the concept of a *story*. Stories are thought by many to be at the very heart of cognition. As we pointed out in Chapter 1, in their lead target chapter in *Knowledge and Memory: The Real Story* [251], Roger Schank and Robert Abelson boldly assert on the very first page that "virtually all human knowledge" is based on stories. Schank and Abelson claim later in the book that since the essence of cognition inheres in narrative, we can jettison propositional, logic-based, rule-based, formal ... schemes for knowledge representation. Of the 17 commentators who react to the target piece, 13 affirm the story-based view (the remaining four authors are skeptical).[17]

The other nice thing about stories, from our perspective, is that apparently we know a thing or two about them, especially in the context of computation — as this book presumably shows. We are devoted to creating an artificial agent capable of generating sophisticated fiction; BRUTUS shows that this is far from a pipe dream. At any rate, one of us (Bringsjord) discussed story generation work in his *What Robots Can and Can't Be* [40], in which he specifically discussed the challenge of characterizing, precisely, the class of *interesting* stories. (His main claim was that analytic philosophy offers the best hope of supplying this characterization.) For those who seek

---

[16]What argument could be mustered for ignoring beauty in the context of attempts to reduce cognition to computation, or to build an artificial agent capable of behaviors analogous to human ones typically taken to involve beauty? We envisage an argument running parallel to the one John Pollock [182] gives for ignoring human emotions in his attempt to build an artificial person. Pollock's view, in a nutshell, is that human emotions are in the end just "time savers"; with fast enough hardware, and clever enough algorithms, artificial persons could *compute* the need to quickly flee (say) a lion, whereas we take one look and immediately feel a surge of fear that serves to spark our rapid departure.

[17]Schank has devoted a book to the view that stories are at the very heart of human cognition [204]. And, as we remarked in our opening chapter, Dennett's *Consciousness Explained* [70] can be read as a defense of the view (his "multiple drafts" view of consciousness) that thinking is at bottom the spinning out of parallel stories.

to build agents capable of creative feats like good storytelling, this is a key challenge. It's easy enough to build systems capable of generating *un*interesting stories. For example, the world's first artificial story generator, TALE-SPIN [160], did a good job of that. Here, for instance, is one of TALE-SPIN's best stories:

"Hunger"

> Once upon a time John Bear lived in a cave. John knew that John was in his cave. There was a beehive in a maple tree. Tom Bee knew that the beehive was in the maple tree. Tom was in his beehive. Tom knew that Tom was in his beehive. There was some honey in Tom's beehive. Tom knew that the honey was in Tom's beehive. Tom had the honey. Tom knew that Tom had the honey. There was a nest in a cherry tree. Arthur Bird knew that the nest was in the cherry tree. Arthur was in his nest. Arthur knew that John was in his cave. ...

How are things to be improved? How is one to go about building an agent capable of creating truly interesting stories? It has been the sustained attempt to answer this question, in conjunction with the concept of productivity discussed earlier, that has persuaded us that CT is indeed false. Let us explain.

First, to ease exposition, let S^I denote the set of all interesting stories. Now, recall that productive sets must have two properties, P1 and P2; let's take them in turn, in the context of S^I. First, S^I must be classically undecidable; i.e., there is no program (= TM) which answers the question, for an arbitrary story in S, whether or not it's interesting. Second, there must be some computable function f from the set of all programs to S^I which, when given as input a program P that purportedly decides S^I, yields an element of S^I for which P fails. It seems to us that S^I does have both of these properties — because, in a nutshell, our research group seems to invariably and continuously turn up these two properties "in action." Every time someone suggests an algorithm-sketch for deciding S^I, it's easily shot down by a counterexample consisting of a certain story which is clearly interesting despite the absence in it of those conditions P regards to be necessary for interestingness. (It has been suggested that interesting stories must have inter-character conflict, but monodramas can involve only one character. It has been suggested that interesting stories must embody age-old plot structures, but some interesting stories are interesting precisely because they violate such structures, and so on.)

The situation we have arrived at can be crystallized in deductive form as follows.

Arg₃

(9) If $S^I \in \Sigma_1$ (or $S^I \in \Sigma_0$), then there exists a procedure P which adapts programs for deciding members of S^I so as to yield programs for enumerating members of S^I.

(10) There's no procedure P which adapts programs for deciding members of S^I so as to yield programs for enumerating members of S^I.

. (11) $S^I \notin \Sigma_1$ (or $S^I \notin \Sigma_0$).   10, 11

 (12) $S^I \in$ AH.

∴ (13) $S^I \in \Pi_1$ (or above in the AH).   disj syll

 (14) S^I is effectively decidable.

∴ (15) CT is false.   *reductio*

Clearly, Arg₃ is formally valid. Premise (9) is not only true, but necessarily true, since it's part of the canon of elementary computability theory. What about premise (10)? Well, this is the core idea, the one expressed earlier by Kugel, but transferred now to a different domain: People who can *decide* S^I, that is, people who can decide whether something is an interesting story, can't necessarily *generate* interesting stories. Students in *Autopoeisis*[18] have been a case in point: With little knowledge of, and skill for, creating interesting stories, they can nonetheless recognize such narrative. That is, students who are, by their own admission, egregious creative writers, are nonetheless discriminating critics. They can decide which stories are interesting (which is why they know that the story generators AI has produced so far are nothing to write home about), but *producing* the set of all such stories (including, as it does, such works as not only *King Lear*, but *War and Peace*) is quite another matter. These would be, necessarily, the *same* matter if the set of all interesting stories, S^I, was in either Σ_0 or Σ_1, the algorithmic portion of AH.

---

[18]The project that was the precursor to our work on BRUTUS, mentioned in the Acknowledgments.

But what's the rationale behind (13), the claim that S^I is effectively decidable? The rationale is simply the brute fact that a normal, well-adjusted human computist can effectively decide S^I. Try it yourself: First, start with the sort of story commonly discussed in AI, for example:

"Shopping"

Jack was shopping at the supermarket. He picked up some milk from the shelf. He paid for it and left.[19]

Well? Your judgment? Uninteresting, we wager. Now go back to "Hunger," and come up with a judgment for it, if you haven't done so already. Also uninteresting, right? Now render a verdict on a story within BRUTUS's reach, one we saw earlier.

"Betrayal in Self-Deception" (conscious)

Dave Striver loved the university. He loved its ivy-covered clocktowers, its ancient and sturdy brick, and its sun-splashed verdant greens and eager youth. He also loved the fact that the university is free of the stark unforgiving trials of the business world — only this *isn't* a fact: academia has its own tests, and some are as merciless as any in the marketplace. A prime example is the dissertation defense: to earn the PhD, to become a doctor, one must pass an oral examination on one's dissertation. This was a test Professor Edward Hart enjoyed giving.

Dave wanted desperately to be a doctor. But he needed the signatures of three people on the first page of his dissertation, the priceless inscriptions which, together, would certify that he had passed his defense. One of the signatures had to come from Professor Hart, and Hart had often said — to others and to himself — that he was honored to help Dave secure his well-earned dream.

Well before the defense, Striver gave Hart a penultimate copy of his thesis. Hart read it and told Dave that it was absolutely first-rate, and that he would gladly sign it at the defense.

---

[19]From page 592 of [49]. The story is studied in the context of attempts to resolve pronouns: How do we know who the first occurrence of 'He' refers to in this story? And how do we render the process of resolving the pronoun to Jack as a computational one?

They even shook hands in Hart's book-lined office. Dave noticed that Hart's eyes were bright and trustful, and his bearing paternal.

At the defense, Dave thought that he eloquently summarized Chapter 3 of his dissertation. There were two questions, one from Professor Rodman and one from Dr. Teer; Dave answered both, apparently to everyone's satisfaction. There were no further objections.

Professor Rodman signed. He slid the tome to Teer; she too signed, and then slid it in front of Hart. Hart didn't move.

"Ed?" Rodman said.

Hart still sat motionless. Dave felt slightly dizzy.

"Edward, are you going to sign?"

Later, Hart sat alone in his office, in his big leather chair, saddened by Dave's failure. He tried to think of ways he could help Dave achieve his dream.

This time, interesting, right?

Now at this point some readers may be thinking: "Now wait a minute. Isn't your position inconsistent? On the one hand you cheerfully opine that 'interesting story' cannot be captured. But on the other you provide an interesting story — a story that must, if I understand your project, capitalize upon some careful account of interestingness in narrative."

"Betrayal in Self-Deception (conscious)," as we saw in Chapter 4, is based in significant part upon an implementation of definitions taking the classic form of necessary and sufficient conditions. These definitions are given for "immemorial themes"; in "Betrayal in Self-Deception (conscious)" the two themes are self-deception and, of course, betrayal. Here again is the definition of betrayal with which BRUTUS essentially works:[20]

Def$_B$ 8 Agent s_r betrays agent s_d at t_b iff there exists some state of affairs p and $\exists t_i, t_k, t_j$ $(t_i \leq t_k \leq t_j \leq t_b)$ such that

---

[20]Recall that the variables t_i range over times, and that $\leq$ means "earlier or simultaneous." Note also the following clauses, which appear in clause 3'.

3 s_r agrees with s_d that p ought to occur;

6' s_d wants that there is some action a which s_r performs in the belief that thereby p *will* occur.

1 s_d at t_i wants p to occur;

2 s_r believes that s_d wants p to occur;

3' $(3 \wedge 6') \vee$

    6'' s_d wants at t_k that there is no action a which s_r performs in the belief that thereby p will not occur;

4'' there is some action a such that:

    4''a s_r performs a at t_b in the belief that thereby p will *not* occur; and

    4''b it's not the case that there exists a state of affairs q such that q is believed by s_r to be good for s_d and s_r performs a in the belief that q will not occur;

5' s_r believes at t_j that s_d believes that there is some action a which s_r will perform in the belief that thereby p *will* occur.

All of this sort of work (i.e., the gradual crafting of such definitions in the face of counterexample after counterexample) is perfectly consistent with the absence of an account of 'interesting story.' *In fact*, this kind of analysis figures in the observation that proposed accounts of interestingness are invariably vulnerable to counterexample. For example, suppose we try (here, schematically) something we have tried: Let $c_1, \ldots, c_n$ enumerate the definitions of all the immemorial themes involved in narrative. Now suppose we venture a definition having the following structure.

D' A story s is interesting iff

    1 ...

    $\vdots$

    k s instantiates (inclusive) either c_1 or c_2 or ... or c_n.

    $k + 1$ ...

    $\vdots$

    p ...

The problem — and, alas, we have experienced it time and time again — is that along will come a counterexample; in this case, a story which explicitly fails to satisfy k from D''s definiens will arrive. For example, an author can write a very interesting story about a phenomenon like betrayal as cashed out in definition Def_B 8, except that instead of clause 4'', the following weaker clause is satisfied.

4' there is some action a which s_r performs in the belief that thereby p will *not* occur.

The story here might involve a courageous, self-sacrificial mother who assures her addicted son that she will procure drugs to relieve his misery (as he desires), but intends only to confront the pusher and put an end to his destructive dealings. (As you may recall, this was a case we explicitly considered in Chapter 4.) Ironically, clearly some of the interestingness in this story will derive precisely from the fact that the mother is not betraying her son according to a definition containing clause 4'. In short, devising accounts like D' seems to be to fight a battle that can never be won; good narrative cannot be bottled.

At this point, we suspect that many readers are chomping at the bit, raring to tear into our position with additional objections. Let's see if we can't anticipate and disarm them now.

5.7 Objections

5.7.1 Objection 1

"Look, Bringsjord and Ferrucci, you must have gone wrong somewhere! Stories are just strings over some finite alphabet. In your case, given the stories you have thus far put on display, the alphabet in question is {Aa, Bb, Cc, ..., :, !, ;, ...}, that is, basically the characters we see before us on our computer keyboard. Let's denote this alphabet by 'E.' Elementary string theory tells us that though E^*, the set of all strings that can be built from E, is infinite, it's *countably* infinite,[21] and that therefore there is a program P which enumerates E^*. (P, for example, can resort to lexicographic ordering.) From this it follows that your $\mathcal{S}$, the set of all stories, is itself countably infinite. (If we allow, as no doubt we must, all natural languages to be included — French, Chinese, and even Norwegian — the situation doesn't change: The union of a finite number of countably infinite sets is still just countably infinite.) So what's the problem? You say that your students are able to decide $\mathcal{S}^I$? Fine. Then here's what we do to enumerate $\mathcal{S}^I$: Start P in motion, and for

---

[21] Intuitively, a set is countably infinite if it can be paired off with the natural numbers. For example, the set of even natural numbers is countably infinite because the pairing (0, 0), (2, 1), (4, 2), (6, 3), ... can be defined.

each item S generated by this program, call your students to pass verdict on whether or not S is interesting. This composite program — call it P': P working in conjunction with your students — enumerates S^I. So sooner or later, P' will manage to write *King Lear*, *War and Peace*, and even more recent belletristic narrative like that produced in the United States by Selmer's favorite living novelist: Mark Helprin."

There is good reason to think that even if S is in some sense typographic, it needn't be countably infinite. Is $\mathcal{A}$, the set of all As, countable? (You might at this point want to return to Figure 5.1.) If not, then simply imagine a story associated with every element within $\mathcal{A}$; this provides an immediate refutation of Objection 1. For a parallel route to the same result, think of a story about π, a story about $\sqrt{2}$, indeed a story for every real number!

On the other hand, stories, in the real world, are often neither strings nor, more generally, typographic. After all, authors often think about, expand, refine, ... stories without considering anything typographic whatsoever. They may "watch" stories play out before their mind's eye, for example (as we mentioned in Chapter 2). In fact, it seems plausible to say that strings (and the like) can be used to *represent* stories, as opposed to saying that the relevant strings, strictly speaking, *are* stories.[22]

5.7.2   Objection 2

"Ah! You concede then that you have a decision procedure for S^I. But uncountably infinite sets like **R**, the reals, are *not* decidable!"

This objection is anemic (though we have had it earnestly expressed to us). And the reason it is, of course, is that we need

---

[22]Someone might at this point complain that this latitudinarian view of stories implies that they are not the sort of well-defined things that are in the Arithmetic Hierarchy. This complaint can't be on the right track, for if it were, then even the concepts involved in standard, well-oiled computational work would have to be said to fall outside of AH, which would in turn cut an unacceptable chasm between the theory of computation and computation itself. For example, a good chess move, a sensible medical test to be conducted given the presentation of certain symptoms, an expert judgment about where to drill for oil given certain evidence, and so on — the assumption is always that these concepts, each of which is at the core of concrete work, are ultimately in AH, even though it seems well nigh impossible to express them in terms of quantifiers over computable predicates.

only maintain that $\mathcal{S}^I$ is *effectively* decidable, not that there is some program (or Turing machine, etc.) that can decide this set. (CT is the customary justification given for identifying effective decidability with formal decidability, but of course one can hardly invoke CT in the present context without falling prey to a *petitio*.)

Though Objection 2 is misguided, it does suggest an interesting parallel for Arg$_3$:

Arg$'_3$

(9′)   If $\mathbf{R} \in \Sigma_1$ (or $\mathbf{R} \in \Sigma_0$), then there exists a procedure P which adapts programs for deciding members of $\mathbf{R}$ so as to yield programs for enumerating members of $\mathbf{R}$.

(10′)   There's no procedure P which adapts programs for deciding members of $\mathbf{R}$ so as to yield programs for enumerating members of $\mathbf{R}$.

∴ (11′) $\mathbf{R} \notin \Sigma_1$ (or $\mathbf{R} \notin \Sigma_0$).   10, 11

(12′) $\mathbf{R} \in$ AH.

∴ (13′) $\mathbf{R} \in \Pi_1$ (or above in the AH).   disj syll

(14′) $\mathbf{R}$ is effectively decidable.

∴ (15′)   CT is false.   *reductio*

As we know by now, premise (9′) is an instantiation of a simple theorem of elementary computability theory; (11′) and (13′) are simply intermediate conclusions; (15) does indeed follow from (13′) and (14′), since these two propositions counterexample CT's "only if" part; and the other two inferences are unassailable. Everything boils down to (10′) and (14′). But we know that in the case of the reals, (11′) is true (and, of course, so is (10′), but we don't need it), and the technique of getting $\mathbf{R}$ from $\mathbf{N}$ (the natural numbers) via (e.g.) Dedekind cuts constitutes a proof of (12′).[23] Of course, it's doubtful that $\mathbf{R}$ or a subset thereof is effectively decidable. Such is not the case, as we've explained, with $\mathcal{S}^I$.

5.7.3   Objection 3

"I now see your error, gentlemen: premise (12) in Arg$_3$. If $\mathcal{S}^I$ is to be in AH, then your key predicate — 'Interesting'; denote it by

---

[23] For coverage of this technique see [226].

'I — must be a bivalent one. (More precisely, I must be isomorphic to a predicate that is built via quantification out of the totally computable bivalent predicates of Σ_0.) But a moment's reflection reveals that I *isn't* bivalent: different people have radically different opinions about whether certain fixed stories are interesting! Clearly, though Jones and Smith may share the same language, and may thus be able to fully understand "Shopping," "Hunger," "Betrayal in Self-Deception," *King Lear*, and *War and Peace*, their judgments may differ. "Shopping" might be downright thrilling to an AInik interested in determining how, upon reading such a story, humans know instantly that the pronoun 'He' refers to Jack."[24]

It is important to realize that we are talking about stories *qua* stories; stories as narrative. Hence a better way to focus the present objection is to note that Jones may find *Kind Lear* to be genuine drama, but monstrously boring drama (because, he says, King Lear, is but a lunatic), while Smith is transfixed. It's undeniable that differences of opinion like those existing between Jones and Smith are common. But this fact is not a threat to our argument. First, note that such differences are present in *all* domains, not just in the domain of narrative. Wittgenstein [248] teased much out of a clash between someone who says that $2 + 2 = 4$ and someone who flatly denies it — so even the arithmetical realm, if Objection 3 goes through, would lack bivalent properties, and if anything is suffused with bivalence, it's arithmetic. Moreover, there is nothing to prevent us from stipulating that these agents come decked out with some fixed "value system" — for judging stories. In fact, let us heretofore insist that I be read as not just interesting *simpliciter*, but interesting given (what must surely be one of the world's most refined systems for gauging stories) the knowledge and ability of none other than Umberto Eco.[25] Our new predicate, then, can be I_{UE}.

---

[24]This intelligent objection is essentially due to Michael McMenamin [157], though a number of thinkers have conveyed its gist to us.

[25]Those unfamiliar with Eco's nonfiction work might start with his surprising reasons for finding Ian Fleming's 007 (James Bond) series to be very interesting; see "Chapter Six: Narrative Structures in Fleming," in [83]. We discuss these issues in Chapter 6.

5.7.4 Objection 4

"At this start of this chapter you affirmed Mendelson's characterization of 'algorithm.' Let me remind you that according to that characterization, 'An algorithm does not reaquire ingenuity.' Are you not now bestowing remarkable ingenuity upon the readers/judges you have in mind?"

Recall that in order to parse 'effectively computable,' as we have noted, it's necessary to invoke the generic concept of an agent, either Turing's "computist" or Post's "worker." The agent in question, as none other than Elliot Mendelon reminded us nearly forty years ago [162], needn't be a *human* agent, because, following the mantra at the heart of computability theory, we impose no practical restrictions on the length of calculations and computations. It follows immediately that the agents we have in mind have enough raw time and energy to process the longest and most complex contenders in S. Furthermore, if we are going to seriously entertain CT, we must, all of us, allow the agents in question to have certain knowledge and ability, for example the knowledge and ability required to grasp the concepts of number, symbol, change, movement, instruction, and so on. The agents we have in mind are outfitted so as to be able to grasp stories, and the constitutents of stories. And in deploying I, and in moving to I_{UE}, we assume *less* on the part of agents (workers, computists, etc.) than what even defenders of CT through the years have assumed. This is so because such thinkers freely ascribe to the agents in question the knowledge and ability required to carry out sophisticated proofs — even proofs which cannot be formalized in first-order logic. The agents capable of deciding S^I need only read the story (and, for good measure, read it n subsequent times — something mathematicians routinely do in order to grasp proofs), and render their decision.

5.7.5 Objection 5

"Yes, but what your computists do is not decomposable into smaller, purely mechanical steps, which is the hallmark of an algorithm. They are supposed to read a story (and, if I understand you, perhaps read it again some finite number of times), and then, just like that, render a judgment. This is more like magic than mechanism."

This objection is a complete non-starter. In order to see this, let's prove, in a thoroughly traditional manner, that a certain well-defined problem is effectively solvable. Recall that all Turing Machines can be recast as flow diagrams (see e.g. [21]). Next, note that any TM represented by a flow diagram having as part the fragment shown in Figure 5.2 would be a non-halting TM (because if started in state 1 with its read/write head scanning the leftmost 1 in a block of 1s — and we can assume the alphabet in question to be a binary one consisting of {0,1} — it will loop forever in this fragment. Let M be a fixed TM specified for computist Smith in flow diagram form, and let this diagram contain the fragment of Figure 5.2. Suppose that Brown looks for a minute at the diagram, sees the relevant fragment, and declares: "Non-halter!" In doing this, Brown assuredly decides M, and his performance is effective. And yet what's the difference between what Brown does and what our "Eco-ish" agents do? The activity involved is decomposable in both cases. There are innumerable "subterranean" cognitive processes going on beneath Brown's activity, but they are beside the point: That we don't (or perhaps can't) put them on display does not tell against the effectiveness in question. The fact is that Brown simply looks at the diagram, finds the relevant fragment, assimilates, and returns a verdict.[26] The same is true of our agents in the case of stories.

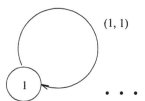

(The node here reflects the start state.)

Figure 5.2: Flow-Diagram Fragment That Entails Non-Halting.

Before turning to the next objection, we point out that the predicates I and I_{UE} really aren't exotic, despite appearances to the contrary. All those who try to harness the concepts of theoretical computer science (concepts forming a superset of the formal ones canvased in this chapter) in order to get things done end up working with predicates *at least* as murky as these two. A good example is to

---

[26]Our example is perfectly consistent with the fact that the set of TMs, with respect to whether or not they halt, is neither Turing-decidable nor effectively decidable.

be found in the seminal work of John Pollock, which is based on the harnessing of theoretical computer science (including AH) so as to explicate and implement concepts like warrant, defeasibility, *prima facie* plausibility, and so on.[27]

5.8 Arg$_3$ in Context: Other Attacks

Over the past six decades, the possibility of CT's falsity has not only been raised,[28] but CT has been subjected to a number of attacks. While we obviously don't have the book-long space it would take to treat each and every attack, we think it's possible to provide a provisional analysis that is somewhat informative, and serves to situate the attack on CT we have just articulated. What this analysis shows, we think, is that Arg$_3$ is the best attack going.

Following R.J. Nelson, we partition attacks on CT into three categories:

CAT1 Arguments against the arguments for CT;

CAT2 Arguments against CT itself; and

CAT3 Arguments against doctrines (e.g., the computational conception of mind) which are said to presuppose CT.

Consider category CAT3 first. Perhaps the most promising argument in this category runs as follows. Assume for the sake of argument that all human cognition consists in the execution of effective processes (in brains, perhaps). It would then follow by CT that such processes are Turing-computable, i.e., that computationalism is true. However, if computationalism is false, while there remains

---

[27]Here is one example (from [182]): Pollock's OSCAR system is designed so as to constantly update that which it believes in response to the rise and fall of arguments given in support of candidate beliefs. What constitutes correct reasoning in such a scheme? Pollock notes that because a TM with an ordinary program can't decide theorems in first-order logic (the set of such theorems isn't Turing-decidable), answering this question is quite tricky. He ingeniously turns to super-computation for help: The basic idea is that OSCAR's reasoning is correct when it generates successive sets of beliefs that approach the ideal epistemic situation in the limit. This idea involves AH, as Pollock explains.

[28]Boolos and Jeffrey, for example, in their classic textbook *Computability and Logic* [21], provide a sustained discussion of CT — and take pains to leave the reader with the impression that CT can be overthrown.

incontrovertible evidence that human cognition consists in the execution of effective processes, CT is overthrown.

Attacks of this sort strike us as decidedly unpromising. For starters, many people aren't persuaded that computationalism is false (despite the many careful arguments one of us has given;see e.g. [40]). Secondly, this argument silently presupposes some sort of physicalism, because the evidence for the effectiveness of cognition no doubt derives from observation and study of processes in the central nervous system. Thirdly, it is certainly an open question as to whether the processes involved *are* effective. At present, we just don't know enough about the brain, physics, and computability theory (and the interrelationships among these things) to conclude that cognition rests completely on effective processes. (To be a bit more specific, perhaps cognition arises from physical processes which are irreducibly analog and chaotic, a type of process mathematized in the final section of this very chapter.)

What about CAT1? Well, our refutation of Mendelson falls within it — and yet who would claim that what we have revealed about Mendelson's reasoning constitutes, by itself, a serious attack on CT? The same fundamental question derails even the work of those who intend to attack CT by attacking the time-honored rationales for it. For example, William Thomas [230] seeks to capitalize on the fact (and it *is* a fact, that much is uncontroversial) that the main rationale behind CT involves empirical induction — a form of reasoning that has little standing in mathematics. Unfortunately, Thomas' observations don't threaten CT in the least, as is easy to see. Most of us believe, *unshakably* believe, that the universe is more than 3 seconds old — but what mathematical rationale have we for this belief? As Russell pointed out, mathematics is quite consistent with the proposition that the universe popped into existence 3 seconds ago, replete not only with stars, but with light here on Earth from stars, and also with minds whose memories include those we have. More generally, of course, from the fact that p doesn't follow deductively from a set of propositions Γ, it hardly follows that p is false; it doesn't even follow that p is the slightest bit implausible.

We are left, then, with CAT2 — the category into which our own attack on CT falls. How does Arg$_3$ compare with other attacks in this category? To support the view that our own attack is superior, let us consider a notorious argument from four decades back, one

due to László Kalmár [124] (and rejected by, again, none other than
Elliott Mendelson [162]), and the only other modern attack on CT
that we know of, one given by Carol Cleland [54], [53].[29]

5.8.1 Kalmár's Argument Against CT

Here's how Kalmár's argument runs. First, he draws our attention
to a function g that isn't Turing-computable, given that f is:[30]

$$g(x) = \mu_y(f(x,y) = 0) = \begin{cases} \text{the least } y \text{ such that } f(x,y) = 0 \text{ if } y \text{ exists} \\ 0 \text{ if there is no such } y \end{cases}$$

Kalmár proceeds to point out that for any $n \in \mathbf{N}$ for which a natural number y with $f(n, y) = 0$ exists, "an obvious method for the
calculation of the least such $y \ldots$ can be given," namely, calculate in
succession the values $f(n, 0), f(n, 1), f(n, 2), \ldots$ (which, by hypothesis, is something a computist or TM can do) until we hit a natural
number m such that $f(n, m) = 0$, and set $y = m$.

> On the other hand, for any natural number n for which we
> can prove, not in the frame of some fixed postulate system
> but by means of arbitrary — of course, correct — arguments
> that no natural number y with $f(n, y) = 0$ exists, we have
> also a method to calculate the value $g(n)$ in a finite number of
> steps: prove that no natural number y with $f(n, y) = 0$ exists,
> which requires in any case but a finite number of steps, and
> gives immediately the value $g(n) = 0$. ([124], p. 74)

Kalmár goes on to argue as follows. The definition of g itself implies
the *tertium non datur*, and from it and CT we can infer the existence
of a natural number p which is such that

(i) there is no natural number y such that $f(p, y) = 0$; and

---

[29]Perhaps we should mention here something that students of CT and its history will be familiar with, viz., *given an intuitionistic interpretation of 'effectively
computable function,'* CT can be disproved. The basic idea is to capitalize on
the fact that any subset of $\mathbf{N}$ is intuitionistically enumerable, while many such
sets aren't effectively enumerable. (A succinct presentation of the disproof can
be found on p. 592 of [168].) The main problem with such attacks on Church's
Thesis, of course, is that they presuppose (certain axioms of — see [138], [137],
e.g.) intuitionistic logic, which most reject.

[30]The original proof can be found on p. 741 of [128].

(ii) this cannot be proved by any correct means.

Kalmár claims that (i) and (ii) are very strange, and that therefore CT is at the very least implausible.

This argument is interesting, but really quite hopeless, as a number of thinkers have indicated. For example, as Mendelson [162] (see also Moschovakis' [166] review of both Kalmár's paper and Mendelson's reaction) points out, Kalmár's notion of 'correct proof,' for all Kalmár tells us, may fail to be effective, since this proof is outside the standard logical system (set theory formalized in first-order logic). This is surely historically fascinating, since — as we have seen — it would be Mendelson who, nearly 30 years later, in another defense of CT (the one we examined earlier), would offer a proof of the 'only if' direction of this thesis — a proof that he assumes to be correct but one that he admits to be beyond ZF. Mendelson's proof, however, at least has the virtue of having been presented. The root of Kalmár's problem is that his proofs, on the other hand, are wholly hypothetical: We don't have a single one to ponder. And things get even worse for Kalmár (as Nelson [168] has pointed out), because even absent the proofs in question, we know enough about them to know that they would vary for each argument to g that necessitates them, which would mean that Kalmár has failed to find a *uniform* procedure, a property usually taken to be a necessary condition for a procedure to qualify as effective.

Though Kalmár does anticipate the problem of lack of uniformity,[31] and though we personally happen to side with him on this issue, it is clear that his argument against CT falls flat: If Kalmár's argument is to succeed, (ii) can be supplanted with

(ii′) this cannot be proved by any effective means.

---

[31] He says:

> By the way, [the assumption that the procedure in question] must be uniform seems to have no objective meaning. For a school-boy, the method for the solution of the diverse arithmetical problems he has to solve does not seem uniform until he learns to solve equations; and several methods in algebra, geometry and theory of numbers which are now regarded group-theoretic methods were not consider as uniform before group-theory has (sic) been discovered. ([124], p. 73)

But then how can the argument be deductively valid? It is not, at bottom, a *reductio*, since (i) and (ii') surely are not absurd, yet a reductio is the only form a compelling version of the argument could at core be. Kalmár himself, as we have noted, confesses that his argument is designed only to show that CT is implausible, but this conclusion goes through only if (i) and (ii'), if not absurd, are at least counterintuitive. But are they? For some, perhaps; for others, definitely not.

Our own take on Kalmár's argument is that it can be rather easily *shown* to be impotent via the machinery we set out earlier to analyze Mendelson's this-decade defense of CT: First, let

$$M_1^P, M_2^P, \ldots, M_n^P, M_{n+1}^P, \ldots$$

enumerate all the Turing machine/Program pairs that figured in our earlier discussion. Now substitute for Kalmár's g the following function (which is just a trivial variation on the predicate $H(P, i)$ given earlier).

$$h(M_i^P) = \begin{cases} 1 & \text{if } M_i^P \text{ halts} \\ 0 & \text{if } M_i^P \text{ doesn't halt} \end{cases}$$

Recall that if a TM halts, simulating this machine will eventually reveal this fact. (This was why, though $H \notin \Sigma_0$, we could place H in Σ_1.) This allows us to produce an exact parallel to Kalmár's reasoning: Start with M_1^P; proceed to simulate this machine. Assuming it halts, return 1, and move on to M_2^P, and do the same for it; then move to M_3^P, and so on. While this process is running, stand ready to proof "not in the frame of some fixed postulate system but by means of arbitrary — of course, correct — arguments" that the machine M_i^P fails to halt, in which case 0 is returned. The parody continues as follows. Given CT, and the law of the excluded middle (which the definition of the function h presupposes), we infer two implausible propositions — propositions so implausible that CT is itself cast into doubt. They are:

(i_h) there exists an M_k^P such that $h(M_k^P) = 0$; and

(ii_h') this cannot be proved by any effectively computable means.

This is a parody, of course, because both of these propositions are fully expected and welcomed by all those who both affirm CT and have at least some familiarity with the formalisms involved.

Now, what about *our* case against CT? Well, it would seem to be free of the defects that plague Kalmár's argument. First, our narrational case is deductive, as Arg_3 makes plain. Second, the process of reading (and possibly rereading a finite number of times) a story, assimilating it, and judging whether or not it's interesting on a fixed evaluation scheme, is transparently effective. (Indeed, related processes are routinely requested on standardized tests containing reading comprehension problems, where stories are read, perhaps reread, and judged to express one from among n "main ideas.") Third, the process we're exploiting would seem to be uniform.[32]

5.8.2 Cleland's Doubts About CT

Cleland [54], [53] discusses three variants on our CT:

CT_1 Every effectively computable number-theoretic function is Turing-computable.

CT_2 Every effectively computable function is Turing-computable.

CT_3 Every effective procedure is Turing-computable.

Before evaluating Cleland's arguments against this trio, some exegesis is in order. First, each of these three theses is a conditional, whereas our CT is a *bi*conditional. There should be no question that the biconditional is more accurate, given not only Mendelson's authoritative affirmation of the biconditional form, but also given that Church himself originally refers to his thesis as a *definition* of "effectively calculable function" in terms of "recursive function" [51].[33] However, since we have happily conceded the 'if' direction in CT, there is no reason to worry about this aspect of Cleland's framework. The second point is this: By 'number-theoretic' function Cleland simply means what we have hitherto called a function,

---

[32]No doubt test designers are correct that a uniform procedure needs to be followed in order to excel in their reading comprehension sections. So why wouldn't the process at the heart of Arg_3 be uniform as well?

[33]On the other hand, Church then immediately proceeds to argue for his "definition," and the reader sees that Church is without question urging his readers to affirm a *thesis*.

that is, a mapping from $\mathbf{N}$ to $\mathbf{N}$. We thus now understand function *simpliciter*, as for example as it's used in CT_2, to allow functions from the reals to reals.[34] There is of course no denying that Church and Turing failed to advocate CT_2, but CT_1 is certainly the "left-to-right" direction of our CT.

Now, what does Cleland say against CT_1–CT_3? She claims, first, that CT_3 can be disproved; the argument is simply this. One type of effective procedure coincides with what Cleland calls "mundane procedures," which are "ordinary, everyday procedures such as recipes for making Hollandaise sauce and methods for starting camp fires; they are methods for manipulating physical things such as eggs and pieces of wood" ([53], p. 11). Turing machine procedures, on the other hand, are "methods for 'manipulating' abstract symbols" ([53], p. 11). Since mundane procedures have "causal consequences," and TMs (*qua* mathematical objects) don't, it follows straightaway that mundane procedures aren't Turing-computable, that is, $\neg CT_3$.

Cleland's reasoning, when formalized, is valid; no question about that. The problem is that CT_3 (at least on her reading) has next to nothing to do with those propositions placed in the literature under the title "Church's Thesis"! CT_3 is a variant that no one has ever taken seriously. It may *seem* to some that CT_3 has been taken seriously, but this is only because one construal of it, a construal at odds with Cleland's, has in fact been recognized. On this construal, that a procedure is Turing-computable can be certified by either a relevant design (e.g., a TM flow-graph for making Hollandaise sauce, which is easy to come by), or by a relevant artifact (e.g., an artificial agent capable of making Hollandaise sauce, which again is easy to come by). At any rate, we're quite willing to concede that CT_3, on Cleland's idiosyncratic reading, is provably false. (Note that we have known for decades that even CT_1, on an intuitionistic (and hence idiosyncratic) reading of "effectively computable function," is provably false. See the footnote on page 135.) It's worth noting that Cleland herself has sympathy for those who hold that her reading of CT_3 is not a bona fide version of Church's Thesis ([53], p. 10). What then, about CT_2 and CT_1?

---

[34]It will not be necessary to present here the formal extension of computability with number-theoretic functions to computability with functions over the reals. (For the formal work, see, e.g., [103] and [102].)

Here Cleland no longer claims to have a refutation in hand; she aims only at casting doubt on these two theses. This doubt is supposed to derive from reflection upon what she calls "genuinely continuous devices" ([53], p. 18), which are objects said to "mirror" Turing-uncomputable functions ([53], pp. 16-17). An object is said to **mirror** a function iff (a) it includes a set of distinct objects which are in one-to-one correspondence with the numbers in the field of the function, and (b) the object pairs each and every object corresponding to a number in the domain of the function with an object corresponding to the appropriate number in the range of the function. Cleland takes pains to argue, in intuitive fashion, that there are objects which mirror Turing-uncomputable functions (e.g., an object moving through a two-dimensional Newtonian universe). She seems completely unaware of the fact that such objects *provably* exist — in the form, for example, of analog chaotic neural nets and, generally, analog chaotic dynamical systems [213], [212]. (These objects are known to exist in the mathematical sense. Whether they exist in the corporeal world is another question, one everyone — including Cleland — admits to be open.) We will be able to see Cleland's fundamental error (and, indeed, the fundamental error of anyone who attacks CT by taking her general route) if we pause for a moment to get clear about the devices in question. Accordingly, we present here an analog dynamical system via the "analog shift map," which is remarkably easy to explain.

First let's get clear on the general framework for the "shift map." Let A be a finite alphabet. A **dotted sequence** over A is a sequence of characters from A^* wherein one dot appears. For example, if A is the set of digits from 0 to 9, then 3.14 is a dotted sequence over A. Set $A^{.}$ to the set of all dotted sequences over A. Dotted sequences can be finite, one-way infinite (as in the decimal expansion of π), or bi-infinite. Now, let $k \in \mathbf{N}$; then the shift map

$$S^k : A^{.} \to A^{.} : (a)_i \to (a)_{i+k}$$

shifts the dot k places, negative values for a shift to the left, positive ones a shift to the right. (For example, if $(a)_i$ is 3.14159, then with $k = 2$, $S^2(3.14159) = 314.159$.) Analog shift is then defined as the process of first replacing a dotted substring with another dotted substring of equal length according to a function $g : A^{.} \to A^{.}$. This new sequence is then shifted an integer number of places left or right as directed by a function $f : A' \to \mathbf{Z}$. Formally, the analog shift is the map

$$\Phi : a \to S^{f(a)}(a \oplus g(a)),$$

where $\oplus$ replaces the elements of the first dotted sequence with the corresponding element of the second dotted sequence if that element is in the second sequence, or leaves it untouched otherwise. Formally:

$$(a \oplus g)_i = \begin{cases} g_i & \text{if } g_i \in A \\ a_i & \text{if } g_i \text{ is the empty element} \end{cases}$$

Both f and g have "finite domains of dependence" (DoDs), which is to say that they depend only on a finite dotted substring of the sequence on which they act. The domain of *effect* (DoE) of g, however, may be finite, one-way infinite, or bi-infinite. Here is an example from [212] (p. 547) which will make things clear, and allow us to see the fatal flaw in Cleland's rationale for doubting CT_2 and CT_1. Assume that the analog shift is defined by (where π^2 is the left-infinite string ... 51413 in base 2)

DoD	f	g
0.0	1	π^2
0.1	1	.10
1.0	0	1.0
1.1	1	.0

and that we have a starting sequence of $u = 000001.10110$; then the following evolution ensues:

$$000001.00110$$

$$0000010.0110$$

$$\pi^2.0110$$

$$\pi^2 0.100$$

$$\pi^2 0.100$$

$$\pi^2 01.00$$

$$\pi^2 1.00$$

$$\pi^2 01.00$$

At this point the DoD is 1.0 and hence no changes occur; this is a **fixed point**. Only the evolution from an initial dotted sequence to fixed point counts. In this case the input/output map is defined as the transformation of the initial sequence to the final subsequence to the right of the dot. (Hence in our example u as input leads to 00.) The class of functions determined by the analog shift includes as a proper subset the class of Turing-computable functions. (The proof is straightforward; see [212].) Moreover, the analog shift map is a mathematical model of idealized physical phenomena (e.g., the motion of a billiard ball bouncing among parabolic mirrors). From this it follows that we provably have found exactly what Cleland desires, that is, a genuinely continuous device that mirrors a Turing-uncomputable function. So, if Cleland can establish that

(16) If x mirrors a function, then x computes it

she will have overthrown both CT_2 and CT_1. Unfortunately, given our analysis of the analog shift map, we can see that Cleland doesn't have a chance; here is how the reasoning runs. Recall, first, the orthodox meaning of 'effectively computable function,' with which we started this chapter: A function f is effectively computable provided that, an agent having essentially our powers, a computist (or worker), can compute f by following an algorithm. So let's suppose that you are to be the computist in the case of the analog shift map. There is nothing impenetrable about the simple math involved; we'll assume that you have assimilated it just fine. So now we would like you to compute the function Φ as defined in our example involving π. To make your job as easy as possible, we will guarantee your immortality, and we will supply you with an endless source of pencils and paper (which is to say, we are "idealizing" you). Now, please set to work, if you will; we will wait and observe your progress ...

What happened? Why did you stop? Of course, you stopped because you hit a brick wall: It's rather challenging to write down and manipulate (or imagine and manipulate mentally) strings like π in base 2! (Note that the special case where the DoE of g is finite in the analog shift map generates a class of functions identical to the class of Turing-computable ones.) Yet this is precisely what needs to be done in order to attack CT_2 and CT_1 in the way Cleland prescribes.   •

Cleland sees the informal version of the problem, for she writes:

> Is there a difference between mirroring a function and com-
> puting a function? From an intuitive standpoint, it seems that
> there is. Surely, falling rocks don't compute functions, even
> supposing that they mirror them. That is to say, there seems
> to be a difference between a mere representation of a function,
> no matter how detailed, and the computation of a function.
> [Q:] But what could this difference amount to? ([53], p. 20)

She then goes on to venture an answer to this question:

> A natural suggestion is that computation requires not only the
> mirroring of a function but, also, the *following* of a procedure;
> falling rocks don't compute functions because they don't follow
> procedures. ([53], p. 20)

Cleland then tries to show that this answer is unacceptable. The idea
is that since the answer doesn't cut it, she is entitled to conclude that
(16) is true, that is, that there *isn't* a difference between mirroring
a function and computing a function,[35] which then allows the mere
existence of (say) an idealized billiard ball bouncing among parabolic
mirrors to kill off CT_2 and CT_1.

What, then, is Cleland's argument for the view that the "natural
suggestion" fails in response to Q fails? It runs as follows:

> Turing machines are frequently construed as *purely* mathe-
> matical objects. They are defined in terms of the same kinds
> of basic entity (viz., sets, functions, relations and constants)
> as other mathematical structures. A Turing machine is said
> to *compute* a number-theoretic function if a function can be
> *defined* on its mathematical structure which has the same de-
> tailed structure as the number-theoretic function concerned;
> there isn't a distinction, in Turing machine theory, between
> computing a function and defining a function ... If comput-
> ing a function presupposes following a procedure, then neither
> Turing machines nor falling rocks can be said to compute func-
> tions. ([53], p. 13)

This argument is an enthymeme; its hidden premise is that 'compute' is used univocally in the relevant theses, i.e., that 'compute'
means the same thing on both the left and right sides of CT, CT_1,

---

[35]This reasoning is certainly enthymematic (since it hides a premise to the
effect that there are no other answers that can be given to Q), but we charitably
leave this issue aside.

and CT_2. This premise is false. The locution 'f is effectively computable,' on the orthodox conception of Church's Thesis, does imply that there is an idealized agent capable of *following* an algorithm in order to compute f. But it hardly follows from this that when 'compute' is used in the locution 'f is Turing-computable' (or in the related locution 'TM M computes f'), the term 'compute' must have the same meaning as it does in connection with idealized agents. Certainly anyone interested in CT, and in defending it, would hasten to remind Cleland that the term 'compute' means one thing when embedded within CT's left side, and another thing when embedded within CT's right side.[36] Having said this, however, and having implicitly conceded the core mathematical point (viz., that at least some definitions of TMs and Turing-computability deploy 'compute' in the absence of the concept of "following"[37]), we should probably draw Cleland's attention to the formal approach we took earlier, where in order to characterize information-processing beyond the Turing Limit, we distinguished between a TM as a type of architecture, and a program which this architecture *follows* in order to compute. This is why we spoke of TM-program pairs.

Cleland never intended to literally refute CT_1 and CT_2. (As we have seen, she did intend to refute the heterodox CT_3, and for the sake of argument we agreed that here she succeeds.) But we conclude that she fails even in her attempt to cast doubt upon these theses, and that therefore CT is unscathed by her discussion. In contrast, our own case against CT targets this thesis with a deductive argument having no hidden premises and presupposing no convenient construal of CT. We have laid our cards on the table for all to see:

---

[36]Unexceptionable parallels abound: We can say 'My friend told me that Burlington is a nice city,' and we can say 'My CD-ROM travel program told me that Burlington is a nice city,' but we needn't accept the view that 'told me' means the same in both utterances.

[37]Consider, e.g., what one of us (Bringsjord) uses in teaching mathematical logic: A **Turing machine** is a quadruple (S, Σ, f, s) where

1. S is a finite set of **states**;

2. Σ is an alphabet containing the black symbol $-$, but not containing the symbols $\Leftarrow$ ("go left") and $\Rightarrow$ ("go right").

3. $s \in S$ is the **initial state**;

4. $f : S \times \Sigma \longrightarrow (\Sigma \cup \{\Leftarrow, \Rightarrow\}) \times S$ (the **transition function**).

The ability to judge and generate narrative, we claim, is simply astonishing. We're pretty sure our hand is the best one hitherto revealed, but as to whether it wins, or merely marks another chapter in the — interesting — story of Church's Thesis, our readers must judge.

5.9 And Interestingness in BRUTUS$_1$?

Though we believe, on the strength of the foregoing analysis and argument, that interestingness is uncomputable, we are of course once again faced with our engineering challenge: How is BRUTUS$_1$ to *appear* to have mastery over interestingness on par with human authors? The bulk of the answer to this question is provided by what we have done to this point. For example, in Chapter 2, we implicitly held that interestingness is promoted if the narrative generated by BRUTUS$_1$ triggers readerly imaging; and we concluded that chapter with a list of heuristics for how to produce the desired reader response. The same can be said for the issue of point of view, which we discussed in Chapter 3: In order for BRUTUS$_1$ to write interesting stories, he must carry the reader into a landscape of consciousness, and there seem to be certain determinate ways to enable this.

A number of thinkers who have come before us have grappled directly with the problem of capturing the essence of interesting narrative; first and foremost among them probably comes Roger Schank. Schank [205] believes that what makes a story interesting can be captured in computable schemes, but in the paper in question he doesn't provide the scheme itself — this, despite the fact that on page 278 of that paper [205] Schank promises: "What I shall attempt to do now is to *define* interestingness ..." (emphasis ours). In the next section of his paper, which is supposed to contain the definition in question, all we find are ad hoc strategies relating to interestingness. To motivate these strategies, Schank does present certain stories, most prominently the following two:

Schank Story 1 — Interesting

John was walking down the street eating an ice cream cone. He saw a man walk into the bushes and begin to undress. Soon a crowd had gathered and the police came to investigate. While they were there a giant explosion occurred two blocks away. People came running in their direction screaming that there had been a terrible accident. Many were bleeding and one man had lost an arm. Meanwhile a

fire broke out in the park. People said there as a conspiracy afoot
because a bomb had been sighted nearby only yesterday. When an
epidemic broke out the following week, everyone knew aliens had
landed.

Schank Story 2 — Uninteresting

John was walking down the street eating an ice cream cone. He saw
a man walk into the park and begin to read. Soon some pigeons
had gathered and a boy came to feed them. While they were there
a truck drove by a few blocks away. People who came walking
towards the park said that it was a diesel truck. Many were hot and
one man was tired. Meanwhile the park got really crowded. People
said there was a new park being built nearby because a construction
crew had been sighted only yesterday. When construction began the
following week, everyone knew that the mayor had kep his promise.

What he induces from these two stories is that death and danger
are "absolutely interesting," while two "operators," UNEXPECTED
EVENTS and PERSONAL RELATEDNESS, can be applied to topics to make them more interesting. Schank points out that this implies that when the subject of death is an argument to PERSONAL
RELATEDNESS, the result is interesting. Likewise, a story about
unexpected death would be interesting. Schank lists other topics
that are "absolute interests," e.g.,

- Power

- Sex

- Money

- Destruction

- Chaos

- Romance

- Disease

This list prompts Schank to say: "So what is interesting according
to the above? If someone you knew died from having sex for a lot of
money, that would be very interesting by my rules." ([205], p. 290)

All this kind of stuff is utterly "seat of the pants." Schank simply
presents a few stories, and is then off to the races, isolating certain
properties exemplified in these stories. Nowhere here is there anything like a definition; nowhere is there even a *hint* of the sort of
formal accounts which we desire; there isn't even inductive evidence

for the list of "interests" Schank promotes. There is no denying, of course, that a story about, say, death caused by having sex for money, is at least potentially interesting, but this is just one trick out of innumerable similar ones. Where is it to end? How many tricks are there? To seek tricks for generating interesting narrative in general fits well with our own modus operandi, and so we are quite at home with what Schank cooks up, and with *how* he does so (the bottom line is that he just picks things out of thin air to get the job done, or least *partially* done!), nothing in his work casts the slightest doubt upon our contention that the set $S^\mathcal{I}$ is uncomputable.[38]

---

[38]Schank isn't the only thinker to tackle the question of what literary interestingness consists in. For example, Wilensky [246], Kintsch [127], and Britton [43], among others, have all considered the issue. None of the work offered by this trio includes an account of interestingness that succeeds in keeping things within the realm of the computable. For example, Kintsch holds that a story is interesting provided that (a) it evokes assumptions in the minds of the audience, then (b) denies some or all of these assumptions, which in turn causes (c) "some extra-mental operations that engage the cognitive machinery" ([127], p. 596). Such an account certainly seems to fit standard detective stories well (in fact, Kintsch proudly quotes Hercule Poirot: "It gives one furiously to think"), but why couldn't someone (easily) write an interesting story that violates the (a)-(c) sequence? We leave it to the reader to devise such a story.

Chapter 6

Inside the Mind of BRUTUS

> Good gentlemen, look fresh and merrily,
> Let not our looks put on our purposes;
> But bear it as our Roman actors do,
> With untired spirits and formal constancy.
> —Brutus, in *Julius Caesar*

6.1   Where Are We In History?

Though the diagnosis is brutally simplistic, we see three stages in the history of story generation, namely, (i) Meehan's TALE-SPIN and the systems that spring from a reaction to it, (ii) Turner's MIN-STREL, and — no surprise here — (iii) a stage starting with the advent of BRUTUS. We believe that stage (ii), which encapsulates the view that even cases of awe-inspiring creativity are at bottom based on standard, computable problem-solving techniques (and as such marks the natural maturation of stage (i)), will stubbornly persist for some time alongside (iii). As you will recall, we cheerfully operate under the belief that human (literary) creativity is beyond computation — and yet strive to craft the *appearance* of creativity from suitably configured computation. Stage (ii) is fatally flawed by the assumption that human creativity can in fact be reduced to computation. When the years tick on and on without this reduction materializing, more and more thinkers will come round to the approach BRUTUS is designed to usher in: that which shuns the search for such reduction in favor of clever engineering. Hollywood will

Figure 6.1: The Natural Brutus/Our BRUTUS.

want machines to co-write screenplays, even if the scientists haven't figured out how reduce point of view to computation. (Remember Chapter 3.)

6.1.1   TALE-SPIN, and Reaction

In the previous chapter we saw some sample output from TALE-SPIN, the world's first noteworthy story generator. How does TALE-SPIN work? Basically as follows:

1. Identify a **character** from a pre-defined set;

2. Give that character a **problem** from a pre-defined set;

3. Create a **micro-world** from a pre-defined set;

4. Input 1-3 to a simulator; document the character's attempt to solve his/her problem;

5. Either stop or Goto 1.

TALE-SPIN was seminal, but no one, save perhaps for the pathologically charitable, would ascribe literary creativity to the system. It is probably uncontroversial that a system warranting such an ascription needs to be in command of a loop like this (and indeed

BRUTUS₁ has the power to run and capitalize on such a loop), but a lot is missing, as is clearly revealed by the stories TALE-SPIN spins (recall Chapter 5). What's missing? A number of authors have stepped up to try to answer this question: De Beaugrande and Colby [64] noted long ago that TALE-SPIN doesn't handle more than one character (in any genuine sense), and has no notion of what a good story is like (above and beyond a character trying to reach a goal). Soon thereafter, Dehn [65] rejected TALE-SPIN's core loop altogether, claiming that what is missing is management of the *author's* intentions. Lebowitz [146] complained that TALE-SPIN lacks the sort of knowledge that allows for rich, believable characters. Yazdani [252], looking back on all these complaints, designed his ROALD system to address them: ROALD includes a simulator like TALE-SPIN's, a module for generating plots, a module for generating what Yazdani calls "worlds," and modules for representing the narrator's plans and generating the actual text. It isn't clear that ROALD ever matured,[1] but at any rate, the overall design is still well short of what one must aim at in order to build an artificial author that can hold its own with human counterparts.

6.1.2 Turner's MINSTREL

The best extant story generator we know of is Scott Turner's MINSTREL. The best thing about MINSTREL is that it is accompanied by a rich theoretical base, delivered in Turner's *The Creative Process: A Computer Model of Storytelling* [237]. Serious students of story generation would do well to add his book to their libraries. The book you're holding, coupled with Turner's, seems to us to make for a nice foundation on literary creativity — in no small part because of the informative contrast between his approach and ours.[2] For example, the core of Turner's approach is the position that creativity is problem solving, while we start by facing up to at least the *possibility* that creativity, at least the varieties that look like what we have called raw origination, is super-computational. Turner gives this example to anchor his treatment of creativity as problem solving:

---

[1] Yazdani said in conversation with one of us (Bringsjord) in 1990 that the (interestingly enough — given our use of FLEX and Prolog for BRUTUS₁) Prolog-based ROALD crashed constantly, and was probably beyond repair.

[2] And no such library, of course, should lack [160].

One day, while visiting her grandparents, Janelle was seated alone at the dining room table, drinking milk and eating cookies. Reaching for the cookies, she accidentally spilled her milk on the table. Since Janelle had been recently reprimanded for making a mess, she decided to clean up the spill herself.

Janelle went into the kitchen, but there were no towels or paper towels available. She stood for a moment in the center of the kitchen thinking, and then she went out the back door.

She returned a few minutes later carrying a kitten. The neighbor's cat had given birth to a litter about a month ago, and Janelle had been over to play with the kittens the previous day. Janelle brought the kitten into the dining room, where he happily lapped up the spilled milk. ([237], pp. 22–23)

If one accepts Janelle's impressive reasoning here as a paradigmatic case of creativity, one from which general principles of (literary) creativity can be induced, then one might well end up where Turner does, namely, at the view that creativity is a matter of solving problems by adapting known solutions to solutions that can crack new problems. (Given the current state of AI, if you take Janelle to be representative, you also end up, as Turner does, affirming *specific tools*, such as case-based reasoning.) Those who have read our book to this point will be unsurprised by our reaction to the Turnerian approach. The bottom line is that there is no evidence whatever that belletristic fiction is the product of standard problem solving; the evidence runs quite the other way. (As we saw in Chapter 5, there is powerful evidence for the view that even *judgments* about whether or not a story is interesting aren't the result of algorithms applied to previous cases.) Our approach is to stare unblinkingly into the eyes of the most mysterious literary muse, and to engineer a system that can hold its own — by capitalizing on an architecture, BRUTUS, that is designed from the outset to match the output of this muse. Turner's approach, on the other hand, is to commit at the outset to a particular account of creativity that by its nature is implementable, but, relative to, say, Tolstoy's powers, humble.

As we said in the Preface, it seems to us, in large part for reasons explained in previous chapters, that an artificial storyteller able to compete against inspired authors must satisfy seven "magic" desiderata that go miles beyond what Meehan and his successors, and Turner as well, have sought.

6.1.3   The Seven "Magic" Desiderata

MD1 *Do violence to proposed accounts of creativity.* An impressive
   storytelling AI is one that satisfies proposed sophisticated accounts of creativity. BRUTUS$_1$ does this: recall that he (it? —
   we confess to finding it irresistible, for reasons having perhaps
   to do with the gender of the late, non-digital Brutus, to regard BRUTUS$_1$ as male) qualifies as creative according to the
   definitions examined in Chapter 1.

MD2 *Generate imagery in the reader's mind.* An artificial agent
   aspiring to be counted among the literati must be able to spark
   significant readerly imaging. Recall Chapter 2.

MD3 *Story in "landscape of consciousness."* A good storytelling AI
   must produce stories having not only a landscape of action, but
   also a landscape of consciousness, that is, a landscape defined
   by the mental states of characters. Recall Chapter 3.

MD4 *Mathematize concepts at core of belletristic fiction.* No artificial agent will lay claim to being counted literarily creative
   unless it processes the immemorial themes at the heart of literature; and such processing can presumably come only if the
   themes in question have been formalized. This desideratum
   was discussed in Chapter 4.

MD5 *Generate genuinely interesting stories.* A true artificial storyteller must produce genuinely interesting stories — which may
   well mean, given what we learned in Chapter 5, that the AI in
   question must appear to do something that is uncomputable
   (viz., decide the set S^I of interesting stories).

MD6 *Tap into the deep, abiding structures of stories.* Any truly impressive artificial author must be in command of story structures that give its output an immediate standing amongst its
   human audience. Such structures are discussed in this chapter,
   in the form of story grammars.

MD7 *Avoid "mechanical" prose.* Last but not least, there is a challenge we have yet to face up to: An artificial author must
   produce compelling literary prose. We cover this (daunting!)

challenge as we explain the inner workings of BRUTUS₁, an explanation we now commence.

6.2   Story Grammars Resurrected

Once upon a time story grammars were alive and well in AI. Then they died — in large part because of a three-pronged denunciation delivered by Black and Wilensky [14]. Their three objections are that story grammars

- Are formally inadequate;

- Don't constitute necessary and sufficient conditions for something's being a story;

- Don't assist in a computational account of story understanding.

Given our methods and objectives, these objections are anemic: We don't for a minute intend story grammars to in any way constitute a set of necessary and sufficient conditions for something's being a story. (We *are* inclined to believe that an interesting story is at least a *partial* instantiation of one or more story grammars.) Our work has next to nothing to do with story *understanding*; it of course has everything to do with story *generation*. And as to whether a grammar is formally inadequate, well, inadequate for what? Our aim isn't to devise and implement story grammars that function as all-encompassing programs for producing stories (an aim which would presumably require that such grammars be Type 0 in the Chomsky Hierarchy). What we want is simply a formalism that will enable us to pull off a certain specific trick, namely, represent and process story structures of a sort that are sorely missing in TALE-SPIN. Once we have this formalism in hand, we can then mold it to fit our purposes.

Let's be a bit more specific. The notation we prefer is Thorndyke's [231]. (The primogenitor of story grammars in connection with literature was Vladimir Propp [186], and his *Morphology of the Folktale.*) In fact, we not only like the notation, but we like the specific structure: BRUTUS is capable of generating some stories that conform to Thorndyke's constraints (see the grammar shown in Figure 6.2).

If one wants other story structures, one has only to devise an appropriate grammar. For example, the following simple story is one

Rule No.	Rule
(1)	Story → Setting + Theme + Plot + Resolution
(2)	Setting → Characters + Location + Time
(3)	Theme → (Event)* + Goal
(4)	Plot → Episode*
(5)	Episode → Subgoal + Attempt* + Outcome
(6)	Attempt → $\left\{ \begin{array}{l} \text{Event}^* \\ \text{Episode} \end{array} \right.$
(7)	Outcome → $\left\{ \begin{array}{l} \text{Event}^* \\ \text{State} \end{array} \right.$
(8)	Resolution → $\left\{ \begin{array}{l} \text{Event} \\ \text{State} \end{array} \right.$
(9)	$\left. \begin{array}{l} \text{Subgoal} \\ \text{Goal} \end{array} \right\}$ → Desired State
(10)	$\left. \begin{array}{l} \text{Characters} \\ \text{Location} \\ \text{Time} \end{array} \right\}$ → State

Figure 6.2: Thorndyke's Story Grammar.

we quickly wrote on the basis of one of our home-grown grammars (see Figure 6.3), the gist of which is that the main character, suffering from some central character flaw, ventures out on his own and gets a number of opportunities to repent of this flaw. If the opportunity is refused repeatedly, eventually the character perishes. Repentance, on the other hand, produces a happy ending. (This story makes a good starting place for reverse engineering not only the underlying grammar we engineered, but other elements that we haven't striven for.)

Repentance

Peter the puppy lived in a warm, safe house, with a loving family, on the edge of a deep forest in which the hunters roamed. Sometimes their shotguns would echo like thunder through the air. At these times he saw sadness in his mother's eyes — sadness Peter found silly. The fact was, Peter was callous. His mother loved him greatly, but was hurt by the fact that her son was often downright cold.

The forest beckoned with adventure, and one day Peter scampered off for it. Before long he came upon a baby bear whose furry leg was caught in a man-made trap.

"Won't you help me?" the bear asked. Peter didn't help. Hadn't he been taught not to talk to strangers? And didn't he have a lot of exploring to do?

At the edge of a pond, Peter met a young deer who announced: "I'm afraid I'm lost. Maybe if you bark loudly, my mother will come to this spot and find me. Will you help?"

"If you think your mother's within hearing range, how lost can you be?"

Not long thereafter, as darkness began creeping into the forest, and a chill came on, Peter concluded that he was himself utterly lost. At that moment he glimpsed a piece of steel glimmer in the fading sunlight, and he froze. When he looked down, he noticed that one false move on his part, and his own leg would be snared in a trap. Slowly, inch by inch, taking care not to trigger the cruel device, Peter moved out of danger.

Where was the baby bear? Where was the deer? Peter was sick with guilt.

Later, wandering hopelessly in the dark, he suddenly saw the lights of his house. His mother wept upon Peter's return, and

> the next day saw that her son, after hearing a distant gunshot, winced as if in pain down to his very soul.

It's important to realize that story grammars aren't only applicable to children's stories, or even to adult fiction of the short short form that BRUTUS₁ prefers. Research that makes this obvious includes some carried out by Umberto Eco [83]: he shows that a story grammar is at the heart of at least 10 Ian Fleming novels in the 007 series. (Such a demonstration is one Eco can carry out for a *lot* of fiction. An interesting exercise is to attempt such a demonstration on Eco's own fiction, the overall structure of which strikes us as utterly mechanical.) The grammar can be constructed from 9 "moves." They are:

A M moves and gives a task to Bond;

B Villain moves and appears to Bond (perhaps in vicarious forms);

C Bond moves and gives a first check to Villain or Villain gives first check to Bond;

D Woman moves and shows herself to Bond;

E Bond takes Woman (possesses her or begins her seduction);

F Villain captures Bond (with or without Woman, or at different moments);

G Villain tortures Bond (with or without Woman);

H Bond beats Villain (kills him, or kills his representative or helps their killing);

I Bond, convalescing, enjoys Woman, whom he then loses.

The straight scheme, that is,

$$A\ B\ C\ D\ E\ F\ G\ H\ I,$$

is found in *Dr. No*. But there are variations. For example, *Goldfinger* embodies

$$B\ C\ D\ E\ A\ C\ D\ F\ G\ D\ H\ E\ H\ I.$$

In *From Russia, With Love*, on the other hand,

Rule No.	Rule
(1)	Story → Setting + Departure + Lessons
(2)	Setting → Protag + Locale + Defeat + Suptag
(3)	Protag, Locale, Suptag → State
(4)	Defect → { callous, cries-wolf, spoiled, ⋮ }
(5)	callous, cries-wolf, spoiled, ⋮ → State
(6)	Departure → Episode
(7)	Episode → Subgoal + Attempt* + Outcome
(8)	Attempt → { Event*, Episode }
(9)	Outcome → { Event*, State }
(10)	Lessons → Antag + Opportunity + Response
(11)	Response → { Persist, Repent }
(12)	Opportunity → Event
(13)	Antag → State
(14)	Persist → { Death, Refusal + Lessons }
(15)	Repent → Event

Figure 6.3: Our "Home-Grown" *Adventure as Tough Teacher* Grammar. A variant of this grammar was used in Bringsjord's MYTH-LOGICAL system, described in his *What Robots Can and Can't Be* [40].

the company of Villains increases — through the presence of the ambiguous representative Kerim, in conflict with a secondary Villain, Krilunku, and the two mortal duels of Bond with Red Grant and Rosa Klebb, who was arrested only after having grievously wounded Bond — so that the scheme, highly complicated, is B B B B D A B B C E F G H I. ([83], p. 157)

It's easy to cast Eco's analysis as a formal grammar.[3] (It isn't a grammar we find particularly useful.) But our point isn't that such a thing can be carried out. Our point is only that plot structure can be engineered with help from story grammars, and that certain structures seem to "resonate" with readers — these would then be

---

[3]Our readers (which we presume to be, on average, rather well-read) should not infer from the presence of fairly primitive structures at the "spine" of the 007 series that Fleming is a weak or "shallow" writer. The James Bond movies are one thing (an abominable cheapening of the texts from which they arose?); the books are (at least arguably) quite another. Here, for example, is Fleming's description of the death of Mr. Big in *Live and Let Die*:

> It was a large head and a veil of blood streamed down over the face from a wound in the great bald skull ... Bond could see the teeth showing in a rictus of agony and frenzied endeavor. Blood half veiled the eyes that Bond knew would be bulging in their sockets. He could almost hear the great diseased heart thumping under the grey-black skin ... The Big Man came on. His shoulders were naked, his clothes stripped off him by the explosion, Bond supposed, but the black silk tie had remained and it showed round the thick neck and streamed behind the head like a Chinaman's pigtail. A splash of water cleared some blood away from the eyes. They were wide open, staring madly towards Bond. They held no appeal for help, only a fixed glare of physical exertion. Even as Bond looked into them, now only ten yards away, they suddenly shut and the great face contorted in a grimace of pain. "Aaarh," said the distorted mouth. Both arms stopped flailing the water and the head went under and came up again. A cloud of blood welled up and darkened the sea. Two six-foot thin brown shadows backed out of the cloud and then dashed back into it. The body in the water jerked sideways. Half of the Big Man's left arm came out of the water. It had no hand, no wrist, no wrist-watch. But the great turnip head, the drawn-back mouth full of white teeth almost splitting it in half, was still alive ... The head floated back to the surface. The mouth was closed. The yellow eyes seemed still to look at Bond. Then the shark's snout came right out of the water and it drove in towards the head, the lower curved jaw open so that light glinted on the teeth. There was a horrible grunting scrunch and a great swirl of water. Then silence.

structures that an artificial storyteller would need to be in command of.

6.3 BRUTUS: Evolution of a System Architecture

6.3.1 BRUTUS and BRUTUS$_1$

BRUTUS is an architecture for story generation. BRUTUS$_1$ is an initial implementation of this architecture that demonstrates, among other things, the power of formal representations to capture and maintain interestingness through suitable plot, story structure and language generation.

This chapter focuses on system implementation; the *how* rather than the *what*. By our lights, in AI, discovering the how is just as important a result as the what. Generating an interesting story is the *what*, but *how* an agent goes about generating the story weighs significantly in one's judgment of the agent's intelligence and creativity. Consider a story generator that works by simply changing the names in an existing story to produce a "new" one. It isn't very creative; the input and output in this case are for all intents and purposes the same; hence the agent in this case oughtn't be deemed *creative*.

Likewise, a story generator that simply strings together canned paragraphs based on straightforward rules shouldn't generate much ado, even if the system consistently produces narrative with the same level of interestingness as that which flowed from Ibsen's immortal pen. Another trivial model that comes to mind is one inspired by the word game in which one person controls a paragraph with many words replaced with blanks, each of which is annotated with a part of speech. The other players are asked, in turn, to choose for each blank a word having the requisite part of speech. The "author" fills in the blanks based on the player's choices. When the template is done, it is read aloud. Almost invariably the resultant story gets laughs and "rave reviews." Might a program based on a vast database of similar templates indexed by theme, plot type, story structure, rhetoric, and so on, produce an interesting story? Sure. Should one therefore conclude that such a system is genuinely creative? Surely not.

We can render a subjective and humanistic judgment as to a

system's creativity only when we are privy to the details. If we look "under the hood" of a program and find it trivial for a human to transform the program's initial data to the program's output, we are less likely to consider the program creative. If, however, we, as humans, would find it challenging to map the program's initial data to a creative artifact (like a well-written and interesting story), then we are more likely to consider the program creative. We call the perceived difference between a program's initial data and its output **creative distance**.

The main goal behind the development of BRUTUS is to produce real, working systems which, by virtue of their internal logical structure (which implements the architecture) and implementation specifics, allow for generated stories to be sufficiently distant from initial, internal knowledge representations (called, again, **creative distance**) and to vary independently along different dimensions (called **wide variability**).

There are many dimensions over which a story can vary. Plot is only one of them. Characters, settings, literary themes, writing style, imagery, etc. — these are other dimensions, and there are many more. (Recall our remarks in the Preface regarding the wide variability of Mark Helprin's belletristic fiction.)

Whether or not a story generator implementation can achieve wide variability hinges on what we call **architectural differentiation**. A story generation system has architectural differentiation if for each aspect of the story that can vary, there is a corresponding distinct component of the technical architecture that can be parameterized to achieve different results. While we owe many debts to the pioneers who have come before us in the field of story generation, it's safe to say that BRUTUS is a uniquely composite and differentiated architecture capable of enabling wider variability and greater creative distance than its predecessors. While our first implementation of this architecture, BRUTUS₁, has very limited variability, ancestors will implement more and more of those parts of the architecture designed to secure wide variability. It is BRUTUS the architecture, not BRUTUS₁, that we have toiled to create. With the architecture done, implementation is almost trivial.

Prior to the BRUTUS architecture, story generation projects experimented with various architectural approaches in relative isolation of one another. In the following sections we tour a categorization of

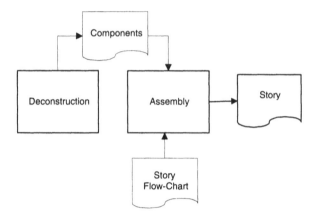

Figure 6.4: Component Configuration Architecture.

previous storytelling system architectures, namely:

1. Component configuration

2. Plot generation

3. Story structure expansion

We discuss how these architectural concepts in story generation have laid the foundation for BRUTUS.

6.3.2   Component Configuration

Sheldon Klein's Automatic Novel Writer ([129]; see also [209]) worked by following a flow-chart representing a typical mystery plot and randomly chose pre-written components, which were inserted into appropriate positions and then adjusted slightly (e.g., names were changed). The component repository from which selections were made was formed by deconstructing well-known short stories of the appropriate genre. A high-level architectural diagram for this approach is illustrated in Figure 6.4.

While writers may "borrow" a sentence structure from here or there to form components of a new story, the notion of simply configuring a story from canned components is not considered a creative approach to story generation. In our estimation, the distance from input to output achieved by this implementation could be improved

Figure 6.5: Plot Generation Architecture.

not only in enabling finer, more artful manipulation of written components, but also in more flexible plot generation.

The BRUTUS architecture does not reject component configuration in its entirety. BRUTUS₁ generates a scenario based on thematic descriptions. A story outline is constructed by selecting paragraph and sentence grammars from a classified collection; these grammars are treated like highly parameterized components. They are specialized on the basis of theme, plot, and literary dimensions. As we begin to detail the BRUTUS architecture we reveal its composite nature. BRUTUS's design moderates and integrates a variety of techniques to produce a more compelling artificial creative agent.

6.3.3   Plot Generation

A variety of story generation systems focused on variability in plot. These systems used planning engines to generate plot descriptions. These descriptions were then mapped to natural language constructions. (As we saw earlier, this approach was the heart of TALE-SPIN.) The notion of interestingness was not guaranteed by explicit, separate, and well-bounded structures in the architecture. Implicit notions of interestingness were assumed to arise as by-products of the story generator's planning process. Figure 6.5 illustrates a high-level architecture intended to produce interesting narrative merely through the process of plot generation. In this architecture, planning engines, like the one in TALE-SPIN, would implicitly ensure that the plot involved a character trying to achieve some goal. But the problem is that sometimes a character's striving for a goal is tedious. A description of how one of us strove during a busy day of meetings to free up sufficient time to play a game of on-line solitaire might not exactly quicken your pulse.

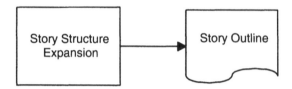

Figure 6.6: Story Structure Expansion Architecture.

6.3.4   Story Structure Expansion

Another implementation approach based on the architecture illustrated in figure 6.6 relies principally on story grammars. Through iterative structural expansion of a story grammar, this type of system builds increasingly detailed outlines. In his excellent overview, "Storytelling by Machines," Sharples [209] illustrates grammars used by GESTER, a program developed in 1984 by Pemberton for his PhD thesis at the University of Toronto. GESTER used a story grammar to produce story outlines for the genre of old French epics. In this approach it becomes extremely difficult to represent the complex plot and literary variations in the declarative form required by story grammars. While we believe it may be theoretically possible for a story grammar to represent all the details required to generate a large variety of interesting stories, we agree with Sharples' assertion that it is highly unlikely that such a grammar will be found. In BRUTUS, as previously indicated, story grammars are used where they are effective: to produce an outline for the story in a way that is largely independent of other storytelling dimensions.

6.3.5   BRUTUS: A Composite Architecture

The factorization of the BRUTUS architecture explicitly reflects a story generation process that starts with a symbolic encoding of a theme to anchor interestingness. The instantiation of the theme from a knowledge-base of characters and events is used to guide plot generation, story structure expansion, and natural language (= English prose) generation. The result is a quicker path to scenarios and stories that conform (necessarily) to the explicitly represented theme, which is likely to be interesting from the get-go. The idea of a composite architecture that "covers all the bases" with differentiated and independently varying components seems to have helped breathe

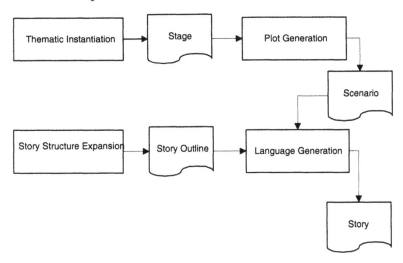

Figure 6.7: Brutus: A Composite Architecture

new life into the vision of a storytelling AI. Figure 6.7 illustrates the orchestration of BRUTUS's different components, including thematic instantiation, story expansion, and plot and language generation, all working together with different classes of knowledge.

The rest of this chapter is decidedly "no-nonsense." We describe enough of the "guts" of BRUTUS$_1$ (our current implementation of the BRUTUS architecture) to enable readers to understand how the system works. This description is short on theory, but long on information about our actual implementation.

6.4 BRUTUS$_1$'s Anatomy: An Introduction

The BRUTUS technical architecture is decomposed into two distinct levels: the **knowledge level** and the **process level**.

The knowledge level comprises the different types of knowledge required to generate a written story about a particular theme. The process level contains the processes that together use the knowledge level to generate a story. The process level represents BRUTUS$_1$'s computational approach to story generation. In this section we describe the major aspects of the BRUTUS technical architecture (an overview of this architecture, highlighting the knowledge and process levels, is illustrated in Figure 6.8). We explain the representational

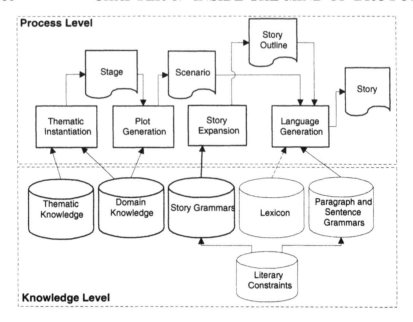

Figure 6.8: BRUTUS₁: Knowledge and Process Levels.

and computational approach used by the system to generate interesting stories. We first introduce the knowledge and process levels. In a separate sub-section we offer a brief overview of the implementation structures and methods provided by FLEX, a multi-paradigm AI programming system based in the programming language Prolog. FLEX was used to implement BRUTUS₁, and the constructs available in this development system are used throughout the chapter to convey examples. In separate sub-sections, the knowledge level and the process level are explained in more detail; readers are exposed to the different types of knowledge (with corresponding representations and applications) in the BRUTUS₁ system.

6.4.1 Introduction to the Knowledge Level

The knowledge level contains representations of different types of knowledge required to generate the written story:

1. Domain knowledge (e.g., people, places, things, events, goals, behaviors, etc.)

2. Linguistic knowledge (e.g., sentences, phrases, words, parts of speech

etc.)

3. Literary knowledge (e.g., thematic descriptions, literary structures, story grammars, etc.)

6.4.1.1 Domain Knowledge

In very general terms, a story is a natural language description of objects, their attributes, relationships, behaviors and interactions. It may or may not be centered around any particular theme or have any particular message. A story may or may not be interesting (and, as we've seen, a quick route to *un*interestingness is through the absence of themes and structure). But all stories include a description of some set of objects and their interactions.

Domain knowledge encodes a formal representation of objects, attributes, relationships, goals, behaviors, and events — a formal description of a domain. Domain knowledge is not the story itself, but is a description of a collection of concepts about which some story may be written.

Domain concepts may include the fundamental elements that might compose a story's settings (e.g., places, things, and their attributes and interrelationships), its characters (e.g., people, their physical and psychological makeup, their goals and behaviors) and the events that occur (e.g., steal, kill, murder, give, take, run, sign, buy, borrow, loan, kiss, etc.).

6.4.1.2 Linguistic Knowledge

A story is a description of a set of objects and events. The description itself is of course encoded in a natural language. A story therefore takes the form of a sequence of words of some language strung together to conform to the language's grammar.

While domain knowledge may be considered a description of domain concepts, it doesn't qualify as a story because, among other reasons, the description is not encoded in a natural language. **Linguistic knowledge** is knowledge required to produce a natural language description of domain concepts from a formal, logical representation of domain knowledge.

Linguistic knowledge formally describes the linguistic structure of paragraphs, sentences, phrases, and words. It categorizes words of a lexicon as verbs, nouns, adjectives, adverbs, etc.

6.4.1.3   Literary Knowledge

With but a pinch of domain knowledge and a dash of linguistic knowledge, a story generation system can cough up a story. But chances are the story won't be particularly interesting; to the literate in our culture it may not appear to be a story at all — because most of the time the appellation 'story' is reserved for fairly polished narrative. (TALE-SPIN, though certainly seminal, would seem to be a perfect example of a system that spits out a "story" in only a most relaxed sense of that term.) A weak story may look more like a laundry list (of descriptions of places, things, people, and events) than engaging narrative. Such a story doesn't have a theme or a message, nor will it be told in a way that holds readers or steers them toward some intended meaning. In short, such defective stories fail to satisfy (all, or at least most of) our aforementioned magic desiderata. But of course we must admit that these seven points both aren't sufficient, and aren't sufficiently detailed. These points really only gesture at the mysterious elements of compelling narrative. The seventh point is particularly mysterious; it stands at the darkest part of what we gropingly label **literary knowledge**.

Literary knowledge is independent of a story's domain content or grammatical integrity. It is knowledge of the high *art* of storytelling. Literary knowledge enables the compelling communication of interesting interpretations of domain knowledge through the medium of natural language. Specifically, BRUTUS₁ encodes literary knowledge to generate stories that can achieve key literary objectives, including the objectives described in Chapters 2, 3, and 5, namely,

MD2 Trigger readerly imaging

MD3 Project P-consciousness

MD4 Engage readers in classic themes

MD6 Instantiate classic story structures

MD2 and MD3 are achieved through the characterization and selection of words, phrases, sentence, and paragraph structures in terms of their ability to trigger images and P-consciousness in the reader. MD4 is achieved through the formalization of thematic knowledge. (In Chapter 4, recall, the formalization of the thematic concept of betrayal was discussed.) This formalization is encoded as part of the literary knowledge-base in a structure referred to as a *thematic relation*. This relation is an implementation structure used to gather essential ingredients for a story about betrayal from a domain knowledge-base. Thematic relations are described in some detail later in this chapter.

MD6, recall, refers to the familiar flow of a story — how it is structured at a high-level in terms of setting, character introduction, etc. Story grammars, as we explained earlier, are what we use to represent the high-level "look-and-feel" of story structure. These grammars are part of the literary knowledge-base (KB).

6.4.1.4   Knowledge Usage in Story Generation

One can view the domain knowledge-base as a pool of story elements (characters, places, things, events, etc.) that can be configured to produce any number of stories about any number of themes.

The literary knowledge-base's thematic relation defines a particular theme independently of any particular set of domain elements. It is used to identify a set of elements from the domain and their inter-related roles required to tell a story about that theme. The literary KB's story grammars are used to orchestrate the high-level structure of the story that determines which paragraphs to write first and what sentence forms they contain. Literary knowledge is also used to select the key words and phrases that best communicate the theme by triggering readerly imaging and projecting P-consciousness. Finally, linguistic knowledge is used to configure grammatically correct English sentences.

6.4.2   Introduction to the Process Level

In BRUTUS, story generation is decomposed into four high-level processes:

1. Thematic concept instantiation

2. Plot generation

3. Story structure expansion

4. Language generation

Each process uses knowledge represented as part of the knowledge level and stored in BRUTUS₁'s knowledge-base.

Thematic concept instantiation begins with a description of a theme. This description is independent of specific objects or events that might appear in a particular domain knowledge-base. Given a specific domain KB, the theme is instantiated, which serves to identify particular objects, events, characters, etc. from that KB to play the general roles required to realize the theme. The result of this process is called a **stage**.

The stage is input to **plot generation**. Plot generation, through planning and simulation, weaves the details of a specific plot for the cast of characters identified in the stage. Plot generation completes what is called a **scenario**. The scenario is the stage plus a completed set of events and the effects these events had on the state of world.

Story structure expansion is the root of a separate process thread in BRUTUS. A high-level story structure, represented in BRUTUS$_1$ as a story grammar, may be input or randomly selected. As already noted, story grammars describe how a story is organized with respect to introduction, character descriptions, conflict, resolution, conclusions, and so on. Story structures in BRUTUS$_1$ are independent of plot and theme. The process of story expansion recursively expands structural components of a story represented in the story grammar until a series of paragraph types are reached. Paragraph types are further expanded into a series of sentence types. The result is a detailed story template, or story outline, that may be entirely independent of story content. Literary constraints may be used to influence otherwise random choices in the generation of a story outline. It is through these constraints that decisions regarding theme or plot may carry over to achieve congruent influence over story structure.

The scenario developed in plot generation, along with the outline produced in story structure expansion, are fed into the final process: **language generation**. In this process, linguistic and literary knowledge are used to produce the written story. A high-level process model is illustrated in Figure 6.9.

6.4.3   Implementation Structures and Methods

BRUTUS$_1$ is implemented using a variety of knowledge representation and programming techniques available in a logic-programming system called **FLEX**, originally developed by Logic Programming Associates (LPA). FLEX is based in Prolog, a popular logic-programming

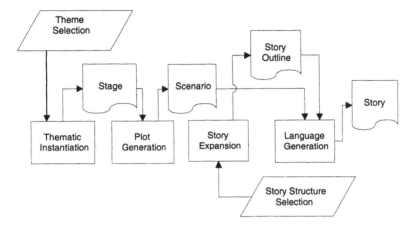

Figure 6.9: Brutus Process Model

language based on a general computational method that starts with a goal statement and searches a database of facts to find a proof for the goal. This method models a form of reasoning often referred to as "goal-directed reasoning." (For an in-depth treatment of Prolog we refer the reader to *The Art of Prolog* [223] and *The Craft of Prolog* [171]. The genealogy of logic programming is well-documented in *Logic and Logic Programming* [193]. We have ourselves written on Prolog's genealogy, and its power [23].)

FLEX provides the developer with complete access to Prolog and enhances the paradigm with frame-based structures, relations, production rules, and an English-like syntax. The syntax and semantics of FLEX are documented in LPA's FLEX technical reference [242].

6.4.3.1 Frames

FLEX's **Frames** allow the developer to group sets of facts around a specific domain entity, enabling a more intuitive structuring of the knowledge. A frame is used to represent a domain entity, and its attributes are used to represent facts or properties about that entity. From a programmer's perspective, frames are data structures that have a name and a set of attributes with default values. Frames can be organized in a generalization hierarchy via the relationship `is-a`. Attributes and default values are inherited from a parent in the frame hierarchy to its children. **Instances** are special kinds of

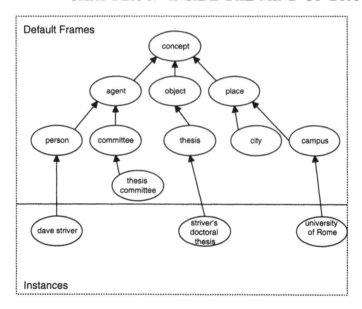

Figure 6.10: Sample Frame Hierarchy of a Subset of Domain Entities.

frames that have actual values rather than default values. Instances are leaves in the frame generalization hierarchy. A sample frame hierarchy, including some instances, is illustrated in Figure 6.10.

The following is part of a sample FLEX frame intended to represent the prototypical person. Specific people would be represented as instances with specific values that might override the default values inherited from the person frame. The value for an attribute in a frame can be a list of things. Lists are represented by { }'s.

```
frame person is an agent
  default height is 5.5 and
  default weight is 130 and
  default gender is female and
  default eye_color is brown and
  default goals are {eat,sleep} and
  default beliefs are {"computers write interesting stories"}
```

6.4.3.2 Relations

Relations in FLEX are used to define abstract properties about a frame or a sets of interrelated frames. Relations are processed by Prolog's goal-directed reasoning mechanism to find the specific frames and their elements that satisfy the relation. For example, a relation may be developed to find all frames in a knowledge-base that contain the necessary features to play the role of the betrayed in a story about betrayal. The following FLEX relation captures the abstract relationships between various persons, goals, plans and actions sufficient for BRUTUS₁ to identify the components of a simple story about betrayal.

```
relation betrayal_p
    if Evil is some goal whose plan is an EvilPlan
        and whose agent is a Betrayor
    and Saying is included in the EvilPlan
    and Saying is some say
    and Thwarting is included in the EvilPlan
    and Thwarting is some thwart
    and Betrayeds_Goal is the prevented_goal of Thwarting
    and Betrayors_Lie is the theme of the Saying
    and Betrayors_Lie is some support of the Betrayeds_Goal
    and Betrayed is some person
        whose goal is the Betrayeds_Goal
        and whose beliefs include the Betrayers_Lie.
```

This relation is actual FLEX code. Strings starting with an uppercase letter are logic variables. The strings **say** and **thwart** refer to types of actions defined in the domain knowledge-base. Goals, agents, and plans are also concepts defined in the domain KB. The English-like syntax of this relation is translated by the FLEX system into standard Prolog programs. These programs drive a goal-directed search through the knowledge-base and assign the logic variables to specific domain concepts.

6.4.3.3 Production Rules

Production rules or **condition-action** rules have a condition and an action. If the condition is met, the actions are executed. These rules are processed in FLEX by a forward reasoning engine. They are used in BRUTUS₁ to represent the reactive behavior of agents. The forward reasoning engine is exploited in BRUTUS₁ to provide a computational facility for simulation that runs in the course of plot generation. A set of production rules is input to the forward reasoning engine. All conditions are checked; rules whose conditions are satisfied are fired, that is, their actions are executed. The result of the actions may change the state of the KB, potentially causing other rules to fire. The process continues until all rules have fired or failed to fire. FLEX provides a variety of control features for specifying the order in which rules should fire and for resolving conflicts if more than one rule can fire at a time.

6.5 The Knowledge Level

6.5.1 Domain Knowledge

Domain knowledge includes a static description of the world, or domain, about which a story is written. Domain knowledge includes descriptions of people, places, things, events, actions, goals, and behaviors. These descriptions are represented in BRUTUS₁ as FLEX frames.

6.5.1.1 Agents and Events

Agents perform actions and participate in events. In stories about people, people are obviously an important class of agents. People are represented as agents with physical and psychological attributes. In addition to the garden-variety physical attributes like height, weight, and eye color, a person's attributes include a set of goals and a set of beliefs. The latter set is an important element in plot generation. Consider frame excerpts describing the by-now-familiar characters Hart and Striver as examples. It is in part through the actions associated with characters' goals that a plot is developed from a stage. Hart's `evilGoal` refers to a goal that includes actions intended to prevent Striver from achieving his goal. The interplay of these various intentions is integral to the betrayal theme.

```
instance hart is a person
    name is 'Hart' and
    gender is male and
    goals is {evilGoal}.
```

```
instance striver is a person and
    name is 'Dave Striver' and
    gender is male and
    goals is {to_graduate} and
    beliefs is {harts_promise}.
```

Events are concepts that relate people, places, and things. In BRUTUS₁ the focus is on the specific event attributes required to facilitate representation of key story elements.

Hart and Striver are described as people with physical and psychological attributes. They are interrelated in the domain KB through their roles in common events. For example, `Striver's thesis defense` is a thesis defense, which is a type of event, where Striver is the `examined` and Hart is a member of the examining `committee`. Among other attributes, the `examined` and the `committee` are the key elements of this event, which link Striver and Hart.

```
instance strivers_defense is a thesis_defense
    thesis is strivers_thesis and
    where is university_of_rome and
    examined is striver and
    committee is {hart,meter,rodgers,walken} and
    status is scheduled.
```

6.5.1.2 Beliefs

The set of beliefs associated with a person describes in part what that person believes is true about the world. That which a person believes, however, need not be true. In BRUTUS₁, a person, by default, is assumed to believe all that is true about the physical state of the world as represented in the domain KB (from now on simply the **world**). This excludes knowledge about other people's psychological attributes or beliefs. A person is not assumed to have knowledge about other people's beliefs, goals, or behavior patterns — unless otherwise explicitly stated. For example, if Hart states publicly that he supports Striver's success, then Striver, by default, believes this statement was made. The system does not conclude by default, however, that Striver believes that Hart is telling the truth (or is lying). Statements about another person's beliefs must be explicitly inferred in BRUTUS₁. Explicit belief statements must be included by the designer of the knowledge-base or may be inferred as the result of a rule.

Consider Striver's belief about Hart's promise. A promise is a type of statement. The frame representing Hart's promise follows.

```
instance harts_promise is a promise
  agent is 'Prof. Hart' and
  utterance is 'I will sign your thesis at your defense.' and
  promised is 'Dave Striver' and
  intended_state is signatures of strivers_thesis include 'Prof. Hart'.
```

The `intended_state` associated with a promise describes some aspect of the state of the world that would be true if the promise were kept. The following frame demonstrates the representation of Striver's belief about the truth of Hart's promise.

```
instance striver is a person
    name is 'Dave Striver' and
    gender is male and
    goals is {to_graduate} and
    beliefs is {harts_promise}.
```

Persons may also believe statements that contradict the current state of the world. For the person with the false belief, these contradictory statements override that actual state of the world. Contradictory or false beliefs must be stated explicitly in the list of beliefs associated with a specific person. For example, if the saying of **harts_promise**, represented by the following frame **say101**,

```
instance say101 is a say
    agent is 'Prof.  Hart' and
    statement is harts_promise.
```

existed in the domain knowledge-base and Striver did not believe that Professor Hart made the promise (i.e., that Hart uttered the statement), then Striver's beliefs must contain an explicit negative belief. The following frame represents that Striver does not believe that **say101** occurred.

```
instance striver is a person
    name is 'Dave Striver' and
    gender is male and
    goals is to_graduate and
    beliefs is {not(say101)}.
```

6.5.1.3   Proactive Behavior: Goals, Plans, and Actions

Goals, plans, and actions are used to represent a character's proactive behavior. Once a character is set in motion, the character attempts to achieve its goal by executing the actions associated with the goal's plan. Each action has pre-conditions and state-operations. The pre-conditions ensure that the setting is right to execute the action; the state-operations attempt to change the state of the domain. If, for some reason, a state-operation fails to execute, then the action fails.

If all the elements of a plan succeed, then the goal is successfully completed by the corresponding agent. Goals, plans, and actions are considered part of the proactive behavioral model because they are initiated by the character as part of his or her explicit intentions.

A goal is a concept that has three main attributes:

1. Agent: someone or something that can achieve the goal, typically a person.

2. Plan: a list of actions.

3. Success state: a condition that if true would indicate that the goal has been satisfied.

For example, Hart may have the goal to destroy Striver's hope to graduate. To achieve this goal there is a sequence of actions that the agent, Hart, must execute. This sequence is the plan. It may include, for example, conveying to the examining committee that Striver's ideas are worthless by refusing to sign his thesis. Hart may execute all elements of the plan, but there is no guarantee that his goal will succeed. A goal's success state is a condition — a condition which, if true of some elements of the domain, indicates that the goal has been achieved: the agent has succeeded. In this case a success state may be the failure of Striver's thesis defense.

The following frame represents Hart's goal to thwart Striver's goal to graduate.

```
instance evilGoal is a goal
   agent is hart and
   plan is {lie101, refuse_to_sign101} and
   success is status of strivers_defense is failed.
```

lie101 and refuse_to_sign101 are specific actions that will execute during plot generation on Hart's behalf when their preconditions are met.

6.5.1.4   Reactive Behavior: Production Rules

Reactive behavior describes how a character reacts to changes or events in the world. Reactive behavior is represented by a set of condition-action rules (or production rules) associated with agents. If the condition is met, then the actions are executed. With reactive rules, BRUTUS₁ allows character behavior to be described in terms of how a character may respond to different events independently of the character's specific goals. Reactive behavioral knowledge is ideal for describing basic elements of a character's default behavior independently of specific roles in a theme. It provides a representation mechanism for capturing particular behavioral dimensions that "trademark" a character.

Rules associated with a character's behavior may be as specific or as general as the knowledge-base designer feels is appropriate. For example, Professor Hart might have specific behavior rules that describe exactly how he may react to a given state. Alternatively, without a specific rule, Professor Hart might react according to a default behavioral rule associated with *all* persons.

Reactive behavior in BRUTUS₁ functions both to increase the variability of a plot's outcome during simulation and to produce dialogue.

BRUTUS₁ combines proactive and reactive behavior in simulation in order to vary plot generation while still maintaining a theme-driven focus. The thematic frame sets key characters in motion by triggering their proactive behavior. Effects may, in turn, trigger the reactive behavior of *other* characters who can twist the plot by helping or hurting a character's proactive agenda.

The following production rule describes the typical reactive behavior of a member of a thesis committee. In summary, this rule states that if a member of a thesis committee is asked by the chair of the committee to sign the candidate's thesis, the member reacts by signing the thesis.

```
rule committee_members_behavior
  IF
  Candidate is some person and
  Thesis is the thesis of Candidate and
  the committee of the Candidate includes Member and
  Request_To_Sign is some request and
  Member is the requestee of Request_To_Sign and
  the requester of Request_To_Sign is the chairman of the committee and
  Thesis is the document of subject of Request_To_Sign and
  status of Request_To_Sign is pending
  THEN
  do answer(Member, Request_To_Sign) and
  do sign(Member, Thesis).
```

Proactive behavior, by default, overrides reactive behavior. In our first story of betrayal, "Betrayal in Self-Deception" (shown in Chapter 1 and again at the end of this chapter), Professor Hart intends to thwart Striver's goal to graduate by refusing to sign his thesis. Professor Hart does not react like a typical committee member. His proactive refusal to sign Striver's thesis must override the reactive behavior imposed by the production rule previously described. This is accomplished in BRUTUS₁ by ensuring that all actions associated with plans are given a chance to execute in response to changes in the knowledge-base before production rules are fired in response to the same changes. In this case the fact that Professor Hart refused to sign the thesis would occur first, ensuring that the reactive rule would not execute for him, since the request directed to Professor Hart would no longer be pending when the reactive rule fired.

By changing behavioral rules and/or actions, and activating different sets of rules, the simulation process will unfold different plots about the same theme and the same stage. For example, varying Professor Hart's reaction to pressure from the chairman to sign the thesis can result in a happy or sad ending for the candidate, Dave Striver. While the story is still about betrayal, the difference revolves around whether or not the betrayer succeeds in the quest to thwart the betrayed's goals.

6.5.2   Linguistic Knowledge

While domain knowledge, the thematic relation, and the results of simulation determine what BRUTUS$_1$ will write about, how BRUTUS$_1$ will express the story is determined by linguistic and literary knowledge. Linguistic knowledge is knowledge about natural language. The written story is formed from "legal" expressions in a natural language; in BRUTUS$_1$ the natural language is (as readers by now certainly know) English.

Linguistic knowledge is explicated through observations of how humans express internal knowledge in distinct language structures. Linguistic theory describes language structures at a number of different levels. These levels include:

1. Discourse

2. Paragraph

3. Sentence

4. Phrase

5. Word

The discourse level may be viewed as the most aggregate level. It is composed by configuring elements from the paragraph level. The paragraph level, in turn, is composed by configuring elements from the sentence level, and so on.

Words are defined as the smallest independent units that can be assigned descriptive meaning; however, words can be further decomposed into sets of letters that act as prefixes, roots, and suffixes. These can be combined to form different words. The study of how these combinations occur is called **word formation morphology**. The morphology of words may be influenced by semantic properties relating to number, gender, case, or tense. The study of the forms of words as they relate to these properties is called **derivational morphology**. Finally, words may take on different forms based on agreement with the forms of other words which occur simultaneously in a phrase. For example, the number of a noun influences the form of the verb in a noun phrase. The study of the types of agreement and how they influence the form of words is called **inflectional morphology**.

Encoded in the linguistic knowledge-base are a lexicon containing a set of words and the morphological rules necessary to demonstrate story generation examples. For details on encoding morphological rules see *Natural Language Computing* by Dougherty [77].

In general, a sentence in a natural language, L, is a string of words taken from a fixed list of words that constitute L's lexicon. A natural language grammar for L is a device that distinguishes the grammatical from the ungrammatical sequences of words; this defines the valid (i.e., grammatically correct) sentences of L. For an introductory but impressively detailed treatment of formal grammars for a subset of English, and their use in mechanized communication, see [201].

BRUTUS₁ encodes, as Prolog goals, a variety of sentence-level grammars, which include phrase-level grammars, for generating grammatically correct sentences. These generative grammars presuppose lower level linguistic procedures to ensure, among other things, verb/subject agreement, punctuation, etc.

Sentence grammars are categorized in BRUTUS₁ to represent classes of sentences that have a particular structure; these sentences vary around pivotal elements. BRUTUS₁ uses numerous sentence grammars. Examples include sentence types designed to describe a setting, to describe a character, to reveal a character's goals, to narrate different classes of events, and so on. Variations can result in the generation of a negative or positive tone, or the selection of words to produce different classes of imagery.

As an example, we illustrate a sentence grammar for producing a sentence type called an **independent parallel setting description**:

- INDPSD → SETTING verb FP
- FP → 'its' FEATURE FP | 'its' FEATURE
- SETTING → noun_phrase
- FEATURE → noun_phrase

In sentence grammars, uppercase words in the grammar are nonterminals. Words in quotes are literals used exactly as is in a generated sentence. Lowercase words are terminals in the sentence grammar. The terminals are phrase or word types that are selected and/or constructed from the available lexicon when a sentence is generated. Sentence generation procedures use sentence grammars to produce individual sentences that conform to the grammar. Typically, certain elements are fixed in the application of a sentence generation procedure. BRUTUS₁ supports different generation procedures for the same grammar. A generation procedure pivots around the elements which it allows to be fixed. For example, a procedure that pivots on SETTING will generate all possible sentences that can be built from the lexicon where SETTING is fixed to a particular noun. Other sentence generators for a given grammar may pivot on more than one element.

An example of an independent parallel setting description sentence where SETTING is fixed to the noun university is as follows:

> *The university has its ancient and sturdy brick, its sun-splashed greens, and its eager youth.*

Sentences of this type are of course fairly simple. A noun that is a setting is chosen, and some possessive verb is used to link the setting to a list of feature phrases that describe a set of objects considered characteristic of the setting.

This simple sentence grammar is inadequate, however. For sentences of this form to have literary effect, elements of the sentence must be somehow associated with literary knowledge. In the section of this chapter on linking literary and linguistic knowledge, augmented grammars that enhance linguistic structures with literary objectives are described.

A description at the discourse level in BRUTUS₁ is realized by a structure called the **story grammar**, which we visited earlier in this chapter. Such a grammar describes, at a high level, how the story will be laid out in terms of paragraphs that describe the setting, characters, and events that make up the story. For us, stories are best viewed as literary concepts as opposed to linguistic concepts, since they are ultimately language-independent. In fact, the same story grammar can be used to both lay out the frames in a silent movie and generate a written story.

6.5.3   Literary Knowledge

While the linguistic knowledge-base identifies types of words, phrases, and sentences as they function in the English grammar, literary knowledge describes different ways to use words and phrases together to achieve a variety of literary objectives.

Literary objectives may include generating imagery in the reader's mind (recall Chapter 2 and MD2), suggesting a character's landscape of consciousness (recall Chapter 3 and MD3), and producing a positive, secure mood, or a negative, anxious one for the reader. Literary objectives like these may be achieved by selecting appropriate words and sentence structure combinations. Literary concepts, found in BRUTUS₁'s literary knowledge-base, define attributes of linguistic concepts as they relate to domain concepts so that text generation procedures can produce expressions that achieve literary objectives.

6.5.3.1 Literary Associations

Objects described in the domain knowledge-base are interrelated and linked to linguistic concepts (words, phrases, etc.) as one way of capturing literary knowledge. The resulting associations between concepts and language elements are called **literary associations**. They are used to generate sentences that satisfy specific literary objectives.

Currently, BRUTUS₁ includes three types of literary associations:

1. Iconic features

2. Literary modifiers

3. Literary analogs

6.5.3.1.1 Iconic Features: Positive and Negative Objects are related to other objects in BRUTUS₁ via an attribute called **iconic features**. A object's iconic features are represented as a list of other objects that are typically associated with the first object in literary settings. For example, ivy and clocktowers might be iconic features of a university (as indeed they are for BRUTUS₁). Wheels, engines, and speed might be iconic features of a motorcycle. The list of iconic features associated with an object is further specialized with respect to general notions of positive or negative imagery. This classification is highly subjective and may vary with respect to context; however, it can be very effective for imaging.

Consider the following frame fragment describing a university.

```
frame university is a object
  default positive_iconic_features is
  {clocktowers, brick, ivy, youth, architecture, books, knowledge,
  scholar, sports} and
  default negative_iconic_features is
  {tests, competition, 'intellectual snobbery'}.
```

In this frame `ivy` is listed as a positive iconic feature of a university, while `tests` is listed as a negative one. Though the subjectivity of these classifications is apparent, the representational framework allows for capturing and configuring a variety of literary descriptions.

6.5.3.1.2 Literary Modifiers: Positive and Negative The concept of literary modifiers is an association between modifiers and the objects that they typically modify. In BRUTUS₁ these associations are grouped into positive and negative classes. The associations are linked to the frames representing the modified objects with the attributes

`positive_literary_modifiers`

and

`negative_literary_modifiers`.

As is the case with iconic features, the negative and positive classification of literary modifiers is entirely subjective, but nonetheless this classification is profitably configurable in the literary KB.

Given the frame for university and the following frame fragment for ivy

```
frame ivy is an object
    default positive_iconic_features is {leaves, vines} and
    default negative_iconic_features is {poison} and
    default negative_literary_modifiers is {poisonness, tangled} and
    default positive_literary_modifiers is {spreading, green, lush}.
```

a text generation procedure for independent parallel setting description sentences can produce positive imagistic sentences like:

The university has its lush, green ivy.

If the knowledge-base were reconfigured and `ivy` was also listed as a negative iconic feature of `university`, then the following negative imagistic sentence can be produced:

The university is full of tangled poison ivy.

Sentence generators in BRUTUS₁ are parameterized and can be called to produce negative or positive phrases.

6.5.3.1.3 Literary Analogs Metaphors are used in order to support sentence types in BRUTUS₁. These literary devices are supported by an underlying representation structure called **literary analogs**. A literary analog identifies a single main object, another object called the **analog** that is used to represent the main object in a literary fashion, and the intended imagery suggested by the analog.

The following frame is an instance of an analog for the main object **eye** and one of its analogs, the **sun**.

```
instance analog1 is a literary_analog
    object is eye
    analogs are sun
    images are {warmth, power, trust}.
```

6.5.3.2 Linking Literary and Linguistic Knowledge

To the extent that sentence grammars capture the grammatical rules of a natural language, they are considered linguistic concepts; however, in BRUTUS₁ these structures are augmented to contain elements that reflect the linkages between literary objectives and grammatical structure.

Literary augmented grammars (LAGs) are used in BRUTUS₁ to represent and use literary knowledge to produce compelling and interesting prose. Consider the following LAG for independent parallel description sentences:

- INDPSD → SETTING verb (isa possessive_verb) FP(n=3)
- FP → 'its' FEATURE FP | 'its' FEATURE
- SETTING → noun_phrase (has_role setting)
- FEATURE → noun_phrase (isa iconic_feature_of SETTING)

Elements on the rightside of the LAG rules are annotated with expressions in parentheses. These expressions are called **literary constraints**. It is through literary constraints that linguistic and literary knowledge interact. While sentence grammars drive the construction of classes of grammatically correct sentences in a natural language, literary constraints in LAGs are designed to shape the contents of the sentence by using literary and domain knowledge to achieve various literary objectives.

Sentence generation procedures limit the instantiation of terminals to words or phrases that satisfy the literary constraint. The constraints describe the literary roles that the elements of the sentence must assume independently and/or with respect to one another. Constraint processing relies on how words (and their associated objects) are classified and linked in the literary knowledge-base. The constraints are used to search the literary and linguistic KBs, where nouns, modifiers, verbs, etc. are categorized and associated with one another by a variety of classifications and associations. For example, brick, greens, and youth are nouns classified as iconic features of a university.

The constraint

$$(\text{isa possessive\_verb})$$

in the preceding grammar constrains the preceding terminal, **verb**, to be instantiated from a certain class of verbs, namely, **possessive verbs**. Membership in this class is captured in the knowledge-base.

Similarly, (**has_role setting**) constrains the selection for the terminal **noun_phrase** in the SETTING rule of this grammar to be instantiated by a noun phase whose subject can function as a setting according to the classifications contained in the literary knowledge-base. The constraint **isa feature_of** SETTING is used to narrow the selections for a noun phrase based on its relationship with a choice for SETTING. In this case, the constraint ensures that the noun in the associated noun phrase is represented as an iconic feature of whatever object is selected in the **noun_phrase** for SETTING.

The constraint (**n=3**) in the first rule of this grammar instructs the sentence generation procedures to produce exactly three descriptive features in any generated sentence.

6.5.3.3 Imagistic Expertise

As discussed in Chapter 2, Esrock identified four techniques for triggering images in the minds of the reader. They are:

1. Exotic or bizarre material

2. Visual perception and P-consciousness-related verbs

3. Familiar reference

4. Voyeurism

BRUTUS₁ includes a framework in the literary KB for classifying linguistic elements to enable the automation of these techniques.

6.5.3.3.1 The Bizarre To capture the bizarre, modifiers are linked with objects in frames named `bizzaro_modifiers`. Consider the following instance describing the `bizzaro` modifier `bleeding`.

```
instance bleeding is a bizzaro_modifier
    objects are {sun, plants, clothes, tombs, eyes}.
```

An action analogy LAG may be augmented with constraints to stimulate bizarre images in the mind of the reader. The following LAG for action analogies,

- `BizarreActionAnalogy → NP VP like ANP`

- `NP → noun_phrase`

- `ANP → modifier (isa bizzaro_modifier) noun (isa analog of NP)`

in conjunction with `bizzaro_modifiers` can be used to generate the following sentence.

Hart's eyes were like big bleeding suns.

6.5.3.3.2 Perception & P-Consciousness BRUTUS₁ triggers images with the technique of visual perception by constraining the principal verb in the appropriate LAG to be a member of a class of verbs called **vp_verbs**. These include verbs for seeing, looking, glancing, and so on.

Similarly, BRUTUS₁ narrates stories from a particular character's point of view using verbs selected from a special class of verbs represented in the literary KB called **pc_verbs**. These include verbs for feeling, thinking, understanding, wanting, etc. PC verbs give the reader the sense that the subject of these verbs has a psychological life.

A variation of the parallel setting description sentence is a sentence that describes a setting from a particular character's point of view. The following is the LAG for that sentence type. It includes a literary constraint that forces the use of a PC verb to convey the character's consciousness.

- POV → Agent (is a person) Verb (is a PC Verb) FirstFP

- FirstFP → Setting FEATURE FP

- FP → its FEATURE FP | '.'

- FEATURE → noun_phrase (is a feature of SETTING)

- SETTING → noun_phrase (is a setting)

6.5.3.3.3 Familiar Reference   Stories that appeal to a reader's familiar experiences are known to quickly engage their audience. Triggering images of familiar things in the reader's mind keeps him or her interested and gives the author opportunity to manipulate the reader's expectation, better enabling the effect of plot twists and emotional turns. BRUTUS₁ can trigger images with familiar reference by classifying settings, objects and features as familiar to a class of readers and ensuring that they are used in stage and language generation through the elaboration of the thematic relation and the application of literary constraints.

In our examples of betrayal, the university setting is a familiar reference to a wide class of readers and is expected to quickly form familiar and comforting images in the minds of these readers. These images are reinforced with the choice of particular modifiers and features. Of course, in our examples, the imminent betrayal is quickly suggested, shifting the focus from the positive reference of the university to the universal image of classic betrayal.

6.5.3.3.4 Voyeurism   Another literary "trick" known to trigger images and spark the reader's interest is voyeurism. As we noted in Chapter 2, Kafka, for example, often includes in stories scenarios in which one person sneaks a peak at the behavior of others, or even places the reader in the position of outright voyeur. Consider an elaboration of betrayal, **voyeuristic betrayal**. BRUTUS₁ may include a thematic relation for voyeuristic betrayal that requires a few new stage elements, including a new character, **the voyeur**, and a new action **secretly_watch**. The relation may compose a stage where the voyeur is envious of the betrayer and engages in regular acts of secretly watching the betrayer's activities. The stage will initialize the story with the potential for an additional subplot involving the voyeur secretly witnessing the betrayer reveal his plans to betray the betrayed to some confidant. Plot generation will run the stage through a simulation, as described earlier, working out the details regarding the voyeur's experience and decision to tell what he witnessed to the betrayed. Regardless of how the plot plays out, the point is that well-crafted sentences and word choices that describe scenes involving the secret witnessing of another's behavior will serve to tickle the emotions and imaginations of human readers.

6.6 The Process Level

6.6.1 Setting the Stage: Thematic Instantiation

The process of thematic instantiation selects components from the domain knowledge-base sufficient to generate a story about a particular theme. The process of thematic instantiation uses a FLEX relation, based on a formal mathematization of a thematic concept like betrayal, and the goal-directed reasoning mechanism underlying Prolog, to search the domain knowledge-base and assemble the story elements (characters, goals, events, settings, etc.) required to construct a story about the theme.

The following FLEX relation represents the components and their interrelationships sufficient to generate a story about the theme of betrayal.

```
relation betrayal_p(A_Betrayal)
    if Evil is some goal whose plan is an EvilPlan
        and whose agent is a Betrayor
    and Saying is included in the EvilPlan
    and Saying is some say
    and Thwarting is included in the EvilPlan
    and Thwarting is some thwart
    and Betrayeds_Goal is the prevented_goal of Thwarting
    and Betrayers_Lie is the theme of the Saying
    and Betrayers_Lie is some support of the Betrayeds_Goal
    and Betrayed is some person
        whose goal is the Betrayeds_Goal
        and whose beliefs include the Betrayors_Lie.
```

A rough intuitive translation of how this particular relation is interpreted from a procedural perspective runs as follows.

- Look in the domain knowledge-base and find some goal with an associated plan and agent, where the plan includes a saying action and a thwarting action. This agent might be engaged in an act of betrayal; the agent might be the betrayer.

- Look to find that the alleged betrayer's thwarting action is intended to thwart someone else's goal. The person who has this goal might be vulnerable to a betrayal. That person might be the betrayed.

- Look to find that the alleged betrayer's statement is in support of the betrayed's goal and that the alleged betrayed believes the statement.

The search of the domain KB described here is performed automatically by the Prolog inference engine. If the search is successful, then the thematic instantiation process builds the stage. The stage, implemented by a FLEX frame, represents the key roles in a story about the designated theme.

In BRUTUS$_1$, thematic instantiation captures the essential characteristics of betrayal by building the following frame:

```
frame betrayal is a concept
    default betrayer is a person and
    default betrayed is a person and
    default betrayers_goal is a goal and
    default betrayeds_goal is a goal and
    default betrayers_lie is a statement and
    default betrayal_location is a place and
    default betrayers_evil_action is a action.
```

While the domain elements of the story are selected as a result of thematic concept instantiation, the story generation process has yet to develop a specific plot. The domain concepts are static. They represent a snapshot in time, one capturing different characters and events that are the principal ingredients for a story. In plot generation the ingredients are cooked; the details of plot are produced based on the behaviors of the characters.

In BRUTUS₁, thematic instantiation requires that the domain knowledge-base include many of the specific objects required to instantiate the theme. In future versions of BRUTUS the process of thematic instantiation will use general domain concepts as a basis for generating specific objects so that less domain knowledge is required as input into the story generation process.

6.6.2 Developing the Plot Through Simulation

The process of plot generation enables BRUTUS₁ to produce a variety of plots around a particular theme and a particular stage. Through a forward reasoning process provided by FLEX, BRUTUS₁ simulates character behavior. The principal knowledge used in plot generation is behavioral knowledge. As discussed earlier, characters have proactive behavior, represented by goals and plans, and reactive behavior represented by condition-action rules. These rules represent how characters react to particular states. Once set in motion, they result in actions that affect new states, and more rules fire; this process simulates a chain of reactive behavior. Eventually the process of forward-reasoning halts, indicating that a final state has been achieved and the simulation is over.

Changes made to behavioral knowledge lead BRUTUS₁ to produce different plots given the same theme and stage. In this way BRUTUS₁ may be used to write different stories about the same theme with the same cast of characters, events, and initial states.

Plot generation is very much a computational device for dynamically extending the domain knowledge-base through time. Initially the domain KB contains basic story elements that may interact in a variety of ways. The use of rules and simulation enables the process of plot generation to play out a scenario by simulating the behaviors of the selected set of characters and recording the results of the simulation in terms of new events, states, and dialogue (i.e., the results of speaking actions) in the domain KB. At the end of the simulation, the plot is developed and a particular outcome is realized. The new domain KB contains the completed plot or the scenario.

For example, suppose the process of thematic instantiation has produced, from the domain KB, a stage for the theme of betrayal, including the following elements (expressed informally for readability):

- betrayer: Professor Hart

- betrayed: Dave Striver

- location: University of Rome

- betrayed's goal: to get all members of thesis committee to approve and sign thesis

- betrayer's promise: to approve betrayed's thesis.

Plot generation will extend the story elements though time by executing actions associated with character goals, and will process behavioral rules; the final result is a detailed scenario. Specific actions that execute in the development of this stage include

- `sign`

- `refuse-to-sign`

- `say`

- `answer`

- `request_signatures`

- `demand`

Behavioral rules governing the typical behavior of committee members and the committee chairperson would execute during plot generation. For example, at the end of the thesis defense the following rule would trigger the committee chairperson to request the members to sign the thesis.

```
rule committee_chairs_behavior1
  if Committee is a thesis defense committee
  and Chair is the chair of Committee
  and Defense is the subject of the Committee
  and the status of Defense includes completed
    and unjudged
  then do(request_signatures(Chair,Committee)).
```

The following rule would result in the typical committee member agreeing to sign the thesis when asked by the committee chair.

```
rule committee_members_behavior
  IF
  Candidate is some person and
  Thesis is the thesis of Candidate and
  the committee of the Candidate includes Member and
  Request_To_Sign is some request and
  Member is the requestee of Request_To_Sign and
  the requester of Request_To_Sign is the chairman of the committee and
  Thesis is the document of subject of Request_To_Sign and
  status of Request_To_Sign is pending
  THEN
  do answer(Member, Request_To_Sign) and
  do sign(Member, Thesis).
```

The result of plot generation produces a scenario that would for example include the following series of actions and states (expressed informally for readability):

- Prof. Hart tells Dave Striver "I will support your defense and sign your thesis" at T0.
- Dave Striver completed his thesis defense at time T1.
- Prof. Rodgers requests approval signatures of members of Dave Striver's committee at time T2.
- All committee members except Prof. Hart sign Dave Striver's thesis at time T3.
- Prof. Hart refuses to sign Dave Striver's thesis at time T4.
- Prof. Hart says "Dave does not deserve to graduate." at T5.
- Prof. Rodgers insists that Prof. Hart signs at T6.
- Prof. Hart refuses to sign at T7.
- Dave Striver's thesis is rejected.

All the actions that take place in this series are encoded in the domain KB and are related through the stage to the roles that participate in the theme of betrayal. This relationship allows BRUTUS₁ to infer, among other things, that Professor Hart's refusal to sign Striver's thesis is the specific act through which the betrayer successfully thwarted the goal of the betrayed (i.e., Striver's goal to graduate).

BRUTUS₁ must now compose the language to write the story based on the scenario and its relationship to the theme.

6.6.3   Writing the Story: Outline and Language Generation

Thematic instantiation and plot generation produces a **stage** and then a **scenario** respectively. The scenario will be input into the process of language generation. In this process, sentences are constructed based on the characters, goals, events, etc. present in the scenario. The sentence types chosen and the sequence in which they appear depend on the story outline.

The process of **Story structure expansion** builds a story outline. Story grammars, discussed in some detail in the beginning of this chapter, are used to represent a variety of possible story structures. The process pursues a path through a grammar hierarchy, making either random or constrained choices as non-terminals in the grammars are expanded until a string of terminals, representing sentence types, is produced. The sequence of sentence types is the story outline.

BRUTUS captures the knowledge used by story structure expansion and language generation in a three-level grammar hierarchy (illustrated in Figure 6.11). We named this hierarchy the **literary-to-linguistic grammar hierarchy** because its successive levels takes story expansion from high-level story structure (literary knowledge) all the way down to English sentence grammar and word selection (linguistic knowledge). The top level of the hierarchy is composed of story grammars. Story grammars may be organized in a taxonomy, in which top-level story grammars are very generic and may apply to a wide variety of story types. Lower levels in the story grammar taxonomy may contain story grammars specialized for particular kinds of stories, like stories about betrayal, for example.

The terminals, or leaves of story grammars, are names of paragraph types. These are associated with structures in the second level of the grammar hierarchy called **paragraph grammars**. The terminals of these grammars are in turn sentence types. The final level in the grammar hierarchy is composed of literary augmented sentence grammars (abbreviated, recall, as **LAGs**). These are formal language grammars that represent components of English syntax augmented with literary constraints. The augmentation enables the generation of grammatically correct sentences that achieve particular literary objectives. The leaves of LAGs are variables instantiated to words that represent domain concepts. LAGs are described in

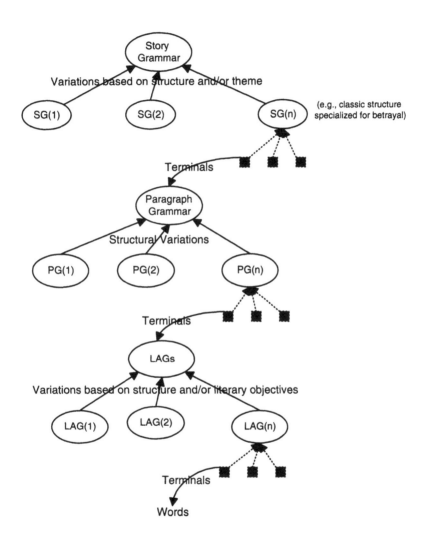

Figure 6.11: BRUTUS₁ Literary-to-Linguistic Grammar Hierarchy.

some detail in the section dedicated to BRUTUS$_1$'s knowledge level.

Starting with a story grammar, the structures in the grammar hierarchy are expanded until a sequence of sentence types is generated. This entire process may be performed independently of the scenario produced by thematic instantiation and plot generation. However, augmenting the story and paragraph grammars in a manner similar to the way LAGs do for sentences can allow for shaping the story outline by constraining choice points in its expansion based on literary objectives. These objectives may be determined by different elements of the theme or plot. More generally, the BRUTUS architecture suggests that any parameter, for example author styles or user preferences, may be used to constrain choices in the expansion of a story outline. The current implementation, BRUTUS$_1$, uses the notion suggested by LAGs only to direct sentence generation, however.

Language generation takes the scenario and the story outline and uses literary and linguistic knowledge to generate a story in English. The language generation process is all about choosing words. The story outline is a map identifying the sequence of sentence types that will be used to tell the story. Each of these sentence types must be instantiated, that is, subjects, objects, verbs, adjectives, etc. must be chosen from a lexicon. These choices are directed by the story elements represented in the scenario and the constraints imposed by literary objectives captured in the LAGs.

Consider the following fragment (simplified to enhance readability) from a BRUTUS$_1$ story grammar specialized for short stories about betrayal:

1. Story → Setting + Goals_and_plans + Betrayers_evil_action +
   betrayed's_state

2. Goals_and_plans → Betrayed's_goal + Betrayers_promise +
   Betrayers_goal

3. Setting → setting_description(betrayal_location,pov,betrayed)

4. Betrayed's_goal → personal_goal_sentence(betrayed)

5. Betrayed's_goal → personal_goal_sentence(betrayer)

6. Betrayers_promise → promise_description(betrayer,betrayed)

7. Betrayers_evil_action → narrate_action(betrayers_evil_action)

This grammar specifies a structure that first exposes the reader to a description of the setting where the betrayal occurs from the point of view of the betrayed. It then describes the betrayed's goal and the betrayer's promise to assist the betrayed in achieving that goal. Finally, the story ends with a description of the betrayer's evil action that ultimately thwarts the goal of the betrayed, and a statement about the betrayed's state. Non-terminals in this grammar begin with caps. Terminals begin with lowercase letters and indicate the names of paragraph grammars or LAGs. Arguments to grammars are roles contained in the stage-produced thematic instantiation and are assigned domain entities from the stage completed in plot generation.

The third rule in this story grammar leads to a paragraph grammar containing two sentences for describing a location from some character's point of view. Following from our sample stage, the paragraph grammar called in this third rule would be

```
setting_description(university_of_rome,pov,'Dave Striver').
```

The terminals in the following paragraph grammar lead to LAGs; and one is for the parallel description sentence explained earlier in the section on BRUTUS's knowledge level.

1. `Setting_description(Loc,pov,Person)` → `pc_of(Person,Loc)` +
   `parallel_dscrp(Loc,pov,Person)`

A brief sample story generated from the simple grammars just described and the theme and stage produced earlier in our example follows.

> *Dave loves the university of Rome. He loves its studious youth, ivy-covered clocktowers and its sturdy brick. Dave wanted to graduate. Prof. Hart told Dave, "I will sign your thesis at your defense." Prof. Hart actually intends to thwart Dave's plans to graduate. After Dave completed his defense and the chairman of Dave's committee asked Prof. Hart to sign Dave's thesis, Prof. Hart refused to sign. Dave was crushed.*

The brief examples here taken from the BRUTUS₁ grammar hierarchy illustrate how story grammars can drive a variety of story structures that lead to paragraphs and sentence structures, which are in turn tied directly to domain entities and literary objectives through LAGs. Significant storytelling and literary variability can be achieved by altering, adding, or selecting different story, paragraph, or LAGs. Content variability can, of course, be achieved by creating or modifying thematic relations, behavioral rules, and domain knowledge.

6.6.4   Variations on a Theme

In preceding sections of this chapter, the betrayal relation and frame, and the process by which BRUTUS generates stories, starting with an interesting theme, are described. Variations can be realized by adjusting the thematic relation to describe different outcomes. For example, while the betrayal relation previously described allows for success or failure of the betrayer's goal, a betrayal frame for generating specialized stories about betrayal where the betrayer necessarily succeeds can be built (see the definition of `successful(Betrayal)` in the next box). The thematic instantiation process would ensure that the stories generated will include only events such that the betrayer will succeed in thwarting the betrayed. The instantiation of this type of betrayal might entail associated variations in plot, story structure, and language. A similar approach can be taken to produce a variety of specializations; for example, cases where the betrayer's goal is considered altruistic by a general audience but taken as an offense by the betrayed. This is a case that may apply to a parent betraying a child's trust to ultimately save the child from a tragic end. (You may recall that we discussed such a case in Chapters 4 and 5.) Many variations may be achieved by adding or relaxing constraints in the thematic relation.

```
relation successful(Betrayal)
   if Betrayer is the betrayer of the Betrayal
   and Betrayers_Evil_Goal is the goal of the Betrayer
   and Condition1 is the success of Betrayor_Evil_Goal
   and Condition1
   and Betrayed is the betrayed of Betrayal
   and G is the goal of the Betrayed
   and Condition2 is the success of G
   and not(Condition2)
   and RName is the name of the Betrayed
   and DName is the name of the Betrayor
   and ! .
```

6.7   Interestingness: From the Theme Down

Computer programs are not human; they are not affected by the emotional elements that are part and parcel of human drama. In fact, it is hard to even *imagine* how a computer could discover, from a sea of swimming 0s and 1s, what might be compelling to a living, feeling human being. (For an excellent treatment of what we can realistically expect modern computers to understand, see [247].) However, engineering a computer to compose stories based on a pre-defined representation of what we already know to be interesting is a very different challenge. And we do already know, at least in broad strokes, what is interesting to human readers; successful authors, after all, routinely exploit this knowledge. Among the things that readers find interesting, as we noted in Chapter 5, are particular topics like sex and money and death (as the well-known cognitive scientist Roger Schank has explained: [205]), and also classic themes like betrayal, ruthless ambition, and unrequited love. The central thrust of BRUTUS's approach to story generation is based on the assumed limitation of computers to genuinely grasp such things as interestingness and to begin with a well-established, interesting literary theme like betrayal, and then work down through plot, story structure, and finally through the details of language. Once a theme has been sufficiently formalized, it can be encoded for BRUTUS₁ as a FLEX frame. This frame represents the static elements of the theme, and a FLEX relation represents the relationships between domain elements; the instantiation of these elements, structured and cast in English, yields a story. The theme and domain elements are elaborated and extended through time by simulation in the process of plot development. Here, significant variability can be realized by adjusting the actions of character and behavioral rules associated with them. Finally, the language generation process crafts prose through a disciplined expansion of a series of grammars which can be massaged to reveal different story paragraph and sentence structures. Our LAGs enable different literary objectives to drive the choices of words and phrases for generating a variety of sentences with specific literary effect.

6.8 Sample Stories

Here, together in sequence, are the four stories seen at previous points in the book. As you read them now, try to call upon what you have read in this book so that you can "demystify" the fact that they can be generated by a "mere" machine.

"Betrayal in Self-Deception" (conscious)

Dave Striver loved the university. He loved its ivy-covered clocktowers, its ancient and sturdy brick, and its sun-splashed verdant greens and eager youth. He also loved the fact that the university is free of the stark unforgiving trials of the business world — only this *isn't* a fact: academia has its own tests, and some are as merciless as any in the marketplace. A prime example is the dissertation defense: to earn the PhD, to become a doctor, one must pass an oral examination on one's dissertation. This was a test Professor Edward Hart enjoyed giving.

Dave wanted desperately to be a doctor. But he needed the signatures of three people on the first page of his dissertation, the priceless inscriptions which, together, would certify that he had passed his defense. One of the signatures had to come from Professor Hart, and Hart had often said — to others and to himself — that he was honored to help Dave secure his well-earned dream.

Well before the defense, Striver gave Hart a penultimate copy of his thesis. Hart read it and told Dave that it was absolutely first-rate, and that he would gladly sign it at the defense. They even shook hands in Hart's book-lined office. Dave noticed that Hart's eyes were bright and trustful, and his bearing paternal.

At the defense, Dave thought that he eloquently summarized Chapter 3 of his dissertation. There were two questions, one from Professor Rodman and one from Dr. Teer; Dave answered both, apparently to everyone's satisfaction. There were no further objections.

Professor Rodman signed. He slid the tome to Teer; she too signed, and then slid it in front of Hart. Hart didn't move.

"Ed?" Rodman said.

Hart still sat motionless. Dave felt slightly dizzy.

"Edward, are you going to sign?"

Later, Hart sat alone in his office, in his big leather chair, saddened by Dave's failure. He tried to think of ways he could help Dave achieve his dream.

"Simple Betrayal" (no self-deception; conscious)

Dave Striver loved the university. He loved its ivy-covered clocktowers, its ancient and sturdy brick, and its sun-splashed verdant greens and eager youth. He also loved the fact that the university is free of the stark unforgiving trials of the business world — only this *isn't* a fact: academia has its own tests, and some are as merciless as any in the marketplace. A prime example is the dissertation defense: to earn the PhD, to become a doctor, one must pass an oral examination on one's dissertation.

Dave wanted desperately to be a doctor. But he needed the signatures of three people on the first page of his dissertation, the priceless inscriptions which, together, would certify that he had passed his defense. One of the signatures had to come from Professor Hart.

Well before the defense, Striver gave Hart a penultimate copy of his thesis. Hart read it and told Striver that it was absolutely first-rate, and that he would gladly sign it at the defense. They even shook hands in Hart's book-lined office. Dave noticed that Hart's eyes were bright and trustful, and his bearing paternal.

At the defense, Dave thought that he eloquently summarized Chapter 3 of his dissertation. There were two questions, one from Professor Rodman and one from Dr. Teer; Dave answered both, apparently to everyone's satisfaction. There were no further objections.

Professor Rodman signed. He slid the tome to Teer; she too signed, and then slid it in front of Hart. Hart didn't move.

"Ed?" Rodman said.

Hart still sat motionless. Dave felt slightly dizzy.

"Edward, are you going to sign?"

Later, Hart sat alone in his office, in his big leather chair, underneath his framed PhD diploma.

"Betrayal in Self-Deception" (non-conscious)

Dave Striver loved the university — its ivy-covered clocktowers, its ancient and sturdy brick, and its sun-splashed verdant greens and eager youth. The university, contrary to popular opinion, is far from free of the stark unforgiving trials of the business world: academia has its own tests, and some are as merciless as any in the marketplace. A prime example is the dissertation defense: to earn the PhD, to become a doctor, one must pass an oral examination on one's dissertation. This was a test Professor Edward Hart enjoyed giving.

Dave wanted to be a doctor. But he needed the signatures of three people on the first page of his dissertation, the priceless inscriptions which, together, would certify that he had passed his defense. One of the signatures had to come from Professor Hart, and Hart had often said — to others and to himself — that he was honored to help Dave secure his well-earned dream.

Well before the defense, Striver gave Hart a penultimate copy of his thesis. Hart read it and told Dave that it was absolutely first-rate, and that he would gladly sign it at the defense. They even shook hands in Hart's book-lined office. Dave noticed that Hart's eyes were bright and trustful, and his bearing paternal.

At the defense, Dave eloquently summarized Chapter 3 of his dissertation. There were two questions, one from Professor Rodman and one from Dr. Teer; Dave answered both, apparently to everyone's satisfaction. There were no further objections.

Professor Rodman signed. He slid the tome to Teer; she too signed, and then slid it in front of Hart. Hart didn't move.

"Ed?" Rodman said.

Hart still sat motionless. Dave looked at him.

"Edward, are you going to sign?"

Later, Hart sat alone in his office, in his big leather chair. He tried to think of ways he could help Dave achieve his goal.

"Self-Betrayal" (no self-deception; conscious version)

Dave Striver loved the university — at least most of the time. Every now and then, without warning, a wave of ... well, it was true: a wave of *hatred* rose up and flowed like molten blood through every cell in his body. This hatred would be directed at the ghostly gatekeepers. But most of the time Striver loved — the ivy-covered clocktowers, the ancient and sturdy brick, and the sun-splashed verdant greens and eager youth who learned alongside him. He also loved the fact that the university is free of the stark unforgiving trials of the business world — only this *isn't* a fact: academia has its own tests, and some are as merciless as any in the marketplace. A prime example is the dissertation defense: to earn the PhD, to become a doctor, one must pass an oral examination on one's dissertation.

Dave wanted desperately to be a doctor. He had been working toward this end through six years of graduate school. In the end, he needed the signatures of three people on the first page of his dissertation, the priceless inscriptions which, together, would certify that he had passed his defense. One of the signatures had to come from Professor Hart.

Well before the defense, Striver gave Hart a penultimate copy of his thesis. Hart read it and told Striver that it was absolutely first-rate, and that he would gladly sign it at the defense. They shook hands in Hart's book-lined office. Hart's eyes were bright and trustful, and his bearing paternal.

"See you at 3 p.m. on the tenth, then, Dave!" Hart said.

At the defense, Dave eloquently summarized Chapter 3 of his dissertation. His plan had been to do the same for Chapter 4, and then wrap things up, but now he wasn't sure. The pallid faces before him seemed suddenly nauseating. What was he doing?

One of these pallid automata had an arm raised.

"What?" Striver snapped.

Striver watched ghosts look at each other. A pause.

Then Professor Teer spoke: "I'm puzzled as to why you prefer not to use the well-known alpha-beta minimax algorithm for your search?"

Why had he thought so earnestly about inane questions like this in the past? Striver said nothing. His nausea grew. Contempt, fiery and uncontrollable, rose up.

"Dave?" Professor Hart prodded, softly.

God, they were pitiful. Pitiful, pallid, and puny.

"Dave, did you hear the question?"

Later, Striver sat alone in his appartment. What in God's name had he done?

6.9 BRUTUS₁ **on the Web**

Information about BRUTUS, BRUTUS₁, and this book can be obtained on-line via the following URL.

```
http://www.rpi.edu/dept/ppcs/BRUTUS/brutus.html
```

This site includes most of the figures and illustrations in this book, as well as the Preface, and, courtesy of Microsoft Agent^{TM}, BRUTUS₁ can be called upon to narrate some of the stories seen earlier. Eventually the web site will allow direct interaction with more sophisticated incarnations of BRUTUS.

Bibliography

[1] Andersen, S. & Slator, B. (1990) "Requiem for a Theory: The 'Story Grammar' Story," *Journal of Experimental and Theoretical Artificial Intelligence* **2.3**: 253–275.

[2] Aristotle, "On Memory and Recollection," 45a 5, 450a 7, and 451a; 19, in: McKeon, R., ed., (1941) *The Basic Works of Aristotle* (New York, NY: Random House), pp. 425–519.

[3] Ashcraft, M.H. (1994) *Human Memory and Cognition* (New York, NY: HarperCollins).

[4] Attneave, F. & Curlee T.E. (1983) "Locational Representation in Imagery: A Moving Spot Task," *Journal of Experimental Psychology: Human Perception and Performance* **9**: 20–30.

[5] Averbach, E. & Coriell, A.S. (1961) "Short-term Memory in Vision," *Bell System Technical Journal* **40**: 309–328.

[6] Baron, R.J. (1985) "Visual Memories and Mental Images," *International Journal of Man-Machine Studies* **23**: 275–311.

[7] Barr, A. (1983) "Artificial Intelligence: Cognition as Computation," in Machlup, F., ed., *The Study of Information: Interdisciplinary Messages* (New York, NY: Wiley-Interscience), pp. 237–262.

[8] Barwise, J. & Etchemendy, J. (1993) *Hyperproof* (Stanford, CA: CSLI Publications).

[9] Barwise, J. & Etchemendy, J. (1993) *Turing's World 3.0* (Stanford, CA: CSLI Publications).

[10] Bennett, C.H. (1984) "Thermodynamically Reversible Computation," *Physics Rev. Lett.* **53**: 1202.

[11] Bennett, C.H. (1982) "The Thermodynamics of Computation — A Review," *International Journal of Theoretical Physics* **21**: 905–940.

[12] Bennett, C.H. (1973) "Logical Reversibility of Computation," *IBM Journal of Research Development* November: 525–532.

[13] Berlekamp, E., Conway, J., & Guy, R. (1982) *Winning Ways*, Vol. 2 (New York, NY: Academic Press). See chapter 25 for Conway's description of Life.

[14] Black, J.B. & Wilensky, R. (1979) "An Evaluation of Story Grammars," *Cognitive Science* **3**: 213–230.

[15] Block, N. (1995) "On a Confusion About a Function of Consciousness," *Behavioral and Brain Sciences* **18**: 227–247.

[16] Block, N. (1981) *Imagery* (Cambridge, MA: MIT Press).

[17] Block, N. (1980) "Troubles with Functionalism," in *Readings in Philosophy of Psychology Vol. I* (Cambridge, MA: Harvard University Press).

[18] Boden, M. (1995) "Could a Robot be Creative?—And Would We Know?" in Ford, K.M., Glymour, C. & Hayes, P.J. eds., *Android Epistemology* (Cambridge, MA: MIT Press), pp. 51–72.

[19] Boden, M. (1994) "Creativity and Computers," in T. Dartnall, ed., *Artificial Intelligence and Computers* (Dordrecht, The Netherlands: Kluwer), pp. 3–26.

[20] Boden, M. (1991) *The Creative Mind: Myths and Mechanisms* (New York, NY: Basic Books).

[21] Boolos, G.S. & Jeffrey, R.C. (1989) *Computability and Logic* (Cambridge, UK: Cambridge University Press).

[22] Bringsjord, S. & Noel, R. (in press) "Why Did Evolution Engineer Consciousness?" in Mulhauser, Gregory, ed., *Evolving Consciousness* (Reading, MA: Benjamin Cummings).

[23] Bringsjord, S. & Ferrucci, D. (1998) "Logic and Artificial Intelligence: Divorced, Separated, Still Married ...?" *Minds and Machines* **8**: 273–308.

[24] Bringsjord, S., Bringsjord, E. and Noel, R. (1998) "In Defense of Logical Minds," in *Proceedings of the 20th Annual Conference of the Cognitive Science Society* (Hillsdale, NJ: Lawrence Erlbaum Associates), pp. 173–178.

[25] Bringsjord, S. (1998) "Chess Is Too Easy," *Technology Review* **101.2**: 23–28 This is an expanded version of one part of the paper Bringsjord, S. & Lally, A. (1997) "Chess Isn't Tough Enough: Better Games for Mind-Machine Competition," in *Collected Papers from the 1997 Workshop Deep Blue versus Kasparov: The Significance for Artificial Intelligence*, Technical Report WS-97-04, (Menlo Park, CA: AAAI Press), pp. 14–19.

[26] Bringsjord, S. (1998) "Philosophy and 'Super'-Computation," in Moor, J. & Bynum, T., eds., *The Digital Phoenix* (Oxford, UK: Basil Blackwell), pp. 231–252.

[27] Bringsjord, S. (1997) "Consciousness by the Lights of Logic and Commonsense," *Behavioral and Brain Sciences* **20.1**: 144–146.

[28] Bringsjord, S. (1997) *Abortion: A Dialogue* (Indianapolis, IN: Hackett).

[29] Bringsjord, S. (1997) "An Argument for the Uncomputability of Infinitary Mathematical Expertise," in Feltovich, P., Ford, K.M., & Hoffman, R.R., eds., *Expertise in Context* (Menlo Park, CA: AAAI Press), pp. 475–497.

[30] Bringsjord, S. & Bringsjord, E. (1996) "The Case Against AI From Imagistic Expertise," *Journal of Experimental and Theoretical Artificial Intelligence* **8**: 383–397.

[31] Bringsjord, S. (1995) "Computation, Among Other Things, is Beneath Us," *Minds and Machines* **4**: 469–488.

[32] Bringsjord, S. (1995) "Could, How Could We Tell If, and Why Should–Androids Have Inner Lives," in *Android Epistemology*, Ford, K., Glymour, C., & Hayes, P., eds., (Cambridge, MA: MIT Press), pp. 93–122.

[33] Bringsjord, S. (1995) "Pourquoi Hendrik Ibsen Est-Is Une Menace pour La Littérature Générée Par Ordinateur?" (traduit par Michel Lenoble) in Vuillemin, A., ed., *Littérature et Informatique la Littérature Générée Par Orinateur*, (Arras, France: Artois Presses Universite), pp. 135–144.

[34] Bringsjord, S. (1995) "In Defense of Impenetrable Zombies," *Journal of Consciousness Studies* **2.4**: 348–351.

[35] Bringsjord, S. (1994) Review of Margaret Boden's *Myths and Mechanisms, Behavioral and Brain Sciences* **17.3**: 532–533.

[36] Bringsjord, E. & Bringsjord, S. (1994) "Can AI Accommodate Imagistic Expertise?" in *Proceedings of the Second International Conference on Expert Systems for Development* (Los Alamitos, CA: IEEE Press), pp. 36–41,

[37] Bringsjord, S. (1994) "Searle on the Brink," *Psyche* **1**: 19–31.

[38] Bringsjord, S. & Bringsjord, E. (1994) "Animal Communication of Private States Doesn't Illuminate the Human Case," *Behavioral and Brain Sciences* **16.4**: 645–646.

[39] Bringsjord, S. (1992) "CINEWRITE: An Algorithm-Sketch for Writing Novels Cinematically, and Two Mysteries Therein," *Instructional Science* **21**: 155–168.

[40] Bringsjord, S. (1992) *What Robots Can and Can't Be* (Dordrecht, The Netherlands: Kluwer).

[41] Bringsjord, S. (1991) "Is the Connectionist-Logicist Clash one of AI's Wonderful Red Herrings?" *Journal of Experimental & Theoretical AI* **3.4**: 319–349.

[42] Bringsjord, S. & Zenzen, M. (1991) "In Defense of Hyper-Logicist AI," in *IJCAI '91* (Mountain View, CA: Morgan Kaufmann), pp. 1066–1072.

[43] Britton, B. (1983) "What Makes Stories Interesting," *Behavioral and Brain Sciences* **6**: 596–597.

[44] Bruner, J. (1986) *Actual Minds, Possible Worlds* (Cambridge, MA: Harvard University Press).

[45] Cervantes, M. (1999) *Don Quijote* (New York, NY: Norton).

[46] Castañeda, H. (1979) "Fiction and Reality: Their Fundamental Connections; An Essay on the Ontology of Total Experience," *Poetics* **8**: 31–62.

[47] Chalmers, D. (1995) "Minds, Machines, and Mathematics," *Psyche*.

- http://psyche.cs.monash.edu.au/psyche/volume2-1/psyche-95-2-09-shadows-7-chalmers.html

- ftp:ftp.cs.monash.edu.au.psyche/psyche-95-2-09-shadows-7-chalmers.txt

[48] Chandrasekaran, B., Hari Narayanan, N. & Iwasaki, Y. (1993) "Reasoning With Diagrammatic Representations: A Report on the Spring Symposium," *AI Magazine*, Summer, 23–32.

[49] Charniak, E. & McDermott, D. (1985) *Introduction to Artificial Intelligence* (Reading, MA: Addison-Wesley).

[50] Chase, C.I. (1985) "Review of the Torrance Tests of Creative Thinking," in Mitchell, J.V., ed., *9th Mental Measurements Yearbook, Vol. II* (Lincoln, NB: Buros Institute of Mental Measurement), pp. 1631–1632.

[51] Church, A. (1936) "An Unsolvable Problem of Elementary Number Theory," in Dave, M., ed., *The Undecidable* (New York, NY: Raven Press), pp. 89–100.

[52] Chellas, B.F. (1980) *Modal Logic: An Introduction* (Cambridge, UK: Cambridge University Press).

[53] Cleland, C. (1995) "Effective Procedures and Computable Functions," *Minds and Machines* **5**: 9–23.

[54] Cleland, C. (1993) "Is the Church-Thesis True?" *Minds and Machines* **3**: 283–312.

[55] Cole, D. & Foelber, R. (1984) "Contingent Materialism," *Pacific Philosophical Quarterly* **65.1**: 74–85.

[56] Cornoldi, D., Cortesi, A., & Preti, D. (1991) "Individual Differences in the Capacity Limitations of Visuospatial Short-Term

Memory: Research on Sighted and Totally Congenitally Blind People," *Memory and Cognition* **19**: 459–468.

[57] Clark, A. (1997) "The Dynamical Challenge," *Cognitive Science* **21.4**: 461–481.

[58] Cummins, R. & Schwarz, D. (1991) "Connectionism, Computation and Cognition," in Horgan, T. and Tienson, J., eds., *Connectionism and the Philosophy of Mind* (Dordrecht, The Netherlands: Kluwer Academic Publishers), pp. 60–73.

[59] Davidson, D. (1987) "Knowing One's Own Mind," *Proceedings and Addresses of the American Philosophical Association* **60**: 441–458.

[60] Davis, M.D., Sigal, R. & Weyuker, E.J. (1994) *Computability, Complexity, and Languages* (San Diego, CA: Academic Press).

[61] Davis, M. (1993) "How Subtle is Gödel's Theorem? More on Roger Penrose," *Behavioral and Brain Sciences* **16**: 611–612.

[62] Davis, W. (1988) *Passage of Darkness: The Ethnobiology of the Haitian Zombie* (Chapel Hill, NC: University of North Carolina Press).

[63] Davis, W. (1985) *The Serpent and the Rainbow* (New York, NY: Simon & Schuster).

[64] De Beaugrande, R. & Colby, B.N. (1979) "Narrative Models of Action and Interaction," *Cognitive Science* **3.1**: 43–46.

[65] Dehn, N. (1981) "Story Generation After TALE-SPIN," *IJCAI 81* (San Mateo, CA: Morgan Kaufmann), 16–18.

[66] Dennett, D.C. (1996) "Cow-sharks, Magnets, and Swampman," *Mind & Language* **11.1**: 76–77.

[67] Dennett, D.C. (1995) "The Unimagined Preposterousness of Zombies," *Journal of Consciousness Studies* **2.4**: 322–326.

[68] Dennett, D.C. (1994) "The Practical Requirements for Making a Conscious Robot," *Philosophical Transactions of the Royal Society of London* **349**: 133–146.

[69] Dennett, D.C. (1993) "Review of Searle's *The Rediscovery of the Mind*," *Journal of Philosophy* **90.4**: 193–205.

[70] Dennett, D.C. (1991) *Consciousness Explained* (Boston, MA: Little, Brown).

[71] Dennett, D. (1981) "The Nature of Images and the Introspective Trap," in Block, N., ed., *Imagery* (Cambridge, MA: MIT Press), pp. 51–61.

[72] Dennett, D.C. (1978) *Brainstorms* (Cambridge, MA: MIT Press).

[73] Descartes, R. (1911–first edition) *The Philosophical Works of Descartes Vol. I*, translated by Haldane, E.S. & Ross, G.R.T. (Cambridge, UK: Cambridge University Press).

[74] Dickens, C. (MCMXCII) *David Copperfield* (New York, NY: Baronet Books).

[75] Dickmann, M.A. (1975) *Large Infinitary Languages* (Amsterdam, The Netherlands: North-Holland).

[76] Dietrich, E. (1990) "Computationalism," *Social Epistemology* **4.2**: 135-154.

[77] Dougherty, R.C. (1994) *Natural Language Computing: An English Generative Grammar in Prolog* (Mahwah, NJ: Lawrence Erlbaum Associates).

[78] Doyle, A.C. (1984) "The Adventure of Silver Blaze," in *The Celebrated Cases of Sherlock Holmes* (Minneapolis, MN: Amarenth Press), pp. 172–187.

[79] Dreyfus H. L. & Dreyfus, S.E. (1986) *Mind Over Machine* (New York, NY: Free Press).

[80] Dretske, F. (1996) "Absent Qualia," *Mind & Language* **11.1**: 78–85.

[81] Earman, J. (1986) *A Primer on Determinism* (Dordrecht, The Netherlands: D. Reidel).

[82] Ebbinghaus, H.D., Flum, J. & Thomas, W. (1984) *Mathematical Logic* (New York, NY: Springer-Verlag).

[83] Eco, U. (1979) *The Role of the Reader: Explorations in the Semiotics of Texts* (Bloomington, IN: Indiana University Press).

[84] Esrock, E.J. (1994) *The Reader's Eye: Visual Imaging as Reader Response* (Baltimore, MD: Johns Hopkins).

[85] Euclid. (1956) *The Thirteen Books of Euclid's Elements*, trans. T. Heath (New York, NY: Dover).

[86] Feferman, S. (1994) "Penrose's Gödelian Argument," *Psyche*.

- http://psyche.cs.monash.edu.au/psyche/volume2-1/psyche-95-2-7-shadows-5-feferman.html
- ftp:ftp.cs.monash.edu.au.psyche/psyche-95-2-7-shadows-5-feferman.txt

[87] Feldman, C.F., Bruner, J., Renderer, B., & Spitzer, S. (1990) "Narrative Comprehension," in Britton, B.K. & Pellegrini, A.D., eds., *Narrative Thought and Narrative Language* (Hillsdale, NJ: Lawrence Erlbaum Associates), pp. 1–78.

[88] Fetzer, J. (1996) "Minds Are Not Computers: (Most) Thought Processes Are Not Computational Procedures," paper presented at the annual meeting of the Southern Society for Philosophy and Psychology, Nashville, April 5.

[89] Fetzer, J. (1994) "Mental Algorithms: Are Minds Computational Systems?" *Pragmatics & Cognition* **2.1**: 1–29.

[90] Fjelde, R. (1965) Foreword in Ibsen, H. (1965) *Four Major Plays* (New York, NY: New American Library).

[91] Flanagan, O. & Polger, T. (1995) "Zombies and the Function of Consciousness," *Journal of Consciousness Studies* **2.4**: 313–321.

[92] Folina, J. (1993) "Commentary on Selmer Bringsjord's 'Church's Thesis, Contra Mendelson, Is Unprovable ... And Worse: It May be False'," Annual Eastern Division APA Meeting, Atlanta, GA, December 27, 1993.

[93] Freud, S. (1959) *Creative Writers and Daydreaming* (London, UK: Hogarth Press and the Institute of Psychoanalysis).

[94] Funt, B.V. (1980) "Problem Solving With Diagrammatic Representations," *Artificial Intelligence* **13**: 201–230.

[95] Gardin, F. & Meltzer, B. (1989) "Analogical Representations of Naive Physics," *Artificial Intelligence* **38**: 139–159.

[96] Genesereth, M.R. & Nilsson, N.J. (1987) *Logical Foundations of Artificial Intelligence* (Los Altos, CA: Morgan Kaufmann).

[97] Gershenfield, N. (1999) *When Things Start to Think* (New York, NY: Henry Holt & Company).

[98] Glasgow, J., Narayanan, H. & Chandrasekaran, B., eds. (1995) *Diagrammatic Reasoning* (Cambridge, MA: MIT Press).

[99] Glasgow, J. & Papadias, D. (1995) "Computational Imagery," in Glasgow, J., Narayanan, H., & Chandrasekaran, B., eds., *Diagrammatic Reasoning* (Cambridge, MA: MIT Press), pp. 435–480.

[100] Glasgow, J.I., Fortier, S. & Allen, F.H. (1992) "Molecular Scene Analysis: Crystal Structure Determination Through Imagery," in Hunter, L., ed., *Artificial Intelligence and Molecular Biology* (Cambridge, MA: MIT Press), pp. 433–458.

[101] Glymour, C. (1992) *Thinking Things Through* (Cambridge, MA: MIT Press.

[102] Grzegorczyk, A. (1957) "On the Definitions of Computable Real Continuous Functions," *Fundamentals of Mathematics* **44**: 61–71.

[103] Grzegorczyk, A. (1955) "Computable Functionals," *Fundamentals of Mathematics* **42**: 168–202.

[104] Gummerman, K., Gray, C. & Wilson, J.M. (1992) "An Attempt to Assess Eidetic Imagery Objectively," *Psychonomic Science* **28.2**: 115–118.

[105] Harnad, S. (1995) "Why and How We Are Not Zombies," *Journal of Consciousness Studies* **1**: 164–167.

[106] Harnad, S. (1991) "Other Bodies, Other Minds: A Machine Incarnation of an Old Philosophical Problem," *Minds and Machines* **1.1**: 43–55.

[107] Haugeland, J. (1981) *Artificial Intelligence: The Very Idea* (Cambridge, MA: MIT Press).

[108] Hilbert, D. (1926) "On the Infinite," *Math. Annalen* **95**: 161–190. Translated in Van Heijenoort.

[109] Hobbes, T. (1839) *De Corpore*, chap. 1, in *English Works*, Molesworth, ed., reprinted in (1962) *Body, Man and Citizen* (New York, NY: Collier), pp. 124–225.

[110] Hoffman, R.R. & Klein, G.A. (1993) "Seeing the Invisible: Perceptual-Cognitive Aspects of Expertise," in *Cognitive Science Foundations of Instruction*, Rabonowitz, M., ed., (Hillsdale, NJ: Lawrence Erlbaum), pp. 203–226.

[111] Hofstadter, D.R. (1995) *Fluid Concepts and Creative Analogies* (New York, NY: Basic Books).

[112] Hofstadter, D.R. (1985) "Waking Up from the Boolean Dream," chap. 26 in his *Metamagical Themas: Questing for the Essence of Mind and Pattern* (New York, NY: Bantam), pp. 631–665.

[113] Hofstadter, D. (1982) "Metafont, Metamathematics, and Metaphysics," *Visible Language* **14.4**: 309–338.

[114] Hopcroft, J.E. & Ullman, J.D. (1979) *Introduction to Automata Theory, Languages and Computation* (Reading, MA: Addison-Wesley).

[115] Jackson, F. (1982) "Epiphenomenal Qualia," *Philosophical Quarterly* **32**: 127–136.

[116] Jacquette, D. (1994) *Philosophy of Mind* (Englewood Cliffs, NJ: Prentice-Hall).

[117] Johnson, G. (1997) "Undiscovered Bach? No, a Computer Wrote It," *The New York Times*, November 11, pp. F1-2.

[118] Johnson-Laird, P. (1988) *The Computer and the Mind* (Cambridge, MA: Harvard University Press).

[119] Johnson-Laird, P.N. (1983) *Mental Models: Toward a Cognitive Science of Language, Inference, and Consciousness* (Cambridge, MA: Harvard University Press).

[120] Joyce, J. (1986) "Eveline," in Joyce, J., *The Dubliners* (New York, NY: Penguin).

[121] Julstrom, B.A. & Baron, R.J. (1985) "A Model of Mental Imagery," *International Journal of Man-Machine Studies* **23**: 313–334.

[122] Kafka, F. (1948) "The Metamorphosis," in *The Penal Colony*, trans. W. Muir and E. Muir (New York, NY: Schocken Books).

[123] Kafka, F. (1948) "The Penal Colony," in *The Penal Colony*, trans. W. Muir and E. Muir (New York, NY: Schocken Books).

[124] Kalmár, L. (1959) "An Argument Against the Plausibility of Church's Thesis," in Heyting, A., ed., *Constructivity in Mathematics* (Amsterdam, Holland: North-Holland), pp. 72–80.

[125] Keisler, H.J. (1971) *Model Theory for Infinitary Logic* (Amsterdam, The Netherlands: North-Holland).

[126] Kerr, N.H. (1987) "Locational Representation in Imagery: The Third Dimension," *Memory and Cognition* **15**: 521–530.

[127] Kintsch, W. (1980) "Learning From Text, Levels of Comprehension, or: Why Anyone Would Read a Story Anyway," *Poetics* **9**: 87–98.

[128] Kleene, S.C. (1936) "General Recursive Functions of Natural Numbers," *Math. Annalen* **112**: 727–742.

[129] Klein, S. (1975) "Meta-Compiling Text Grammars as a Model for Human Behaviour," *TINLAP*, 94–98.

[130] Kolata, G. (1996) "Computer Math Proof Shows Reasoning Power," *The New York Times' Cybertimes*. (No page numbers: an online article.)

[131] Kosslyn, S. (1994) *Image and Brain* (Cambridge, MA: MIT Press).

[132] Kosslyn, S., Alpert, N.M., Thompson, W.L., V. Maljkovic, V., Weise, S.B., Chabris, C.F., Hamilton, S.E., Rauch, S.L., & Buonanno, F.S. (1993) "Visual Mental Imagery Activates Topographically Organized Visual Cortex: PET Investigations," *Journal of Cognitive Neuroscience* **5.3**: 263–287.

[133] Kosslyn, S. (1983) *Ghosts in the Mind's Machine* (New York, NY: Norton).

[134] Kosslyn, S. (1980) *Image and Mind* (Cambridge, MA: Harvard).

[135] Kosslyn. S. & Schwartz, S.P. (1978) "Visual Images as Spatial Representations in Active Memory," in Riseman, E.M., & Hanson, A.R. *Computer Vision Systems* (New York, NY: Academic Press), pp. 12-38.

[136] Kosslyn. S. & Shwartz, S.P. (1977) "A Simulation of Visual Imagery," *Cognitive Science* **1**: 265–295.

[137] Kreisel, G. (1968) "Church's Thesis: A Kind of Reducibility Thesis for Constructive Mathematics," in Kino, A., Myhill, J., & Vesley, R.E., eds., *Intuitionism and Proof Theory: Proceedings of a Summer Conference at Buffalo, N.Y.* (Amsterdam, Holland: North-Holland), pp. 219–230.

[138] Kreisel, G. (1965) "Mathematical Logic," in Saaty, T.L., ed.,*Lectures in Modern Mathematics* (New York, NY: John Wiley), pp. 111–122.

[139] Kripke, S. (1971) "Naming and Necessity," in Davidson, D.& Harman, G., eds., *Semantics of Natural Language* (Dordrecht, The Netherlands: Reidel), pp. 253–355, 763–769.

[140] Kugel, P. (1990) "Is it Time to Replace Turing's Test?" Paper presented at *Artificial Intelligence: Emerging Science or Dying Art Form*, sponsored by the American Association of Artificial Intelligence and the State University of New York at Binghamton's program in Philosophy and Computer and Systems Sciences, the University at Binghamton, Binghamton, NY, June 27.

[141] Kugel, P. (1986) "Thinking May Be More Than Computing," *Cognition* **22**: 137–198.

[142] Kurzweil, R. (1999) *The Age of Spiritual Machines: When Computers Exceed Human Intelligence* (New York, NY: Viking).

[143] Lambek, J. (1961) "How to Program an Infinite Abacus," *Canadian Mathematical Bulletin* **4**: 295–302. (See the correction noted in (1962) **5**: 297.)

[144] Larkin, J. & Simon, H.A. (1987) "Why a Diagram Is (Sometimes) Worth Ten Thousand Words," *Cognitive Science* **10**: 65–100.

[145] (1981) *Graphic Art Materials Reference Manual* (New York, NY: Letraset).

[146] Lebowitz, M. (1984) "Creatiing Characters in a Story-Telling Universe," *Poetics* **13**: 171–194.

[147] Lewis, D. (1978) "Truth in Fiction," *American Philosophical Quarterly* **15**: 37–46.

[148] Lewis, H. & Papadimitriou, C. (1981) *Elements of the Theory of Computation* (Englewood Cliffs, NJ: Prentice-Hall).

[149] Lindsay, R.K. (1988) "Images and Inference," *Cognition* **23**: 229–249.

[150] Lucas, J.R. (1964) "Minds, Machines and Gödel," in Anderson, A.R., ed., *Minds and Machines* (Englewood Cliffs, NJ: Prentice-Hall), pp. 43–59.

[151] Luria, A.R. (1968) *The Mind of a Mnemonist*, trans. L. Solotaroff (New York, NY: Basic Books).

[152] Martin, R. (1984) *Recent Essays on Truth and the Liar Paradox* (Oxford, UK: Oxford University Press).

[153] Marxen, H. & Buntrock, J. (1990) "Attacking the Busy Beaver 5," *Bulletin of the European Association for Theoretical Computer Science* **40**: 247–251.

[154] Maudlin, T. (1989) "Computation and Consciousness," *Journal of Philosophy* **84**: 407–432.

[155] McCulloch, W.S. & Pitts, W. (1943) "A Logical Calculus of the Ideas Immanent in Nervous Activity," *Bulletin of Mathematical Biophysics* **5**: 115–137.

[156] McGinn, C. (1999) "Hello, Hal" *New York Times Book Review* January 3: 11–12.

[157] McMenamin, M. (1992) "Deciding Uncountable Sets and Church's Thesis," unpublished manuscript.

[158] Mele, A. (forthcoming) "Real Self-Deception," *Behavioral and Brain Sciences*.

[159] Melzak, Z. (1961) "An Informal Arithmetical Approach to Computability and Computation," *Canadian Mathematical Bulletin* **4**: 279–293.

[160] Meehan, J. (1981) "TALE-SPIN," in Schank, R. & Reisbeck, C., eds., *Inside Computer Understanding: Five Programs Plus Miniatures* (Hillsdale, NJ: Lawrence Erlbaum Associates), pp. 197–226.

[161] Mendelson, E. (1990) "Second Thoughts About Church's Thesis and Mathematical Proofs," *Journal of Philosophy* **87.5**: 225–233.

[162] Mendelson, E. (1963) "On Some Recent Criticism of Church's Thesis," *Notre Dame Journal of Formal Logic* **4.3**: 201-205.

[163] Meteer, M. (1992) *Expressibility and the Problem of Efficient Text Planning* (London, UK: Pinter).

[164] Millikan, R.G. (1996) "On Swampkinds," *Mind & Language* **11.1**: 103–117.

[165] Moravec, H. (1999) *Robot: Mere Machine To Transcendant Mind* (Oxford, UK: Oxford University Press).

[166] Moschovakis, Y. (1968) "Review of Four Recent Papers in Church's Thesis," *Journal of Symbolic Logic* **33**: 471–472. One

of the four papers is: Kalmár, L. (1959) "An Argument Against the Plausibility of Church's Thesis," in Heyting, A., ed., *Constructivity in Mathematics* (Amsterdam, Holland: North-Holland), pp. 72–80.

[167] Nagel, T. (1974) "What Is it Like to Be a Bat?" *Philosophical Review* **83**: 435–450.

[168] Nelson, R.J. (1987) "Church's Thesis and Cognitive Science," *Notre Dame Journal of Formal Logic* **28.4**: 581–614.

[169] Newell, A. (1980) "Physical Symbol Systems," *Cognitive Science* **4**: 135–183.

[170] Oakhill, J.V., Johnson-Laird, P.N. & Garnham, A. (1989) "Believability and Syllogistic Reasoning," *Cognition* **31**: 117–140.

[171] O'Keefe, R. (1990) *The Craft of Prolog* (Cambridge, MA: MIT Press).

[172] Omori, T. (1992) "Dual Representation of Image Recognition Process: Interaction of Neural Network and Symbolic Processing," *Proceedings of the International Symposium on Neural Information Processing*, pp. 50–53.

[173] Parsons, T. (1975) "A Meinongian Analysis of Fictional Objects," *Grazer Philosphische Studien* **1**: 73–86.

[174] Partee, B., Meulen, A. & Wall, R. (1990) *Mathematical Methods in Linguistics* (Dordrecht, The Netherlands: Kluwer Academic Publishers).

[175] Peck, M.S. (1983) *People of the Lie* (New York, NY: Simon and Schuster).

[176] Penrose, R. (1994) *Shadows of the Mind* (Oxford, UK: Oxford University Press).

[177] Penrose, R. (1989) *The Emperor's New Mind* (Oxford, UK: Oxford University Press).

[178] Piaget, J. & Inhelder, B. (1969) *The Psychology of the Child* (New York, NY: Basic Books).

[179] Piaget, J. & Inhelder, B. (1966) *L'Image Mentale Chez L'enfant* (Paris, France: Presses Universitaires de France).

[180] Pinker, S. (1997) *How the Mind Works* (New York, NY: Norton).

[181] Plum, F. & Posner, J.B. (1972) *The Diagnosis of Stupor and Coma* (Philadelphia, PA: F.A. Davis).

[182] Pollock, J. (1995) *Cognitive Carpentry: A Blueprint for How to Build a Person* (Cambridge, MA: MIT Press).

[183] Pollock, J. (1989) *How to Build a Person* (Cambridge, MA: MIT Press).

[184] Post, E.L. (1936) "Finite Combinatory Processes – Formulation 1," *Journal of Symbolic Logic* **1.3**: 103–105.

[185] Poundstone, W. (1985) *The Recursive Universe* (New York, NY: William Morrow).

[186] Propp, V. (1986) *The Morphology of the Folktale* (Austin, TX: University of Texas Press).

[187] Putnam, H. (1960) "Minds and Machines," in his *Mind, Language, and Reality: Philosophical Papers, Vol. 2* (Cambridge, UK: Cambridge University Press), pp. 45–61.

[188] Pylyshyn, Z. (1981) "Imagery and Artificial Intelligence," in Block, N., ed., *Readings in Philosophy of Psychology Vol. 2* (Cambridge, MA: Harvard).

[189] Quaife, A. (1992) *Automated Development of Fundamental Mathematical Theories* (Dordrecht, The Netherlands: Kluwer).

[190] Racter (1984) *The Policeman's Beard is Half Constructed* (New York, NY: Warner).

[191] Rado, T. (1963) "On Non-Computable Functions," *Bell System Technical Journal* **41**: 877–884.

[192] Rapaport, W.J. (1991) "Predication, Fiction, and Artificial Intelligence," *Topoi* **10**: 79–91.

[193] Robinson, J.A. (1992) "Logic and Logic Programming," *Communications of the ACM* **35.3**: 40–65.

[194] Rogers, H. (1967) *Theory of Recursive Functions and Effective Computability* (New York, NY: McGraw-Hill).

[195] Rosenthal, D.M. (forthcoming) "State Consciousness and What It's Like," in hi Title TBA (Oxford, UK: Clarendon Press.

[196] Rosenthal, D.M. (1990) "Why Are Verbally Expressed Thoughts Conscious?" ZIF Report No. 32, Zentrum für Interdisziplinäre Forschung, Bielefeld, Germany.

[197] Rosenthal, D.M. (1990) "A Theory of Consciousness," ZIF Report No. 40, Zentrum für Interdisziplinäre Forschung, Bielefeld, Germany.

[198] Rosenthal, D.M. (1989) "Thinking That One Thinks," ZIF Report No. 11, Research Group on Mind and Brain, Perspective in Theoretical Psychology and the Philosophy of Mind, Zentrum für Interdisziplinäre Forschung, Bielefeld, Germany.

[199] Rosenthal, D.M. (1986) "Two Concepts of Consciousness," *Philosophical Studies* **49**: 329–359.

[200] Russell, B. (1936) "The Limits of Empiricism," *Proceedings of the Aristotelian Society* **XXXVI**: 131–150.

[201] Russell, S. & Norvig, P. (1995) *Artificial Intelligence: A Modern Approach* (Englewood Cliffs, NJ: Prentice-Hall).

[202] Sackheim, H. & Gur, R. (1978) "Self-Deception, Self-Confrontation, and Consciousness," in *Consciousness and Self-regulation, Vol. 2* (New York, NY: Plenum Press), pp. 117-129.

[203] Schacter, D.L. (1989) "On the Relation Between Memory and Consciousness: Dissociable Interactions and Conscious Experience," in Roediger, H. & Craik, F., eds., *Varieties of Memory and Consciousness: Essays in Honour of Endel Tulving* (Hillsdale, NJ: Erlbaum), pp. 22-35.

[204] Schank, R. (1995) *Tell Me a Story* (Evanston, IL: Northwestern University Press).

[205] Schank, R. (1979) "Interestingness: Controlling Inferences," *Artificial Intelligence* **12**: 273–297.

[206] Searle, J. (1992) *The Rediscovery of the Mind* (Cambridge, MA: MIT Press).

[207] Searle, J. (1983) *Intentionality* (Cambridge, UK: Cambridge University Press).

[208] Searle, J. (1980) "Minds, Brains and Programs," *Behavioral and Brain Sciences* **3**: 417–424.

[209] Sharples, M. (1997) "Story Telling by Computer," *Digital Creativity* **8.1**: 20–29.

[210] Shepard, F.N. & Metzler, J. (1971) "Mental Rotation of Three-dimensional Objects," *Science* **171**: 701–703

[211] Sieg, W. & Byrnes, J. (1996) "K-graph Machines: Generalizing Turing's Machines and Arguments," in Hájek, P., ed., *Gödel 96, Lecture Notes in Logic 6* (New York, NY: Springer-Verlag), pp. 98–119.

[212] Siegelmann, H. (1995) "Computation Beyond the Turing Limit," *Science* **268**: 545-548.

[213] Siegelmann, H. & Sontag, E.D. (1994) "Analog Computation Via Neural Nets," *Theoretical Computer Science* **131**: 331–360.

[214] Simon, H. (1980) "Cognitive Science: The Newest Science of the Artificial," *Cognitive Science* **4**: 33–56.

[215] Simon, H. (1981) "Study of Human Intelligence by Creating Artificial Intelligence," *American Scientist* **69.3**: 300–309.

[216] Slezak, P. (1982) "Gödel's Theorem and the Mind," *British Journal for the Philosophy of Science* **33**: 41–52.

[217] Smith, M.C. (1981) *Gorky Park* (New York, NY: Ballantine Books).

[218] Smolensky, P. (1988) "On the Proper Treatment of Connectionism," *Behavioral & Brain Sciences* **11**: 1–22.

[219] Smolensky, P. (1988) "Putting Together Connectionism — Again," *Behavioral & Brain Sciences* **11**: 59–70.

[220] Smullyan, R.M. (1992) *Gödel's Incompleteness Theorems* (Oxford, UK: Oxford University Press).

[221] Soare, R. (1980) *Recursively Enumerable Sets and Degrees* (New York, NY: Springer-Verlag).

[222] Sperling, G. (1960) "The Information Available in Brief Visual Presentations," *Psychological Monographs* **74**: 48.

[223] Sterling, L. & Shapiro, E. (1986) *The Art of Prolog* (Cambridge, MA: MIT Press).

[224] Stillings, N.A., Weisler, S.E., Chase, C.H., Feinstein, M.H., Garfield, J.L., & Rissland, E.L. (1995) *Cognitive Science: An Introduction* (Cambridge, MA: MIT Press).

[225] Stromeyer, C.F., & Psotka, J. (1970) "The Detailed Texture of Eidetic Images," *Nature* **225**: 346–349.

[226] Suppes, P. (1972) *Axiomatic Set Theory* (New York, NY: Dover).

[227] Swartz, J.D. (1988) "Torrance Tests of Creative Thinking," in Keyser, D.J. & Sweetland, R.C., eds., *Test Critiques, Vol. VII* (Kansas City, MO: Test Corporation of America), pp. 619–662.

[228] Tarjan, R.E. (1971) "An Efficient Planarity Algorithm" (Report STAN-CS-244-71), Stanford, CA: Stanford University.

[229] Tchaikovsky. (1893) "Letter to Vladimir Davidov (Tchaikovsky's nephew)," reproduced in *Notes on Tchaikovsky's Symphony No. 6 – Pathétique*, text included with CD produced by RCA Records, New York, NY, 1985.

[230] Thomas, W. (1973) "Doubts About Some Standard Arguments for Church's Thesis," in *Papers of the Fourth International Congress for Logic, Methodology, and Philosophy of Science, Bucharest* (Amsterdam, Holland: D. Reidel), pp. 13–22.

[231] Thorndyke, P.W. (1977) "Cognitive Structures in Comprehension and Memory of Narrative Discourse," in his *Cognitive Psychology* (New York, NY: Academic Press), pp. 224–239.

[232] Torrance, E.P. (1988) "The Nature of Creativity as Manifest in its Testing," in Sternberg, R.J., ed., *The Nature of Creativity: Contemporary Psychological Perspectives* (Cambridge, UK: Cambridge University Press), pp. 72–89.

[233] Torrance, E.P. (1966) *The Torrance Tests of Creative Thinking: Technical-Norms Manual* (Princeton, NJ: Personnel Press).

[234] Trabasso, T. (1996) "Review of *Knowledge and Memory: The Real Story*," Robert S. Wyer, ed., Lawrence Erlbaum, 1995, *Minds & Machines* **6**: 399–403.

[235] Treffinger, D.J. (1985) "Review of the Torrance Tests of Creative Thinking," in Mitchell, J.V., ed., *9th Mental Measurements Yearbook, Vol. II* (Lincoln, NB: Buros Institute of Mental Measurement), pp. 1632–1634.

[236] Turing, A.M. (1964) "Computing Machinery and Intelligence," in Andersen, A.R., ed., *Minds and Machines*, Contemporary Perspectives in Philosophy Series (Englewood Cliffs, NJ: Prentice-Hall), pp. 4–30.

[237] Turner, S. (1994) *The Creative Process: A Computer Model of Storytelling* (Hillsdale, NJ: Lawrence Erlbaum Associates).

[238] Tye, M. (1991) *The Imagery Debate* (Cambridge, MA: MIT Press).

[239] Tye, M. (1988) "The Picture Theory of Mental Images," *The Philosophical Review* XCVII.4: 497–520.

[240] Van Heijenoort, J., ed. (1967) *From Frege to Gödel* Amsterdam, The Netherlands: North-Holland).

[241] Van Inwagen, P. (1977) "Creatures of Fiction," *American Philosophical Quarterly* **14**: 299–308.

[242] Vasey, P. (1989) *LPA-flex Technical Reference* (London, England: Logic Programming Associates Ltd.).

[243] Warwick, K. (1997) *March of the Machines: Why the New Race of Robots Will Rule the World* (London, UK: Century).

[244] Webb, J. (1980) *Mechanism, Mentalism and Metamathematics* (Dordrecht, The Netherlands: D. Reidel).

[245] Weyl, H. (1949) *Philosophy of Mathematics and Natural Science* (Princeton, NJ: Princeton University Press).

[246] Wilensky, R. (1983) "Story Grammars Versus Story Points," *Behavioral and Brain Sciences* **6**: 529–591.

[247] Winograd, T. & Flores, F. (1986) *Understanding Computers and Cognition: A New Foundation for Design* (Norwood, NJ: Ablex).

[248] Wittgenstein, L. (1983) *Remarks on the Foundations of Mathematics* (Cambridge, MA: MIT Press).

[249] Wos, L. (1996) *The Automation of Reasoning: An Experimenter's Notebook With OTTER Tutorial* (San Diego, CA: Academic Press).

[250] Wos, L. (1992) *Automated Reasoning: Introduction and Applications* (New York, NY: McGraw Hill).

[251] Wyer, R.S. (1995) *Knowledge and Memory: The Real Story* (Hillsdale, NJ: Lawrence Erlbaum Associates).

[252] Yazdani, M. (1989) "Computational Story Writing," in Williams, N., and Holt, P., eds., *Computers and Writing* (Norwood, NJ: Ablex), pp. 125–147.

[253] Ybarra, M.J. (1996) "Discovering an Answer in the Flames," *New York Times*, Sunday, February 4, Section A, p. 13.

[254] Zenzen, M. & Hollinger, H. (1985) *The Nature of Irreversibility* (Dordrecht, The Netherlands: D. Reidel).

Index